EDUCATING MUSLIM GIRLS

feminist educational thinking

Series Editors:
Kathleen Weiler, Tufts University, USA
Gaby Weiner, Umea University, Sweden
Lyn Yates, La Trobe University, Australia

This authoritative series explores how theory/practice and the development of advanced ideas within feminism and education can be fused. The series aims to address the specific theoretical issues that confront feminist educators and to encourage both practitioner and academic debate.

Published titles:

Kaye Haw: *Educating Muslim Girls*
Petra Munro: *Subject to Fiction*

Titles in preparation include:

Jill Blackmore: *Troubling Women*
Jacky Brine: under*Educating Women: Globalizing Inequality*
Kathleen Weiler and Sue Middleton (eds): *Telling Women's Lives*

EDUCATING MUSLIM GIRLS

Shifting discourses

KAYE HAW

with contributions from SAEEDA SHAH and
MARIA HANIFA

OPEN UNIVERSITY PRESS
Buckingham · Philadelphia

Open University Press
Celtic Court
22 Ballmoor
Buckingham
MK18 1XW

email: enquiries@openup.co.uk
world wide web: http://www.openup.co.uk

and
325 Chestnut Street
Philadelphia, PA 19106, USA

First Published 1998

A catalogue record of this book is available from the British Library

ISBN   0 335 19773 6 (pb)   0 335 19774 4 (hb)

Library of Congress Cataloging-in-Publication Data
Haw, Kaye
    Educating Muslim girls: shifting discourses / by Kaye
Haw with contributions from Saeeda Shah and Maria Hanifa.
        p.   cm. — (Feminist educational thinking series)
    Includes bibliographical references (p. 185) and index.
    ISBN 0-335-19774-4. — ISBN 0-335-19773-6 (pbk.)
        1. Muslim women—Education—Great Britain.   2. Feminism and education—Great Britain.   3. Teacher-student relationships—Great Britain.   4. Muslims—Cultural assimilation—Great Britain.
    I. Shah, Saeeda.   II. Hanifa, Maria.   III. Title.   IV. Series.
    LC2047.H39   1998
    371.828'82971-dc21

Typeset by Type Study, Scarborough
Printed in Great Britain by Biddles Ltd, Guildford and King's Lynn

Contents

Series editors' preface

At the end of the twentieth century it is not a new idea to have a series on feminist educational thinking – feminist perspectives on educational theory, research, policy and practice have made a notable impact on these fields in the final decades of the century. But theory and practice have evolved, and educational and political contexts have changed. In contemporary educational policy debates, economic efficiency rather than social inequality is a key concern; what happens to boys is drawing more interest than what happens to girls; issues about cultural difference interrupt questions about gender; and new forms of theory challenge older frameworks of analysis. This series represents feminist educational thinking as it takes up these developments now.

Feminist educational thinking views the intersection of education and gender through a variety of lenses: it examines schools and universities as sites for the enacting of gender; it explores the ways in which conceptions of gender shape the provision of state-supported education; it highlights the resistances subordinated groups have developed around ideas of knowledge, power and learning; and it seeks to understand the relationship of education to gendered conceptions of citizenship, the family and the economy. Thus feminist educational thinking is fundamentally political; it fuses theory and practice in seeking to understand contemporary education with the aim of building a more just world for women and men. In so doing, it acknowledges the reality of multiple 'feminisms' and the intertwining of ethnicity, race and gender.

Feminist educational thinking is influenced both by developments in feminist theory more broadly and by the changing global educational landscape. In terms of theory, both post-structuralist and post-colonial theories have profoundly influenced what is conceived of as 'feminist'. As is true elsewhere, current feminist educational thinking takes as central the intersecting forces that shape the educational experiences of women and men. This emphasis on the construction and performances of gender through both discourses and material practices leads to an attitude of openness and questioning of accepted assumptions – including the underlying assumptions of the various strands of feminism.

In terms of the sites in which we work, feminist educational thinking increasingly addresses the impact of 'globalization' – the impact of neo-laissez-faire theories on education. As each of us knows all too well, the schools and universities in which we work have been profoundly affected by the growing dominance of ideas of social efficiency, market choice, and competition. In a rapidly changing world in which an ideology of profit has come to define all relationships, the question of gender is often lost, but in fact it is central to the way power is enacted in education as in society as a whole.

The books in this series thus seek to explore the ways in which theory and practice are interrelated. They introduce a third wave of feminist thinking in education, one that takes account of both global changes to the economy and politics, and changes in theorizing about that world. It is important to emphasize that feminist educational thinking not only shapes how we think about education but what we do *in* education – as teachers, academics, and citizens. Thus books within the series not only address the impact of global, national and local changes of education but what specific space is available for feminists within education to mount a challenge to educational practices which encourage gendered and other forms of discriminatory practice.

Kathleen Weiler
Gaby Weiner
Lyn Yates

Preface

I am delighted to see this work in print; work that has been so painstakingly and thoughtfully carried out and which I have seen at various stages – in conference papers, articles and thesis examination. The reason for this relatively long journey to publication has been not only because the research undertaken by Kaye Haw, Saeeda Shah, Maria Hanifa and their colleagues, is rigorous, thoughtful, and theoretically well grounded. It is also because the researchers have not been afraid to confront some of the most difficult questions for what have long been regarded as contentious and problematic issues in education – those of race, ethnicity and gender. For example, what are the ethical issues of researching an ethnic group, social class (or gender, for that matter) to which the researcher does not belong? How is it possible to research educational conditions and inequalities concerning race and gender without prioritizing one or the other or without forgetting that individuals constitute entities where race, ethnicity, gender and class etc. come together and which are, therefore, experienced as a unity? How is it possible to write about theoretical frameworks such as that offered by the French philosopher Michel Foucault, in a way that has relevance to the non-academic reader?

This book is a welcome addition to the *feminist educational thinking* series because on the one hand, it articulates many of the most popular concerns of feminism, both nationally and internationally: for example, of carrying out research that is non-exploitative of the researched; of illuminating gender relations without privileging white, western feminism; of writing meaningful texts without claiming possession of exclusivity and authenticity in accounts and explanations of events and narratives; and of recognizing that girls' and women's experience is as diverse as it is common.

On the other hand, it opens up new possibilities and prospects for feminist researchers. The authors are conscious of the risk they are taking in critically questioning how Muslim girls are being educated in Britain in the 1990s; in particular, in suggesting that independent single-sex girls' schools might be able to offer benefits to Muslim girls that state co-educational schools cannot. They also explore how to work and write collaboratively, yet retain distinctive styles and viewpoints which show not only where they have each, individually, come from but also where they are individually and collectively going to. In particular, Kaye Haw, the main author of the book, has had both to 'unlearn privilege' of being a white, non-Muslim academic, working with Muslim academics, teachers, parents and pupils, and to confront and challenge sensationalist media constructions and polarities of Muslims, as foreigners rather than British, them rather than us, and dangerous as opposed to safe.

So this book can be read at a number of levels: as a study of Muslim girls' schooling in Britain, and their range of options; as an example of how feminist research has developed since the 1970s and 1980s, empirically and theoretically; and/or as evidence of a new consciousness of how gender, or class, or ethnicity individually, are adequate to explain school experience or achievements. It is to the credit of the authors (and to the series) that all this complexity is fully portrayed, yet with a lucidity and frankness that also makes the book a good read.

Gaby Weiner

Foreword

If an observer waited at an appropriate point on a coastline and watched the sea continually for months, they would see the ocean in many different states, from flat and calm to stormy and wild. At some time during the vigil they may see 'perfect waves', which result when sets of waves generated hundreds of miles out at sea meet the coast and there is a gentle breeze blowing from the land.

Given these conditions each wave will be seen to peel as the foaming broken part chases, the ever steepening, as yet unbroken face across the ocean's floor. The six or so waves making up a set may appear identical, but when the first arrival is nearly spent near the shoreline, the last will be further out and just beginning to break. Each individual wave is continually changing while appearing to be the same as its antecedents in the set.

With a view from the water the observer may see that no two waves are the same, they may come from slightly different directions, some may be bigger than others and the breeze may vary its effects. As the tide and the wind changes the phase of the 'perfect waves' may change imperceptibly until the ocean has entered a new state.

(The musings of a surfer, Mark Linsell 1997)

Acknowledgements

To the people whose 'story' this is, I hope that I have done them justice in the telling.

Thank you to everyone who helped me reach this point. They know who they are but especially to Morwenna Griffiths and Marie Parker-Jenkins who supervised the PhD on which this book is based. Also special thanks to those in C30, Mark Hadfield and Rob Watling and to Steve Bennett of the University of Nottingham who read and commented on the draft.

This work would not have been possible without the help and advice of the head teachers and staff of City State and Old Town High. I am indebted to them for their confidence in me and the openness and warmth they showed in working with me. This is especially so for the head teacher of the Muslim girls' school who welcomed me into her school and to Maria Hanifa who has contributed to this book in sections of Chapters 1 and 3.

Saeeda Shah came to Britain a year after the completion of the research and the finished PhD. The opportunity of re-writing the PhD as a book fortuitously happened at this same time and, with it, the chance to ask Saeeda Shah if she would like to incorporate her perspective into parts of the book. This perspective is a unique one, for Saeeda Shah has grown up and worked as a College Principal in the region where the Muslim communities with whom I was working originated. Her contributions are from an eastern Islamic background and focus, and I believe this adds an original insight into the issues raised in this book in sections of Chapters 1 and 7 and as sole author of Chapter 2.

The author and publishers would also like to thank the Muslim Educational Trust for their permission to reproduce copyright materials.

Introduction

Kaye Haw

The way through the book

The focus of this book is the complexity of the interrelationship between 'race' and gender. One of the aims is to provide an insight into the educational experiences of Muslim girls. Another is to explore the issues which need to be considered in an acknowledgement of feminisms and the tensions of equality and difference which shape feminist discourses in education. The educational needs of Muslim girls and the establishment of private Muslim schools for girls encapsulate many of these issues.

On one level the book is a study of the relationships between teachers (often white and non-Muslim) and their Muslim students. It is a book which looks at how these relationships are affected by their different educational settings and experiences. It is a book based on my research into the educational experiences of Muslim girls in two schools: those in a single-sex state school with a high percentage of Muslim girls, City State, and those in a private Muslim girls' school, Old Town High. As a white non-Muslim person working in this area a primary concern of my research was to study how white power and privilege are exercised, through an exploration of the relationships between Muslim girls and their teachers.

On another level I see this book as an opportunity to move on from this narrow focus on one particular context. Through looking back from the vantage point of embarking on another piece of research, focusing on the career prospects and destinations of Muslim women, and having spent some time living with families in Pakistan, a wider perspective is made possible. To use a metaphor, I now see that research as the washing line from which to hang clothes and cloth of different forms and hues. It is this washing which will give the line its meaning and reason for being. Throughout the research I asked myself many questions, but there were two which remained significant:

Why was I doing the research and what purpose would it serve?

and

How could I as a white non-Muslim woman work with and write about Muslim girls and women?

For me they were, and continue to be, questions of fundamental importance. To answer them I felt I had to hold on to the things I was clear about. I can only tell my 'truth' and I can never be sure that the 'stories' that I am told are not merely 'stories' for my benefit (as a white, western, non-Muslim woman) or whether they are even the 'truths' of the people telling them. Also, the background to any piece of work consists of historically determined positions, practices, concepts and assumptions; the work is never fixed (Watling 1995). It is constructed as much by the present as by the past, so that there are many incidents and influences that occur before, during and after the course of a piece of research that shape it, while the research in turn colours and affects certain aspects of its background.

Two incidents

The first incident happened early on in the research. I watched a Channel Four documentary called 'Cannibal Tours' (O'Rourke *et al.* 1993). It followed a group of tourists on a tour of villages along the Sepik River in Papua New Guinea where the people had practised cannibalism. The film focused on interviews with the tourists on their view of the tribespeople and interviews with the Papua New Guineans on their views and impressions of the tourists. The tourists took photographs, had their faces painted, bartered for and bought 'the culture' as cheaply as possible. The villagers wanted and needed the tourists' money for clothes, food and schooling. For this the tourists were accepted, and the villagers posed for photographs and performed dances for them. The Papua New Guineans believed that the reason the tourists travelled to the villages was to 'gaze' at a people that had practised cannibalism. While they felt exploited they nevertheless needed the tourists for what little revenue they generated. For the head man the ultimate irony was receiving a postcard from one of his sons that was a picture of their own spirit house. He also expressed the desire for money to travel. The tourists 'appropriated' the selected and carefully prepared slices of the culture and left. For me, the overriding irony of the film was the 'cannibalism' of the tourists.

The second incident happened further into the research. At a Women's Studies Network Conference a group of black women were angry with one of the conference organizers who had announced that there was to be a meeting for the black and ethnic minorities delegates. Consequently some white Jewish women had arrived for the meeting. The black women felt that they had been faced with the difficult situation of deciding whether they wanted the Jewish women at the meeting and whether they could ask them to leave.

These incidents can be analysed in terms of intentionality. The tourists were positioned and caught up in a web of relationships about differing economic groups and the power relationships inherent in them. At the same time, expressed in the notion of tourism is a western discourse concerning a culture which requires one to travel. It is both aspirational and functional, with its roots in the Grand Tour and colonial notions of enrichment through buying and collecting cultural sophistication. Even though the tourists in the film approached their journey with goodwill (and I have to give them the benefit of the doubt here) their room for manoeuvre was blocked by this complex web and how they were positioned by it. In the second incident the intentionality of the black women was explicit. By choosing to open up a space for themselves they were closing down the options of the white Jewish women. Both these events made me feel uncomfortable about myself and the research I was undertaking.

And an influence

For me, those were critical incidents. As far as influences on the research were concerned the work of Foucault stands out. I was clear about my theoretical interest in how the discourses of gender and 'race' articulate with each other and the need for a methodology which would enable an analysis of the complexity and interrelatedness of these discourses and which would be sensitive to the issues of power. Given this, and the fact that I was doing the work in the early 1990s, it was almost inevitable that I would come across the work of Foucault. My first encounter was through reading *Madness and Civilization* (Foucault 1967) and *Discipline and Punish* (Foucault 1979). In *Madness and Civilization* I was immediately struck by the Ships of Fools and Foucault's exploration of the stigma of madness, so that the birth of the asylum can be read as an allegory of how we are constituted as subjects. The notion of Panopticism in *Discipline and Punish* struck me with equal force. This theorizes the transition to disciplinary power from sovereign power and is epitomized in a description of the Panopticon, a circular building of cells with a central watchtower so that no prisoner can be sure that they are not watched. They therefore gradually begin to 'police' themselves; their behaviour becomes self-normalizing. From this point on I was effectively hooked and interested in how others, particularly feminists, interpreted Foucault's work.

Pignatelli (1993) argues that throughout Foucault's work the question of freedom was his central preoccupation, and that a consideration of how 'power, identity, subjectivity and freedom intersect and inform each other' (Pignatelli 1993: 412) can usefully be explored using the insights and perspectives offered by Foucault. For Foucault this is not a common-sense notion of freedom based on personal or civic liberty or the power of self-determination. Instead it is a notion of being able to critically question and reassess our inherited identities and values so that: 'the practice of freedom embraces both an "inner" critical engagement of self-constituting practices as well as an outer questioning of the conditions within which the self is constituted, an ongoing individual and collective challenge to fabricate alternatives' (Pignatelli, 1993: 419).

According to Pignatelli (1993: 418), for Foucault a strand which underpins his understanding of freedom is **risk** so that his concern is about the attendant consequences of not risking oneself, one's truth, one's beliefs.

Reading this paper and Foucault's later interviews and work helped to make the answers to my questions clearer at that time, Sawicki argues that:

> As feminists I believe that we have good reason to appeal to Foucault's negative freedom, that is, the freedom to disengage from our political identities, our presumptions about gender differences, and the categories and practices that define feminism. We must cultivate this freedom because feminism has developed in the context of oppression. Women are produced by patriarchal power at the same time as they resist it.
>
> (Sawicki 1991: 101)

This is effectively an appeal for a continuing endeavour of disengagement of the self and self-invention. Such an appeal both attracted and fascinated me. For myself and the participants in the research I could only produce a piece of work which would take responsibility for its limitations. I would need to make these limitations explicit and take the 'risk' of attempting to critically question and reassess our inherited identities and values, representing these 'truths' in a way that would contribute to the pattern of 'truths' already told. In this way and for these reasons I felt that the research could contribute to theoretical debate.

My intention for the research became to open up spaces for critical dialogue and for the 'voices' of Muslim women. I did not want to speak 'for' them. They were both capable of making themselves heard and able to do it with more authenticity and conviction than me. The spaces were different and opening up one depended on opening up the other. It became about 'listening' and 'hearing' and this means two things (see also Griffiths 1995b). First, this means that we need to reflect critically on how we hear, how we speak, on the choices we make about which voice to use. It means the development of practices that enable us to pose these 'how' questions and use the various answers to guide those concrete moral choices we are constantly being called upon to make (Razack 1993).

Secondly, this means a more insightful, incisive and complex exploration of our differences than has ever been attempted before. For me, this is

Spivak's 'unlearning privilege' (Spivak 1990: 30) so that 'not only does one become able to listen to that other constituency, but one learns to speak in such a way that it will be taken seriously by that other constituency' (p. 42). To accomplish this Trinh recommends a movement away from defining and boxing ourselves into one subject identity:

> You and I are close, we intertwine; you may stand on the other side of the hill once in a while, but you may also be me, while remaining what you are and what I am not. The differences made between entities comprehended as absolute presences – hence the notion of pure origin and true self – are an outgrowth of a dualistic system of thought peculiar to the Occident.
>
> (Trinh 1989: 90)

The argument is that without absolutes, no true self, no pure origin, it becomes all the more imperative to pay attention to how our multiple identities are constructed and played out in any one time, in any one context (Razack 1993). A commitment to the responsibility 'to trace the other in self' (Spivak 1990: 47) must become central to our practice.

Having 'cleared the ground' as well as I could theoretically, the data collection and analysis proceeded. The nature of research is such that, even as you feel you might have gone some way to answer one set of related questions, this opens up new questions. As I finished the study I was acutely aware that although I had spent a lot of time in different Muslim communities, building my ties and relationships with groups and individuals within them, this is a privilege which goes with working in this area. For many an understanding of Muslim communities in this country is one which is based on what is presented in and filtered through the media so that the role of the media in polarizing issues in the pursuit of sensationalism is a developing theme throughout the book. Such unfamiliarity, which equally extends the other way and in all directions, means that there is fear and mistrust 'beyond the school gates' which has repercussions for what goes on during school hours.

One of the major themes to emerge from the research concerned this unfamiliarity. This allowed for a certain amount of 'blame shifting' to occur and relates to the large question which focuses on how regimes of power are perpetuated. At the time I argued: 'The answer seems to lie in an exploration of this shifting of blame which is a two way process and which allows room for the discourses which perpetuate regimes to manoeuvre and operate' (Haw 1995a: 440).

Having finished the study I met Saeeda Shah who had come to this country from Pakistan to do some research in my university department. She read my work and we had many hours of conversation and debate about the issues that it raised. I have also been back with her to Pakistan where I spent some time working in schools and further education colleges in the region from which either the students participating in the research or their parents originated. In this way I was able to gain an insight into their cultural 'roots' and an understanding of the 'parent context'.

In terms of religion, culture and ethnicity Saeeda Shah and I have different backgrounds but our conversations show that we have much in common with respect to our philosophical beliefs and stances. Our discussions have been fluid and dynamic. They have had the advantage of the immediacy of dialogue so they have not been fixed or degenerated into snapshots where we remain 'locked' into our own 'space'. During these discussions we have been able to contextualize our perspectives. We have been able to develop key ideas through applying these perspectives to ourselves individually in order to bring about a critical exploration of our own worlds and each other's. We have explored these ideas from two vantage points:

1 What do these ideas mean to us individually?

and

2 Whether these ideas work for us individually, how they work for us, or don't they work for us, and what implications this has for our aim in working towards a clearer understanding of our own worlds.

A similar dimension also provides a valuable contribution to this book: a perspective from me (British and white) and from Saeeda Shah who has grown up and always lived and worked in an Islamic context, who has three children born and brought up in Pakistan but who are now being educated in all sectors of the British state school system. A different perspective comes from Maria Hanifa, who came to Britain in her early teens, completed her education in the state school system and who has taught in both state schools and private Muslim schools. These are the perspectives which provide other items of 'washing on the line'.

The problem is how to make this work through the mediation of a flat 'text'. We can only make an attempt through painting rich detail of ourselves. This allows for the discussion to pinpoint for you, the reader, as well as for ourselves, our critical explorations of each other's experiences from our own contexts. There is then the possibility that these perspectives can be altered both individually and reciprocally. This also means a requirement on you, as readers, to look behind and through a text which is open and dynamic, engage with it and hang your own washing on the line.

The book features each 'voice' in discrete and identifiable sections in the main body of the text. Saeeda Shah writes in sections of Chapters 1 and 7: first, in Chapter 1 by introducing herself through a discussion of why she decided to contribute to the book; secondly, in Chapter 7 through an analysis of some of the data. She also provides part of the background of the book as the author of Chapter 2. Maria Hanifa adds her voice as someone who came to Britain when she was ten years old. I met her in Old Town High, the

Muslim girls' school where the research was carried out. She contributes through a dialogue with me in Chapter 1 and through a section which discusses education for Muslim girls in British Muslim schools in Chapter 3. There is therefore a perspective from me concerning a set of issues and from Saeeda Shah and Maria Hanifa over these same issues. The aim is to provide a richer understanding of the educational experiences of Muslim girls in the British context through an exploration of our own different worlds and that of the 'other'. The 'voices' of the participants in the research provide other features and are introduced as and where appropriate.

Signposting the way

The structure of the book is as follows. I have already said that it can be read on different levels and I have been told by people who have read it in draft form that I have high expectations of its readers. I make no apologies for this, in the belief that there are parts which should challenge and cause reflection. With this in mind it is presented in two parts. Part One entitled 'Contexts and Themes: Negotiating the Maze', is divided into four chapters: 'Framing the issues from the margins', 'Flash-backs-and-forth: re-searching the roots', 'Schooling for Muslim students in contemporary Britain', and 'Gender, Islam and single-sex schooling'.

The first chapter covers the question, why this research? It discusses professional and personal concerns in the area of social justice and poses the questions which the book aims to answer. It also introduces Saeeda Shah and myself more fully as well as Maria Hanifa. The second section of Chapter 1 provides the theoretical context and framework for the book, as well as for the research, and is concerned to explore feminisms and post-structuralisms. It defines the ontological and epistemological framework of the research through a discussion of post-structuralisms and how this articulates with feminist theories. It discusses Foucauldian notions of power-knowledge and why I chose to incorporate a post-structural analysis seen through the lens of feminism for this piece of work. The reasons for my choice of feminist methodology are also considered in depth. It also outlines the implications that these epistemological considerations have for the practical element of the study. It focuses on the ethical difficulties that arise in the course of any piece of research, and its central concern is to make the process of the research explicit. The third section features Maria Hanifa. She outlines her background, how she felt about the research and her reactions to it.

The aim of this chapter is to provide a detailed insight into the personal, historical and political bases of the research, how they contributed to its conception, how they influenced its development, and how the research in its turn affected certain features of these foundations. It also provides the theoretical background from which to explore further the answers to the research questions. Above all it highlights my assertion that feminist engagement with post-structuralism is analytically useful because this illuminates and reveals how power is exercised through discourse, how oppression works and how, through an examination of discursive relationships and positionings, resistance might be possible. This is the theoretical level of the book and as such stands on its own and can be read on its own.

The second chapter, 'Flash-backs-and-forth: re-searching the roots', is the 'parent context' and is written by Saeeda Shah. In this chapter Saeeda Shah discusses what the term 'Pakistani community in Britain' means for her and why she considers such a discussion to be pivotal to any work which focuses on the educational experiences of Muslim girls in this country. First, there is a discussion of the Muslim *Ummah*[1] in broad terms. The second section discusses the concept of a Muslim, Pakistani, immigrant community in Britain and explores the influences and processes contributing to its constructions. The third section concerns itself with the Islamic concept of emigration, patterns of immigration as directly determined by the British 1962 Immigration Act, and the consequent shaping of a Pakistani community in Britain with a particular socio-economic background. This section concludes by relating these processes to educational issues. The fourth and final section briefly explains the Islamic concept of education/knowledge for all, with specific reference to female education and sex segregation.

The third chapter: 'Schooling for Muslim students in contemporary Britain' is divided into three sections and offers **my** perspective. The first section provides the context for this chapter through a general review of the issues which arise in the education of British Muslims in the state school system in contemporary Britain. This provides the framework for the second section of the chapter which explores the debates concerning Muslim schools in the context of multicultural/antiracist initiatives and the moves to obtain voluntary-aided status. This section also has a discussion of the aims of Islamic education as interpreted by me through readings of the literature in this area. Having provided this theoretical background the concluding section again features Maria Hanifa. She gives an account of how and why the school which participated in the research was established, why she thinks there is a need for Muslim schools, and ends with a more general discussion of her views on educational opportunities for Muslim girls in Britain.

Chapter 4, 'Gender, Islam and single-sex schooling', is subdivided into three sections. Again it is **my** perspective. The first section discusses and explores feminisms and education. The second section considers feminisms and Islam so that from this framework Muslim and feminist responses to single-sex schooling can be analysed in the third and final section. The focus here is the placing of these debates within the context of the move of some sections of Muslim communities in Britain to establish Muslim girls' schools.

The aim of each chapter in this part is to provide a broad overview of the general field and the relevant concepts through an analysis of the main literature. This is of course influenced by my personal positioning in the research and for Saeeda Shah and Maria Hanifa, by their perspectives. The concept of social justice[2] forms the linkage between each chapter. It is in these chapters that the discursive possibilities of the new ethnicities and feminisms are explored. Also it is here, in the analysis of the existing literature, that the implications that these possibilities have for issues of social justice are initially discussed.

The second part of the book, 'Re-searching the research: disentangling the dynamics', also has four chapters, which are written by me as the researcher, with the exception of Chapter 7 which has a section written by Saeeda Shah. It focuses on the schools and presents an analysis of the empirical data so that the 'voices' of the staff and students are introduced and given precedence. It is quite possible to read this part of the book first, or on its own. The first chapter in this part, Chapter 5: 'City State and Old Town High', introduces the schools to the reader and focuses on the research method, direction and design so that it is concerned to make both the process and progress of the research more explicit. This chapter also describes each school, their establishment, management/governance, and background of staff and the curriculum.

Chapter 6, 'Equality in difference', is presented in three sections. It is **my** analysis of the educational experiences of Muslim girls in two British schools. The first section of this chapter considers the ethos and philosophy of the schools from the perspectives and perceptions of the head teachers and staff. This highlights some differences between the two schools which are picked up in the second section of the chapter. Consequently, this section explores the tensions that became apparent as the staff of City State reflected on their relationships with their Muslim students in the context of their commitment to encourage the students to question gender stereotyping. The third and final section of the chapter discusses the different strategies that City State has adopted to accommodate the needs of their Muslim students in the hope that they go some way towards providing 'equality in difference'.

Chapter 7, 'The Nazrah story' introduces the 'voices' of the students through an imaginative story and reintroduces the 'voice' of Saeeda Shah. The chapter has three sections: the first short section includes both my overall analysis of the stories and my reasons for including them in their entirety; the second section of the chapter features the stories preceded by my analytical perspective as an introduction; the third section introduces a different analytical perspective in that Saeeda Shah gives her interpretation of this aspect of the research.

Chapter 8, 'Dancing with the discourses: re-searching the research', is my exploration of different aspects of the approach of the staff in each school to the education of girls in general and Muslim girls in particular. The first section revisits the theoretical underpinning of the work. The second section considers the ongoing debate over single-sex schooling in general and Muslim girls' schools in particular as a dimension of the processes whereby the discourses of education, 'race', gender, religion, culture and age intertwine in the social construction of Muslim girls. It does this through an analysis of two of the discourses apparent in each school, those of liberal and radical feminisms (see also Kenway *et al.* 1994). The third and final section, based on the analysis of the data generated by the research, discusses the implications that this has for Muslim girls, for girls, and for social justice issues. It also makes some suggestions for social justice work in schools.

Conclusion

The book concerns itself with an analysis of contemporary discourses of 'race', religion, culture, ethnicity, class and gender situated within the context of the challenge of some sections of the Muslim community over educational issues within the state school system in Britain and, because of this, their felt need to establish state funded Muslim girls' schools. It takes the latter as symbolic of a challenge to the dominant culture revolving around the construction of a number of competing discourses about 'race', religion, culture and sexism.

It is a book which concerns the interplay of these discourses and their shifting nature where the language of binary oppositions and substitutions does not suffice. What do I mean by binary oppositions? They are a way of seeing, similar to ideologies, so that they draw sharp distinctions between conceptual opposites such as subject/object, space/time, speech (*parole*)/language (*langue*), boy/girl, black/white, 'insider'/'outsider'. They are a way of seeing which can be useful to set out argument and signpost the way to theoretical understanding. **But** they are a way of seeing that has come to dominate western philosophical traditions to the detriment of other ways of thinking, restricting an understanding of a complex multifaceted world with its diverse cultures and histories. By structuring meaning in such a way as to structure human relationships of difference and dominance, one side of the dualism is inevitably defined in a negative relationship to the other, and for whatever reason this strategy is employed it is inherently repressive:

> It is not enough to stand on the opposite river bank shouting questions challenging patriarchal white conventions. A counterstance locks one into a duel of oppressor and oppressed; locked in mortal combat, like the cop and the criminal, both reduced to a common denominator of violence. The counterstance refutes the dominant culture's views and beliefs, and for this it is proudly defiant. All reaction is limited by, and dependent on, what it is reacting against. Because the counterstance stems from a problem with authority – outer as well as inner – it's a step towards liberation from cultural domination. But it is not a way of life.

At some point, on our way to a new consciousness, we will have to leave the opposite bank, the split between the two mortal combatants somehow healed. . .'.

(Anzaldua 1987: 78)

So how do we leave the opposite bank? Derrida[3] argues that these conceptual oppositions should be put under erasure (*sous rature*)[4]. This is to write a word, cross it out and let both word and deletion remain because the word is inadequate but necessary. Derrida suggests that by this means we can leave the opposite bank because one side of the opposition **relies on and exists essentially**[5] in the other. This book is an attempt to leave the opposite bank.

Notes

1 Terms appearing in the glossary appear as bold italic at their first occurrence in the text.
2 For a detailed analysis of this term see Griffiths 1995a and forthcoming in this series.
3 See J. Derrida, *Of Grammatology* (1976); *Speech and Phenomena, and Other Essays on Husserl's Theory of Signs* (1973) and *Writing and Difference* (1978) after reading an *Introduction to Derrida* by D. Wood (1985).
4 Italic is used for foreign words and special terms.
5 Bold is used for emphasis.

Part one

CONTEXTS AND THEMES: NEGOTIATING THE MAZE

1 Framing the issues from the margins

Kaye Haw with contributions from **Maria Hanifa** and **Saeeda Shah**

Introduction

As I write in another time and another place I realize that I am bound by language; it frames. It closes down meaning while opening up space for reinterpretation of meaning. It is a strategic restriction of possible meanings. Every page has a meaning to me, its author, and for you, its reader as you construct meaning for yourself irrespective of my intent. As a reader you will sift, select, ignore and reinterpret. The silences also have significance. I also write at a time when formerly invisible groups of people are becoming increasingly visible and audible, moving to the foreground and challenging and reshaping knowledge. Centres and margins shift (hooks 1984). Foucault (1980a) speaks of 'subjugated knowledges' arising; the silenced are becoming vociferous. It is these debates, issues and limitations which frame this book. As a flat text this makes the dynamics of this context difficult to reproduce. All we can do, you and I and the contributors to this book, is bring our different perspectives to the issues. I shall begin this process through the question 'why did I do this piece of research?'

Why this research? – professional and personal concerns

This research and the perspectives it adopts are, as I have indicated in the Introduction, a product of an interplay and relationship between personal biography, positioning in society, historical period and cultural context. This reflects my assumptions regarding what there is to be known and what is knowable, for these assumptions are rooted in my understanding and experience of the world.

For these reasons the personal account which follows is of direct relevance to this book. This knowledge enables the reader to locate the author within the text. This then is a subjective account and as such contains an inevitable selection of content, for I am attempting to reveal only those parts of my personal and cultural history which I consider to have relevance to my handling of, and approach to, this study and the writing up of it as a book. 'It is a selection, an ordering, a shaping; a complex interplay between the present self and the past self selectively recalled at various stages of personal history' (Weiner 1994: 11).

However the very partiality of this account is of value. A clarification of my personal history and background, from where I stand at this moment and through patterns of experience of my own choosing, is revealing in itself; and it does, I believe, provide a valid means of explaining my approaches to and analysis of the work. Further, it allows the critical reader of the book to judge the knower (as seen by herself) and situate the approach and conclusions within those discursive assumptions and conceptions which have been made explicit.

If categories are useful and comforting (and people seem to find them to be so), then I am a white, middle-class woman who has grown up in a western, (predominantly culturally, if not religiously) Christian, and heterosexual society. As I started an MA in the late 1980s my experience of feminism was never one of a universal 'sisterhood', nor did I ever think of the category 'woman' as being absolute and inviolable. This was underlined by the fierce debate in seminar sessions promoted by the fragmentations quite clearly and explicitly represented by the other women (and two men) on the course. At the time I was not aware that post-structuralisms placed a similar emphasis on fragmentations. This has been a debate which I have explored while doing the research.

From an early age I have always resisted being categorized and for this reason have never formally joined any group of any description. I am however committed to feminism and its concern to understand what has caused women's subordination. I resist being placed in any one feminism because I feel unable to locate myself in one perspective which holds true at all times for all issues. The perspective which I do adopt is one which holds onto commonalities and fragmentations, in the belief that there are times when differences should not be exaggerated because the similarities are more important and vice versa. This stance is reflected in my use of the terms feminism(s) and post-structuralism(s) for example. There are times when I need to refer to them in their overarching sense, and their commonality and 'sameness' is more important. In these circumstances it is **feminism** and **post-structuralism**. In other places where it is necessary to emphasize fracturings and differing interpretations it is **feminisms** and **post-structuralisms**.

This research is founded on and seeks to examine critically a number of failures and a number of needs regarding issues of social justice. I developed these perceptions during my work as a teacher in the 1970s and 1980s and while I was doing my MA and PhD, and as such they are based on a number of personal and professional concerns.

I have always worked in educational settings. My 'first' career was spent as a biology teacher in three mixed comprehensive schools in predominantly white areas. During this time I became gradually disillusioned on several levels. First, in educational terms I was concerned that the science teaching offered failed to engage the majority of the girls. This seemed to be particularly evident in exploratory work when students were asked to put forward and test hypotheses. Secondly, I was concerned that, especially in my last school in the late 1980s when gender and 'race' had come to the forefront, there was no commitment from the school to engage with these issues. In this sense I felt we were failing a number of our students.

I was also concerned on a more personal level in terms of my own career. I had been involved in several interview procedures for promotion and had been asked questions which were clearly discriminatory. I still believe that these practices exist, although I now work in a different academic setting and they are not so blatant. This only makes it more difficult to pin them down, but they have equally powerful effects (as can be seen by the statistics or promotions in universities and schools). I enrolled on my MA in order to gain some theoretical insight into issues such as these.

Whilst preparing for a seminar and essay on 'race' and gender I became aware that the educational needs of Muslim students and the establishment of private Muslim schools for girls encapsulated and focused many of the issues that needed to be considered in any debate concerning social justice issues. I have already said that theoretically I was interested in how the discourses of gender and 'race' articulate with each other.

Having read the literature on issues of 'race' and gender and some local education authority equal opportunity policy documents, I was left confused. Much of this literature and documentation tended to deal with either 'race' or gender but rarely seemed to tackle the complexities of their inter-relationship. My confusion stemmed from the apparent lack of analytical tools to make this process possible. I thought that the consequence of this for women of different backgrounds, in this case Muslim women, had many implications for equal opportunity initiatives and policies implemented by both local authorities and schools in Britain.

For these reasons I decided to research the educational needs and experiences of Muslim girls for a PhD. This study was carried out against the aftermath of the Salman Rushdie affair and the backdrop of the Gulf War. Muslim communities in Britain were targeted for a great deal of media attention. This had many repercussions for these communities. As the work proceeded I became aware that to portray the experiences of the Muslim communities that I was getting to know as entirely those of oppression, would be to fuse together 'race' and racism and that in this case 'race' was not always experienced in a negative way but also provided a positive context for celebration, in the same way that Islam and what it is to be a Muslim woman were also celebrated. It also became obvious that the lives of the Muslim women who participated in the study are multifaceted and as the research unfolded, it became apparent that in certain respects their experiences have some commonality with those of similar class positions in other communities.

The assumptions inherent in the failures and needs I have identified shape the foundations of this research. I needed to develop research which could interrogate and illuminate these and which could be questioned by them in turn. It appeared to me that existing paradigms were inadequate for three reasons: first, because they failed to accommodate the fragmented and shifting nature of categories. Research which relied on the structures of, for example, gender, 'race' and class as analytical tools without acknowledging fragmentation and the fluid and shifting nature of categories such as these, failed to adequately theorize how these categories overlap and intertwine. Second, as we are all positioned differentially within a multiplicity of power relationships, any analysis failing to account for this appeared to me to be somewhat unsophisticated. Third, any piece of research is as much about the researcher(s) as it is about the participants in the research, so that a piece of research which does not give legitimacy to the 'voice' of the researcher closes down the possibilities for critical dialogue and interaction. In summary, much of the previous work suffered from a theoretical inability to combine perspectives which deal with fragmentation, hybridity and pluralism. These perspectives are characteristic of the ever-changing economic, social and cultural context in which Pakistani Muslim and other ethnic minority children are growing up. At the same time there was a failure to root the theoretical frameworks in a set of values which centre on ownership, empowerment and in a commitment to seeking out critical perspectives. These are the perspectives which should be based on open, focused interactions with concrete others (Benhabib 1992; Shackleton 1993).

As I began my research I wanted to construct a theoretical framework of sufficient criticality and complexity to accommodate my attraction to further explore feminist theories and post-structuralisms, and the suggestion contained within them that an account of our position in the social world needs a more complex, more flexible and less deterministic set of analytical tools than we have been familiar with. I needed a framework which could acknowledge the fragmented nature of our society, and the fragmented understandings of individuals within it. I therefore became interested in the possibilities of Foucauldian notions of discourse, in the belief that this might offer the means of redressing some of the analytical failures and ethical problems that I have already referred to.

Underlying these questions concerning the interconnectedness of the discourses of 'race' and gender were additional questions which also shaped the background to the work and which the research in turn made more explicit as it progressed and evolved. These are the questions which relate the

empirical focus of the work and the data which it generated to the broader
theoretical concerns focused around issues of social justice. They arose from
my theoretical positioning during the process of the research. They are the
questions which structured the research which began with an initial interest
in two main areas with regard to Muslim girls' schools: first, whether there
are any areas of agreement between Muslims and feminists concerning the
ethos and purpose of single-sex schools; second, how valid were the objec-
tions that Muslim girls' schools reduce educational opportunities available
to their students. As the research proceeded it became clear that these questions masked other, deeper questions, which were:

1 How do non-Muslim and Muslim teachers interact with their Muslim
   students and vice versa and is there a difference depending on the type of
   school?
2 Do the Muslim students in the private Muslim school feel more 'comfortable' in an environment where being a woman is not an issue, being a
   Muslim is not an issue, but being a Muslim woman is an issue because this
   is the raison d'être of these schools?
3 Are the Muslim students in the Muslim school more empowered to 'read',
   take up or reject the discursive positions offered to them in school in terms
   of 'race' ethnicity, religion, class and gender?
4 Is this different for the Muslim students in the state school, how, why?
5 What implications do these questions have for social justice issues?

It now seems to be a suitable moment for Saeeda Shah to introduce herself.
She is not a British born Muslim girl and her perspective is as a professional,
high-caste[1] Muslim woman who lives and works in Pakistan and who has
had extended study leave in England. It is different, therefore, from mine
and from those of other Muslim women.

Why contribute to this book? – professional and personal concerns

When tentatively asked by Kaye Haw whether I would like to contribute
towards this book my response was something like, 'I need time to think this
over, although I am deeply interested in it because of my particular positioning and subjectivity.' Before committing myself to such an opportunity
I felt some degree of caution:

1 How feasible could it be in my present circumstances to join this venture?
2 Why should I, Saeeda Shah, be joining in at this stage and what ethical
   right did I have to it?
3 What contribution could I make which might have new dimensions?

4 What implications could it have for the researched community, as my interest in this book was motivated mainly by my interest in the researched community?

Answering these questions provides both the rationale for my joining in, and the framework for my contribution.

In answer to the first question I am a Muslim, Pakistani woman and the head of a tertiary college in Pakistan. At the time of writing the book I had a period of study leave to do my PhD at the University of Nottingham in the years from October 1995 to May 1998. My research focus was educational management at further education level, in a particular region of Pakistan. The initial study leave was for one year only, with the plan to get it extended without it posing any threat to my post. This in itself involved much political and professional manoeuvring. Further, it was also a precondition that I complete my PhD work within these academic years. The added strains were looking after three children, an 80-year-old mother-in-law, sharing with a husband in a community-related, highly demanding, management job locally, and trying to run a house for us all in a nearby town, without any domestic help. In the circumstances the question was how feasible would it be for me to take up another demanding responsibility which would certainly add to my workload, and which might jeopardize either my PhD, or my job, or maybe both? In these respects my contribution to this book did not seem feasible but I still felt that I should do it. The discussion around the next three questions is an attempt at self-justification.

The second question: why me, and what ethical right did I have to become involved in the work? This book is based on research focusing on issues relating to the education of Muslim girls, predominantly Pakistani. Why, when and how immigrant communities retain their ethnic identities in a highly complex and strongly debated area, determined by socio-political factors and involving a whole lot more, are my concerns; for it is my belief that there is a relationship between British Muslims and their communities and their educational aspirations. This is a theme which I develop in Chapter 2 from the basis of a discussion of the term 'community'. For now I use the term community with the realization that it is a politically and culturally constructed category.

To identify with people on the basis of social and political categories 'is a process born of rejection and not to be confused with the choosing of such a group because she feels at home in it' (Griffiths 1992: 8). Alternatively, identity is determined by origin and background 'as used by the actors . . . to categorize themselves or others for the purposes of interaction' (Anwar 1979: 13). I think that it is not so simple. Whether it is a case of 'rejection' or 'retention' has different implications, not just for different communities, but also for first and second generations within one community.

In the case of the Pakistani community in Britain, the crucial role of religion in creating ethnic identity cannot be ignored. The religion is a way of life. Further, there is the importance of family, kinship and community in Pakistan, which is a dominant feature of the majority of eastern cultures, but in the case of Muslims it receives very explicit stress from the religion[2] as well. In Pakistani society 'kinship networks are a major element in the . . . [evolution] of the Pakistani community' (Anwar 1979:50). This also holds true for those Pakistani communities in Britain. These people believe themselves to be Pakistani in spite of their British nationality and British passports. It is hard to see it changing at least with this generation, which experienced immigration as children or grown-ups. For people like me, they are 'our people', and the 'relationship' is like giving away a part of your body for one reason or the other, and feeling a 'resentment' as well as a 'concern' for the receiving body, with all the associated implications it has for the 'giver', the 'receiver' and the 'organ' itself. The human nature of the 'organ' in this case, and the continued interaction between the three corners of the 'triangle', has added to the complexity of the 'transplant'.

The problem with British based research into the issues related to Pakistani immigrants (which might also be the case with other ethnic communities) is that it tends to ignore one interacting angle completely, for various reasons and practicalities. This approach is bound to render the whole perspective incomplete and unsatisfactory.

I can appreciate that this transplant was less strongly required by the host body;[3] I believe that it was induced by 'contextual forces' in both the 'bodies' and that once embarked on, it needs to work more for the health of the host body and the organ itself, rather than the parent body. However, for it to be healthy and viable, it is equally important to understand the parent context. This is where I enter – a Muslim, Pakistani woman, coming specifically from an area in Pakistan to which an overwhelming majority of the researched group belonged originally. Additionally the research focus is education, and so another link is forged through my close involvement in education in Pakistan over the last 20 years.

There is certainly the ethical question of justifying my claim to join in the efforts to understand, explore and analyse a context where I was not a part of the immediate research context. My personal experience of the British educational system is limited to my Masters study at Manchester in 1984–5 and more recently as a PhD student at the University of Nottingham. Also, since September 1995 my three children became part of the educational system in Britain, one each at a primary school, a secondary school and a further education college, although in itself this cannot be a basis from which to join in analysing issues related to the educational experiences of Muslim girls in Britain. More importantly my claim is that an understanding of the 'parent body' will facilitate the transplantation process to the 'host body'. I wished, therefore, to provide my understanding of the 'parent body'. This is informed by my knowledge gained through years of interactions with relatives, friends and members of the community, as well as through my shuttling between the two countries. Another source of this knowledge are British Pakistani students, particularly girls, who have been sent back to study in educational institutions in Pakistan, while some further additions have been made during my study leave in Britain through community links.[4]

Regarding the third question: what contribution could I make which adds a new dimension to work in this area? It is my belief that several issues need to be discussed. These are as follows: first, a discussion of the patterns of immigration, which is directly determined by the 1962 Immigration Act, and the consequent shaping of a Pakistani community in Britain with a particular socio-economic background. Second, a brief and relevant introduction to Islam, because of its crucial role in determining the identities and 'way of life' of the local Pakistani community. Third, a discussion of the male/female role because this concept, rightly informed or wrongly interpreted, seems to influence the patterns of education. Fourth, a discussion focusing on Islamic philosophy of education and the concept of sex segregation in Islam. This again appears to interfere in relation to current practices in girls' education and sex segregated schools, and here I argue that the community's attitudes relating to these matters are influenced more by socio-economic background and parent culture rather than the Qur'an. Girls in this 'community of suffering' (Werbner 1991) are doubly suffering as they are faced with 'race' discrimination 'outside' and sex discrimination 'inside' and 'outside' the home.

Lastly, my fourth question: what could my contribution to the book give to the researched community? My aim is to add to existing knowledge in the area, giving new dimensions to the analysis and leading to better insights and enhanced understanding. Through the discussions I have outlined I hope to contribute towards improving conditions for the researched community, and to achieve a change in traditions and practices. In this respect it is my intention that this community should gain an awareness of their 'rights' and 'duties' as Muslims directly from the Qur'an, and through this provide the means for them to free themselves from oppressive practices. I wish them to learn to be self-respecting, confident and emancipated Muslim women able to perform their role in the society in which they live, in accordance with the Qur'anic concepts of equality and difference. Additionally I aim to increase an understanding of the educational needs of Muslim girls among both teachers and education authorities in Britain. My belief is that understanding of an issue is the first step towards resolving it.

Finally, and to end my contribution to this section, I hope this book helps in increasing socio-political adaptation in British society. I do not see these immigrants returning to Pakistan in the near future. Certainly not the second-generation immigrants, who do not feel the 'pull of the soil', and who are experiencing 'a process born of rejection'.

Post-structuralisms and feminisms

The preceding section which ended with Saeeda Shah's perspective has outlined the personal context in which the following sections of this chapter and
the book are rooted. The style of writing will certainly change from the more
personal to the academic, for it is true that as we become more caught up in
the academic world, like chameleons, we adapt ourselves to blend in with
our environment. It is not just a matter of survival. It is a question of making
fine judgements about how best to make a point so that it impacts on the
intended audience. This section, the theoretical framework, can only do that
through recourse to a particular language, that of the academic, which all of
us adapt and use, each in our individual way. It is the theoretical background
which I as a white, non-Muslim researcher adopted for the research, and so
it begins by looking at post-structuralisms and feminisms and then moves to
discuss the implications that post-structuralisms have for the feminist movement. It also discusses whether there is such a thing as post-structural feminism before applying the theoretical perspectives to the practical aspects of
the study. The relationship between the researcher and participants in the
research is a linking theme throughout this section, so that I also discuss
further the questions I raised in the introduction about the reasons for doing
the research and its purpose, and whether I should work with and write
about Muslim women. I argue that through a theoretical consideration of
post-structuralisms and feminisms this enables me to negotiate my way
through these ethical, moral and political mazes.

The relationship between the researcher and participants is, and always
has been, a basic concern of feminist theorists because this relationship is
always one of power regardless of who is doing the researching and who is
participating in the research (Harding 1987; Lather 1988; Edwards 1990;
Stanley and Wise 1990; Cotterill 1992; Opie 1992). It is also apparent that
contemporary feminisms in all their richness and diversity explore certain
concepts in common with post-structuralisms. While realizing that such a
typology is too monolithic to capture the variety of feminisms and post-
structuralisms, for the sake of clarity and the argument weaving through this
discussion, these concepts are:[5]

1 the importance of a de-centred subject;
2 the importance of 'voice';
3 the significance therefore that facts are saturated with moral positions and
  value;
4 the questioning therefore of 'truth' and 'constructs of knowledge';
5 the examination of 'Otherness' and the relation between the 'self' and the
  'Other' as increasingly central themes of feminisms and post-structuralisms.

I began the research believing that dualities, dichotomies, oppositions, both
structure and set limits on our understandings. For these reasons I was

attracted to those aspects of the post-structuralist debate which explore the notion that dualisms which continue to dominate western thought are inadequate for understanding a world of multiple causes and effects: a world in which actions and the motives for actions interact in complex and non-linear ways, all of which are rooted in a limitless array of historical and cultural specificities. This notion is also located within feminist theory, amongst others, so that similarly, and from a feminist standpoint, Jaggar (1988) emphasizes that the insistence on making sharp distinctions between mind and body, reason and passion, knowledge and sense, culture and nature, permanence and change poses insuperable philosophical problems concerning the possibility of knowledge and the relations of mind to body, value to fact and of individuals to each other.

Opposition to male power – structural, institutional, interactional or discursive – is one of the central organizing principles of feminisms. The concern of feminists is that those in positions of power define the knowledge against which all other constructs of knowledge are measured. In exploring these and other related issues I have already explained how and why I was drawn to the work of Foucault and his criticisms of structuralist perspectives, so that the arguments which now follow are based on **my interpretation** of his work. Foucault insisted on the importance of language as constitutive of reality and subjectivity even while its parts shift meaning according to circumstance. Events and situations have to be understood in the interplay of discourse and subjectivity at particular times and places and in terms of power relationships.

A theoretical framework based on post-structuralisms and Foucauldian perspectives is one which places an emphasis on discourses and texts which make up and are reinforced by structures and social institutions. It is also one which explores the possibilities and potentialities of *desire*. It is through discourse that meaning and human subjects are produced and power relations are maintained and changed. At the same time **we are all active producers** of meaning, but the possibilities for meaning and for definition are pre-empted through discursive social and institutional positioning. Meanings arise from regulated practices, from power relations; and as active readers of our worlds we reinterpret and recirculate words and concepts whose meanings are not fixed or immutable. The questions are, are we written or do we write, or are we able to write even as we are written?

Every one of our actions as individuals is intentional, derived as they are from an indication of how we would like to be treated. In Lacanian terms our actions derive from a desire for recognition by the 'other', from a wish for self-recognition in some form or other. However, desire is impossible to satisfy because it refers back to the unconscious and the absolute lack that it conceals. Our actions then are determined by our *desire* for social interaction with others. They are not, and never can be, derived from the notion of an essential nature, because for each individual this is fractured by a variety of accidental and relational features brought about by social forces and motivated by desire. This is where discourses operate.

Foucault uses the term 'discourse' to examine the structures, rules and procedures, exclusions and oppositions which control and restrain what can and what cannot be said, which seek to shape meaning and to represent the 'normal'. He used the term throughout his work and refined it as his thinking progressed. He argued that it is not possible to 'objectively' stand outside of discourse and analyse it and so, rather than ask the question 'what is discourse?', he began to ask the questions 'where is discourse?', 'how does discourse operate?' and 'what does discourse do?' His interest in how discourse operates focused on relationships of power so that in *The Subject and Power* he writes:

> what defines a relationship of power is that it is a mode of action which does not act directly and immediately on others. Instead it acts upon their actions: an action upon an action, on existing actions or on those which may arise in the present or the future . . . In itself the exercise of power . . . is a total structure of actions brought to bear upon possible actions: it incites, it seduces, it makes easier or more difficult; in the extreme it constrains or forbids absolutely; it is nevertheless always a way of acting upon an acting subject or acting subjects by virtue of their acting or being capable of action. A set of actions upon other actions.
>
> (Foucault 1982: 220)

Adopting this Foucauldian notion of discourse, post-structuralist research is about the social; it is about action and how our actions are socially determined and relational, so that: 'Power shapes and informs our psyche. The result is that we are objects of social institutions and processes while we intentionally engage in behaviour' (Cherryholmes 1988: 35).

In other words we are always/already subjects and our everyday lives, socially, culturally and institutionally are made up of webs, spirals, waves of discourses which are fluid and shifting, which compete or co-exist and which are always related through these webs. The positioning of an individual with regard to these competing discourses is discursive; that is, individuals can be placed with reference to a number of discourses and be situated in a number of ways. Foucault suggests that a given discursive formation opens up a certain room for manoeuvre, 'a field of possible options' (Foucault 1972: 66), and he argues that this changing space in which certain possibilities for action emerge, are exploited and then are abandoned, should replace teleological notions of the development of themes and theories. For me, this was the initial attraction of Foucault's work. It provided a useful analytical tool capable of illuminating and revealing how power is exercised through discourse, how oppression works and how resistance might be possible. Also, this is of direct relevance to the relationship between the researcher and the participants in any piece of research, allowing as it does for an understanding that both researcher and participants are active producers of meaning so that this has to be critically explored and placed within the text.

A recognition that we all speak from a particular standpoint, out of a particular experience, a particular history, a particular culture and that this is crucial to our subjectivity does not then imply that we can only research the familiar; on the contrary. The research focus is shifted from a search for formal structures and universal values to how we are constituted as subjects of our own knowledge – a central theme of post-structuralisms and one which implies the necessity for a critical exploration of both commonalities and differences. It allows for the fact that, for example, the name 'woman' does have meaning for the people it names but it has its own specificity constituted within and through historically specific configurations of gender relations (Brah 1991). It is this which provided the basis for a recognition of some shared experience when I talked to Muslim students, their mothers and Muslim teachers. But as Brah says: 'in different womanhoods the noun is only meaningful – indeed only exists – with reference to a fusion of adjectives which symbolise particular historical trajectories, material circumstances and cultural experiences' (Brah 1991: 131).

At this point I also find the idea of a 'changing same' useful (Gilroy 1993), a sameness bound by the tensions of difference, where fractures at one level are transcended by this 'sameness' at another level in a mutual and perpetual dependence. This allows for an exploration of the relationship between gender sameness and gender differentiation, for holding onto commonalities, while giving due consideration to the tensions of difference. It also allows for the commonalities themselves to shift and change, again in a mutual and perpetual, relational dependence so that they are not the same over here as they are over there. These 'samenesses' can be class, or 'race' or culture or community which transcend each other and are transcended by each other in a perpetual, spiralling, curling wave-like motion. Each wave is the same and different and, with and through these, meaning is taken up, rolled over and circulated in a perpetual motion which is neither fixed nor immutable. For me this is a view of relativism which is not nihilistic but which is relational and dependent and which is again directly relevant to the researcher/participant relationship.

So far I have highlighted the possibilities that post-structuralisms, Foucauldian notions of discourse, discursive relations and positioning open up for an analysis of notions of power and dynamic models of identity. The advantage of this theoretical resource is that while it offers an explanation for the pre-existing framework in which I, or any researcher or participant operates, it does not suggest that these are 'set in stone'. On the contrary, the use of discourse requires me to examine the ways in which I engage with the discourses I am subject to (and those of others), and through the research review them, critique them and in this way possibly go beyond their limitations. This necessarily involves the element of **risk** both of myself and of others. For the researcher as traveller, not tourist, prepared with the tools of post-structuralisms and feminisms, the practical means of undertaking the journey become clearer.

Feminisms and post-structuralisms – the implications

The arguments of post-structuralisms have many implications for feminisms or any other marginalized groups. Both feminisms and post-structuralisms challenge traditional power-bases of knowledge from the political perspective in the sense of deployment of power, but the feminist challenge arises from a direct concern – that of the oppression of women. Griffiths (1995a) refers to the 'uneasy love affair' between them, for although they share some common ground, the post-structuralist call to recognize the demise of Enlightenment goals of justice, freedom and equality sweeps away the major objective of feminisms just when these goals appear to be within reach. In this sense many fear that it is especially dangerous for the marginalized (Alcoff 1987; Christian 1987; Hartsock 1987; West 1987). Furthermore it is argued that the appropriation of these ideas is by white, male academics who some would argue have borrowed heavily from (but rarely acknowledged) feminist theory, with its frequent celebrations of 'difference' and specificity, and its critiques of Enlightenment paternalism (Skeggs 1991). For reasons such as these there are those who remain ambivalent to post-structuralisms being attracted to some parts of post-structuralist thought and practice while rejecting others (Giroux 1988; Morris 1988; Best and Kellner 1991; Lather 1991). On the other hand, bell hooks sees no contradiction in valuing the work of Freire (who like Foucault is considered to be no ladies' man) and her commitment to feminist scholarship. She says:

> In talking with academic feminists (usually white women) who feel they must either dismiss or devalue the work of Freire because of sexism, I see clearly how our different responses are shaped by the standpoint that we bring to the work. I came to Freire thirsty, dying of thirst . . . To have work that promotes one's liberation is such a powerful gift – that it does not matter so much if the gift is flawed. Think of the work as water that contains some dirt. Because you are thirsty you are not too proud to extract the dirt and be nourished by the water . . . When you are privileged, living in one of the richest countries in the world, you can waste resources. And you can especially justify your disposal of something that you consider impure, unclean, etc. Look at what most people do with water in this country. Many people purchase special water because they consider tap water unclean and of course this purchasing is a luxury. Even our ability to see the water as unclean is informed by an imperialist consumer perspective.
>
> (hooks 1993: 149)

Feminists too are concerned with multiple subjectivities and a denial of the universal 'woman' **but** it is from the basis of trying to understand and change differences, located in economic and historical material realities, and to identify the commonalities beneath these differences. The aim is to construct theory to explain both differences and commonality and thus to increase understanding and guide action.

In educational settings Jones (1993) argues that what post-structuralism allows for is a conceptual language which transcends agency/structure dualisms, as well as avoiding the simplicities of theories which invoke a monolithic notion of patriarchal power in understanding girls' classroom experiences. She suggests that feminist post-structuralism holds to a view of 'positive uncertainty' (p. 158) in which complexity rather than pattern prevails:

> When girls are seen as multiply located, and not unambiguously powerless, a feminist approach to classroom research must shift away from the 'disadvantage' focus. An interest in the unevenness of power means that . . . studies must focus on the ways in which girls are variously positioned in the classroom.
>
> (Jones 1993: 160–1)

The advantage of this is that it allows for a recognition that all girls (and boys and teachers) are complex human beings and are active readers of their cultures. This theoretical perspective allows for the complicated and ambiguous ways that meaning is made in schools and the highly subjective ways that students and teachers 'read' and 'rewrite' meanings. There is not necessarily a match between the direct and indirect knowledge about gender and Islam that schools and teachers deliver in various ways and its reception and application by the students (see also Kenway *et al.* 1994) because as teachers and students interact with these knowledges, such knowledge is negotiated and re-interpreted.

Feminist engagement with post-structuralisms does offer discursive space in which the individual woman is able to resist her subject positionings – a specific set of fixing of identity and meaning. However, the critique that post-structuralism cannot provide a viable political programme because it rejects absolute values and verges on relativism needs to be further explored.

Research too is a political process and a route guided by feminisms and post-structuralisms does open up for me, possibilities for the notion of a liberatory politics. Foucault argues for: 'an attitude, an ethos, a philosophical life in which the critique of what we are is at one and the same time the historical analysis of the limits that are imposed on us and an experiment with the possibility of going beyond them.' (Foucault 1984: 50).

By working at the intersection of knowledge, power, freedom and ethics this is neither 'for' nor 'against' enlightenment. Rather it is against that which presents itself as authoritarian and finished, and for that which is 'indispensable for the constitution of ourselves as autonomous subjects' (p. 43) – a permanent critique of ourselves, 'always in the position of beginning again' (p. 47). To this end Trinh recommends giving up the quest to definitively 'know' but to question one's point of departure at every turn so that strategies (such as replacing rationality with emotions) do not become end points in themselves (Trinh 1989: 43). This proposal to engage in the ground clearing activity of radically calling into question means that:

> The questions that arise continue to provoke answers but none will dominate as long as the ground-clearing activity is at work. Can knowledge circulate without a position of mastery? Can it be conveyed without the exercise of power? No, because there is no end to understanding power relations which are rooted deep in the social nexus – not merely added to society nor easily locatable so that we can just radically do away with them. **Yes, however, because in-between grounds always exist,** and cracks and interstices are like gaps of fresh air that keep on being suppressed because they tend to render more visible the failures operating in every system. Perhaps mastery need not coincide with power.
>
> (Trinh 1989: 41, emphasis added)

This is not a politics based on modernist approaches such as for example the Right, the Left, Feminisms, Antiracism; but one based on the **immediate,** which is fluid and shifting where alliances are made for a specific purpose and then abandoned, where commonalities and differences are recognized and critically reflected upon so that:

> . . . we can focus on a given context and differentiate between the demarcation of a category as an object of social discourse, as an analytical category, and as a subject of political mobilisation without making assumptions about their permanence or stability across time and space.
>
> (Brah 1992: 131)

It is here that an exploration of post-structuralisms through feminisms provides a basis for a viable political programme because it allows for the possibility of tracing the ongoing commitments behind and beyond the shifting alliances. The task is to articulate those commitments which in some sense underpin the alliances 'without making assumptions' while exploring the tensions holding Gilroy's 'changing same' together; to begin at the interstices and open up the cracks.

Finally, is this then post-structural feminism? I would argue not. I have already argued that different feminisms share certain features of post-structuralisms such as the rejection of the logic of binary oppositions, the principle of the unified subject, the Enlightenment legacy and meta-narratives predicated on unified groups of oppressors and oppressed.

Similarly, different feminisms share linkages with other non-feminist thinking. This is made clear in Chapter 3 which clearly shows for example the cross cutting of Marxist feminism with Marxism, socialist feminism with socialism, and liberal feminism with liberal egalitarianism.

Feminist theoretical traditions are those which seek to understand the differences and dominations between and within femaleness and maleness. This is a central feature of a feminist analysis, together with one which implies a challenge of some sort to any inequitable relationships of power which involve gender or sexuality. For me these shared understandings are the important issues because it is from here that differences can be acknowledged, critically reflected upon and engaged with, so that debate may be pushed forward. For me it is feminism with perhaps a predominantly socialist agenda or a Marxist agenda or a radical agenda or a post-structuralist agenda, each complementing, co-existing with or opposing the others at different times and in different circumstances. Each is to be drawn on in different ways and to different degrees as and when the moment requires it. Each is to be categorized only when it is useful, as in Chapter 3 of this book. All of them are to be critically engaged with but none of them ever to be totally rejected or totally accepted because of the label that they carry. For me and above all it is **feminism**. This is Gilroy's 'changing same'. This, as Spivak (1989) argues is the necessary *essence*, the thing which deconstruction makes you realize that you cannot do without; it is Derrida's notion of *sous rature*, his philosophy of an *absent presence*, so that rather than present an object we employ the sign whose meaning is always postponed or deferred. It is feminism to be used with a criticality, an awareness, and above all sensitivity.

The application of the theoretical framework

I now want to apply this theoretical landscape to my own work. We learn about ourselves through contradictory and shifting patterns of discourses which are produced socially and culturally and through relationships as we participate in everyday life. Therefore Seller (1993) argues:

> I learnt that it is a mistake to aim for **a** dialogue, which will generate agreement out of two systems of thought or cultures. I discovered that people, not belief systems have dialogues, and that these dialogues occur, intermittently, on the basis of common concerns. These concerns, a combination of belief and emotional response, can be over anything from children to architectural styles. So we can be engaged in a wide variety of dialogues with a wide variety of people. I could recognize 'my kind of people' in what appeared to be a wholly alien culture as I recognized common concerns, and I could see how these could break down as we discovered other, different concerns.
>
> (Seller 1993: 246)

With regard to the research this meant that the educational experiences of the Muslim students and their teachers in each school could be seen as a set of discursive relationships (discursive fields) consisting of a number of different and **sometimes** contradictory discourses, such as those of 'race', gender, class, culture and religion. Further, each of these discourses can themselves be considered as a discursive field, consisting of its own different discourses. Impacting on these discourses are other discourses to do with, for example, age, competence, physical ability and sexuality. At any one time these discourses can shift and change places just as the pattern of a kaleidoscope shifts and changes with a twist of the eyepiece. As the pieces which go to make up the patterns of the kaleidoscope remain the same but take their meaning (their perceived colour and shape) from the places that they hold, so also for individuals. The pattern can remain static before it is shifted again in an endless variation of combinations over time which are always subtly different for each individual, even while they belong to groups.

In my work with Muslim girls, women and both Muslim and non-Muslim teachers, we converge and diverge along any of the interstices of these patterns and so does the Muslim researcher working with Muslims, or any other researcher for that matter. The point is, what we are told will depend on how we are perceived and our 'conversations' will be coloured by a host of different factors.

As far as my piece of research was concerned, relationships were established over time. Initially, the Muslim students regarded me as an interesting 'other', an unknown adult so that the discourse of age became another issue to consider. For them I was positioned in several ways. I was not their teacher or their parent. My work and my role in that work intrigued them; after all, what did a researcher do? I was white, not Asian and did not have a background in Islam. They wanted to find out about me and my background, where I bought my clothes, where I had my nose pierced, what I did in my leisure time and my religious background. It was a process of giving and taking. For many I became a confidante, a non-threatening 'other' who was not an 'authority' figure in their educational or home life. In the main our discussions were lively and open because of the lack of these restraints. I gave them room for manoeuvre in this sense. They were unsure about my positioning and therefore not always able to predict the stories that they thought I wanted to hear. This opened up space for me. They explored my opinions and I explored theirs.

My relationship with their parents was much more formal. As a white, non-Muslim female who was an academic I was treated with respect by their fathers. It was not difficult to negotiate access. I was positioned by them in the space normally given to Muslim men, so that in a parents' meeting at the Muslim school where the males were separated from the women I was given a seat in the room with the men. My relationship with their mothers was less formal because we had the experiences of being women in common. I always felt welcomed. I was cooked for, and given cooking lessons, and our discussions were interspersed with stories about our children. These common experiences created space for dialogue for both of us.

My relationship with the teachers was again formal. I let it be known very early on in the research that I had only recently left teaching myself and because of this I was accepted as someone who had experienced and knew the constraints upon them. This mitigated the pressures expressed by some of them who said that they felt they had to converse with me in a powerful and academic way. There were common teaching experiences to draw upon and this was also true for the Muslim teachers who participated in the research. The teachers were given room to talk to someone who was also positioned by the discourse of education but who they now placed differently. The point here is that I was involved in several different types of relationship and was perceived in different ways by all of the participants so that what we talked about was governed by this and I could always recognize, as Seller says, 'my kind of people'.

I have already stated that this theoretical framework means the need for me as researcher to **critically** examine my own positioning and make this explicit. The analysis of the data involves attention to multiplicities, contradictions and relations of power embedded in interpretive structures. It is difficult: partly because it is about critically examining why I wanted to hear the stories of the Muslim women and girls who participated in this research. I have had to ask myself whether I was asking for their accounts for **my** benefit, which I could not **hear** because of the benefit I derived from hearing them (Razack 1993). As I have already said, my intention for my research was, and is, to open up spaces for voices suppressed in traditional education in places where they would not normally be heard, although I recognize that this in itself cannot be enough. To this end, when I was asked to give a paper on the research in a symposium at the 1994 BERA conference I delivered it jointly with the Muslim head teacher of the Muslim girls' school (Haw 1995b). It is also one of the reasons for asking Saeeda Shah and Maria Hanifa to contribute to the book, so the next part of this section is a conversation that I had with Maria Hanifa, a member of staff at Old Town High, after the research was finished. First, I asked her how she felt about the research and how she felt about me as a white non-Muslim person doing the work. I then asked her about her own background. I knew from other conversations that she had come here as a teenager and been educated in the state school system. I also knew that she had taught Science in a girls' state school and now had daughters and sons who were being educated in primary and secondary mainstream schools in the local area.

Conversation with Maria Hanifa

In answer to my question about the willingness of the head teacher, staff and students of Old Town High to participate in the research, Maria Hanifa replied:

> People do stereotype. They make comments and judgements that I find quite difficult. I can remember being in a situation where a man, whom I would describe as a scholar, in the sense that he has probably got more academic knowledge about Islam than me, commented that he could not imagine women wearing the *hijab* unless they had been forced into it. He was looking from a western point of view at something that Muslims have accepted and he could not understand because he was seeing it from a European non-Muslim perspective. His impression was that every woman who covers the hair is suppressed. Yet this person is an intellectual who teaches Islamic Studies. The difference is, I live it and so my feelings are different. My point is that it is possible to study to great depths, but it is not possible to know what individual Muslims think and feel if you approach your study from certain perspectives.

Kaye   I think when I came to this research I really tried to make my limitations very explicit. I came to the research thinking that I wanted Muslim girls and women to 'speak' with their own 'voices' as far as was possible.

Maria   That is right. It is not you, but what they feel, that is the important part. My voice is my voice, no matter how simple it is. My background and the environment I live in somehow determine my thinking. Also, there are many issues within the Muslim community over which I have a different point of view from others. I cannot say that my opinion is better than theirs. It is just a different opinion. With your research you were trying to find out. You did not come with the attitude that you knew it all and were just looking for backing for your ideas. Many people do that – I know it all, I just need some sort of evidence now to make it valid. We did not feel that with your work, and so when you were here we felt quite relaxed. When you feel threatened you close up. Many people had come with the attitude that they knew it all and a comment here and a comment there would fit in nicely. That is something that we did not feel with your presence because of your personality.

   I think the girls had a good experience. They knew you were doing some research. You were an outsider who came in and gave them an opportunity to talk about themselves, their school and issues that affected them. Sometimes it is not until people ask you those questions that you can reflect on it. It was a good opportunity. Maybe that was the reason that we did allow a lot of researchers to come into the school, so that we could look at our own working environment and reflect on our strengths and weaknesses. Outsiders see limitations which are not always obvious to us as we live it. We are still a very enclosed community. These girls do not see anybody else from outside the community except maybe the postman or the delivery man. Some of them are still in a very closed environment and they have no outside influences until something is built in there. That is why we felt we needed to allow outsiders to come in, to open the gates. It is also very important for an institution to be recognized as an institution. That is achieved by showing that the school is doing similar work to other schools. In content it is the same as other schools but in practice it is slightly different because the emphasis is on Islam. The whole foundation of the school is to give signals which are different; GCSEs and A levels[6] are important, but equally important is what you are and how you treat others.

In our community some issues are never raised, except perhaps when people are directly suffering racism. Then they are aware, but otherwise the thoughts are never put into their mind. They never think about these issues, just go along with the wave that is coming along. Islamically you should be aware but I do not think this is to do with Islam; rather it is to do with the community and the way they have come here and the background they have come from. You need to be politically aware. As a minority community we have had to learn what is politically expedient. I think that is important, and that sort of educational process needs to take place in every school because that is what all life is about. It is about your survival and survival in the best possible environment; how do you eliminate certain things, what offends other people, what do you accept, what would others accept. That can only take place when you become aware of people like you bringing in an issue: is there a need for Muslim schools, what is their difference, what are the reasons for being educated in this type of school.

Here we all originated from a particular area and that is also important but people look at us here and think that all Muslims are like us and that in this community we are all the same irrespective of class, caste, language. I have enjoyed this research because I think you have looked at these issues with a balance and in their complexity. Other researchers too have been into the school, have looked at our work, questioned the students on issues and gone away with a much more informed picture. I think that has been a good thing.

Kaye   Yes, I hoped that it would be about giving people a chance to critically reflect on these issues and on themselves. I will never forget when I first said that I wanted to do some work with Muslim schools:

I was told that it would be difficult because I would not be accepted or allowed to spend time in a Muslim girls' school.

Maria The Muslim community is very much closed because of the way it is portrayed. It is better not to say anything than to say anything. A few incidents have made them aware of this. There is the English saying 'once bitten twice shy'. You do not take a second chance. Really deep down there is prejudice and there is hatred. Those people are there. It is their experience because they do not know anything better. You have to move into unknown circles to come towards an under-standing and to know better. In the same way people in my community will sometimes comment that English people have no moral values. I say, 'but English people do have values, it is only what you see. You are talking about the run-down areas where all the problems are, but that is only a small proportion of the community. The rest have values.' It is that type of experience that is limiting the people of our community, which means it is best for them to go out and see other people. I have good friends outside of my community, and I can sit with them, eat with them, speak with them and share things with them. This type of attitude goes with the narrow experience of some of the Muslim community who therefore categorize the host community and vice versa.

Kaye I can remember when we moved to Nottingham we did not know anybody. Immediately we withdrew into ourselves until we felt secure enough to start to move out again. I think that is what happened with Muslim communities.

Maria Obviously the reason we are in pockets is because of the lan-guage. It is no good buying a house ten miles out of the community because you will not find the right type of vegetables and food and spices that you want to buy. You are not going to have a relaxed con-versation. That can only take place in your own mother tongue in which you have been brought up. My children speak fluent English – this is their mother tongue; so when they sit together they are using Eng-lish as their medium. When I sit with my friends it is Punjabi or Urdu and although we can all speak English the main conversation is in that language. It is much easier, less stressful. You are not thinking 'what word shall I use?', 'does this express what I want to say?'. I think that comfort has to be there when you are having a relaxed conversation.

Kaye I think we all like to have that sort of comfort. We all naturally gravitate towards people that are like us.

Maria Yes, it takes courage to move out, and you can only move out once you feel secure. From my experience in mainstream schools I believe that minority communities tend to write descriptive things, for example there is a room with four chairs, but they do not write about how they feel about the room, what is the atmosphere. I think as a Muslim school we now have that other element because we have had the opportunity to reflect. We are saying, yes this is a room with four chairs, but what do we feel about it? This is a school with walls and books but what do we feel about the school? What is the education here, what is its value, how is it going to help us improve and how is it going to disadvantage us? Recently somebody said to me, you might produce excellent grades but will the outside community accept it? That is the question that we have to ask and try to then answer practically by listening to other opinions and also by hearing that we can change the system. It is definitely a hurdle that we have to overcome. We can produce excellent students, but will people outside the community accept it?

Kaye   I can remember you saying that to me at the time as well.

Maria   It is still so. The father of one of the girls said to me that his son had done accountancy and he could not find a job. He went to a mainstream school. I know there is a shortage of jobs but he feels that his son is not getting a job because he is a Muslim. He said my daughter is coming to you, what will happen to her? People do have this real fear that we are making sacrifices. I hope the sacrifices will not continue to be made, that there comes a stage when we will see the benefit of it. I think that question is still there.

We live in a country where there is a lot of tolerance. I think we have a better life here and better understanding. I have friends that I can talk to who are not from my own community, but there are individuals who will always pass a comment without the realization that it hurts. Yet they do not think that they have done it. It is by the way. You will always meet those people but the more understanding there is, the fewer hurtful comments will be passed. Feelings will still be there. People are people and the world will remain good and bad and in-between. I don't think we can transform individuals. Stereotypes and hurdles and problems remain but I think the ground is becoming clearer and more open. The number of Muslim schools in 1997 has grown to 44 or 45. It means that now within England almost every city has come across an institution with some sort of Islamic name to it. Even the mainstream schools as well as the communities have to recognize that they exist. We have a mosque that has just been built. It took about 16 years but now there is a mosque and that is a sign to say that the community is here. It is a permanent mark. Even if the community do not remain here, the sign will remain. I am not saying that we will disappear and go back because *Insha'Allah* this is the community that has now taken up this country as their home. They are born and brought up here, the signs are there. They are permanent signs, that mosque is a mosque until it comes to a state where it needs to be demolished. This assures the community that there is progression and prosperity and they are doing well because otherwise we would not have these symbols.

Kaye   So let us talk about you. When did your family come over here?

Maria   I came in 1967. My mother came in 1965 with three of my brothers and sisters. The rest of us stayed in Pakistan. My elder brother and sister were in Year 10 in secondary school. My mother wanted them to complete that year before coming to England because she thought that it would give them a better chance with their education here. Actually it did not, it disadvantaged them. I stayed behind because I was just about to start my sixth class so my mother thought I should finish that. Her thinking was, if I got reasonable grades it would be useful in case we ever went back to Pakistan. The younger children went with her. She came in 1965.

My father came in 1962 with ten friends by road. He had a business in Pakistan. The idea was that he would stay in England for six months and then he would go back. The whole trip was organized by a friend of his who was married to an English woman. He had brought her back to Pakistan and stayed with us as a good friend of my father. From a Pakistani point of view we are middle class so we had the room and facilities. During that stay he must have convinced my father to go back to England with him. He had a large Transit van so about five or six of them went.

When my father got to Britain he started a business and decided not to go back. He still has the same business now. My father was also very much a community man. He would sort people's social problems and domestic problems. He was always involved with that type of work and he was very much a politician so I think he enjoyed being here.

My mother was worried because she thought he had probably married here and was not coming back. It was a fear that the majority of women left behind had. That was her worry. Then she had four daughters and two sons, there were six in the family. It was not that she wanted to come over here. Without my father knowing, my mother managed to get her passport and visas organized through an agent with the help of her brother. That is how she arrived in 1965. She had a lot of opposition from the rest of the family because they felt that if my mother came to England then that branch of the family would never return. I can understand their anxiety about that.

After two years, when my eldest brother and sister finished their education certificate, we came here. I went to a Language Centre. They were known as immigration centres. It was all right, but I had one experience there that I can never forget. I felt uncomfortable and that is why I cannot forget it. This particular teacher used to make a girl and a boy sit together in the class, a girl and a boy, a girl and a boy. His main reason was to make you feel comfortable, to mix with everyone. But we never did because it was imposed on us. All through your class you sat very stiff next to this person, and that person very stiff next to you. You never spoke to each other but you had to sit in class like that and as soon as the bell went the girls went with the girls and the boys with the boys. I was there for three months and that is where my education started in 1967.

I became ill during that time and had to spend some time in hospital. I was just 13 then. In school I was a very shy child, very placid and timid. I used to sit quietly and just listen. I never had my own views or opinions. I never said anything in class, which also disadvantaged me because the teacher never quite noticed me and never said anything to me. I was not a troublemaker. I did not have many friends. There was one girl who just happened to take up a protective role over me. From the day I walked in, she said 'sit next to me'. I always sat next to her and she would always protect me. If anybody said anything she would be there to fight for me. She remained my friend throughout my school life, not that I spoke to her a lot. Not only was she supportive in terms of this but also she was very good at games and I was hopeless. She was always team leader and she used to pick me, which saved me a lot of embarrassment.

At school I did some O levels and I got a grade B in History. I thought I would do an A level in it. The first day I went to the class the teacher said to me, in front of the class, 'I do not know how you got a B, you cannot come to this class.' Now it would be different. I would say, 'I have got a B, what do you mean? I want to do an A level.' We were taught by a previous generation that you did not question the teacher, so I just walked out. That is exactly what I did. I cried in the toilet, recovered, and life went on. Maybe this experience was valuable, maybe it was worth it.

My sixth form was spent sitting in the sixth form common room. I hardly went to any lessons because I was not allowed to do A levels. There was nothing else available then anyway so I just sat in the common room. I went to registration and then went and sat in the common room and did nothing until I went home in the evening. When I think about it it was pathetic and I think that is why I feel bitter about my schooling here. I was really not advised. The teachers had in mind at that time that I was a Muslim girl who would get married and was not interested in education. I think that was a big factor on their part.

Then I went to college. At college I did my Science O levels and then I did my degree. When I finished my degree in the summer of 1980 there was an advertisement for Urdu teachers in the local state schools. That is how I got into teaching. I never thought that I would become a teacher. My husband was also looking for a job at that time. He was teaching Islamic Studies at lunchtimes for an educational trust. He used to go to five different state schools trying to teach Islamic Studies at lunchtimes. They were supplementary type classes. He was feeling quite depressed because his qualifications from Pakistan were not recognized here. The advert did not specify qualifications so we both applied. I was selected. My first year was teaching Urdu for one year as a tutor because I was not a qualified teacher. Then I realized that if I had been a qualified teacher I would earn twice as much, and so after doing that one year I thought it was better to leave the job and do a PGCE. I also realized that I enjoyed teaching. That was when I thought 'yes I can teach'. I had overcome my fear of the students. That experience straight after my degree gave me another strength and career.

My degree was originally an Ordinary degree and I had a wish to do an Honours degree, so I took one year to do an Honours degree. Then I did one year to get my PGCE. In 1983 I came back as a qualified teacher. I came back again teaching Urdu language, which is quite interesting because I had a degree in Chemistry. I was a qualified Science teacher and I was teaching Urdu. Maybe this is something that you get trapped in, undermining your ability, undermining what people expect from you and so you trap yourself in certain areas. It takes courage to get out from there. I knew with my experience and qualifications and with the lack of qualified Urdu teachers that I would definitely get a job. That is how I got the Urdu.

After one year of teaching Urdu I switched to Science at the same school. I went into Urdu teaching as a guarantee of having a job. If I had felt that I could just as easily have got a job as a Science teacher I would have applied for it, but I did not. This was security. Because I had worked in this school for the first year as a tutor and then as an Urdu teacher I got on with the staff really well so when a science post became available I was encouraged to apply. They rang me to say that tomorrow was the closing date and they had not yet received my application, so I knew I had a chance. That is how I got into Science teaching. My first year was quite tough. I think I was tested by most of the teachers to see how good I would be. This is again another thing: I hope that it no longer exists, because I am talking about 16 years ago, but somehow people never had the confidence in me to say that you can do it.

I felt very happy after the first year. I was teaching fifth formers and the Head of Department said that some of the answers that these students had put down in their exams were unexpectedly detailed. I was teaching them the Chemistry part of the syllabus and I really went into some depth. The students enjoyed it and took a great deal of interest in it which meant that when they took their exams they wrote detailed answers with equations to explain. I know the students really thoroughly enjoyed it because I remember one of the girls saying that they had really enjoyed the lessons. Normally you just stick to a syllabus and you just go through it but my lessons were extended for those who could cope with it. I really enjoyed the comment from the Head of Department. In my first year they asked me to do the exam paper when I had only been in the job for three weeks. I said I could do it but I came home saying it was another pressure and a test. For me it was a test. I remained there until 1989 and I think it was again my own simplicity. I do not blame the school for this but I did not have the right information and I was not guided. I was never given any guidance. I stayed in the same post for nine years. It was a stupid thing to do, to remain on Main Professional Grade for nine years with all the other extra activities that I was doing without recognition. I did religious assemblies, I did lunchtime supervisions, I did prayer times and it was not recognized.

I was the only Muslim teacher in the school initially. When I became a Science teacher obviously they appointed another Urdu teacher and then after that there were two more Muslim teachers so there was a team of three and myself. When I first started at the school it was 50 per cent Muslim 50 per cent white, so then the ratio was very good. Then when I went back after two years it was about 65 per cent Muslim and by the time I became a science teacher I think the ratio was about 40 per cent still non-Muslim, white, which was good because there were also non-Muslim ethnic minorities there. In another two years we were 95 per cent Muslim and only 5 per cent non-Muslim. The majority of the staff felt that this was the Asians' fault. I remember arguing with one of the staff. I said, 'But it is your fault, it is your community's fault. Why are you pulling out of it? Why are you leaving it for the Asians to fill? If you keep sending your children here then it will not become an ethnic minority school. If the places are there and a Muslim child has the desire for it, then why should they not take them? This is a girls' school and Muslim parents want to send their daughters here.'

There was also a Catholic school in the locality which had only a certain percentage of places available to other denominations. These were again filled by a majority of Muslim girls because it was girls-only schooling, and yet as a Catholic school Mass was compulsory. There was no withdrawal option but it was chosen by Muslim parents because it was a girls-only school.

That is how my career started and it was very much a long struggle. I think I have made a more successful career since teaching in Muslim schools. It was in Muslim schools that I became confident, able to speak, to offer my opinion and give my point of view. While I was in mainstream schools I still had that reservation, 'is it worth saying what

I have to say?'. There was some sort of baggage. I just could not say certain things. When I became a manager of a Muslim school it just gave me the opportunity to speak. I had to say what I wanted rather than go through somebody else. I had to do it, and that built my confidence. I still have those feelings of course, but now overall I give the impression that I am confident. I had to learn to deal with the media, parents, governors. I have a lot to thank Muslim schools for in terms of my own personal development, not financially.

Conclusion

This chapter has provided an insight into the personal, historical and political bases of the research, how they contributed to its conception, how they influenced its development, and how the research in its turn affected certain features of these foundations. It has also provided the theoretical background from which to explore further the answers to the research questions. Above all it has highlighted my belief that feminist engagement with poststructuralism is analytically useful because this illuminates and reveals how power is exercised through discourse, how oppression works and how, through an examination of discursive relationships and positionings, resistance might be possible.

So has this theoretical perspective enabled me to solve my moral, ethical and political difficulties and have I managed to persuade you, the reader, that it has? Furthermore, have I persuaded you that it is an adequate theoretical framework within which to contextualize and analyse this particular work with Muslim girls? For me, parts of the debate are answered more satisfactorily and clearly than others, and even then, all it does is represent my thinking at this particular time.

I have chosen a perspective which incorporates both feminisms and poststructuralisms as a response to the critique of existing work which I offered at the beginning of this chapter concerning the issues of fragmentation and hybridity, the necessity of a consideration of power relationships, and the legitimacy of 'voice'.

First, because a framework constructed from post-structuralisms and feminisms moves us away from crude dichotomies constructed around notions of similarities and differences and opens up the way to critically explore the commonalities and differences inherent in any researcher/participant relationship. It allows for hybridity and fragmentation.

Second, and practically and perhaps more importantly with regard to the development of a critical praxis, it allows for the generation of a multiplicity of political agendas and an exploration of the relationships of power inherent in the research process. In this sense it is about travelling with sensitivity, judiciously, continually being aware of your limitations, reflecting critically, making your limitations explicit and admitting when you are wrong. It is about **risk** and being prepared to use the experiences of other cultures and environments to critically examine your own so that others can be included.

Finally, it is about opening up any piece of research so that its perspective breaks away from the 'ghettoization' of the research process. This process is not and never could be about 'safe havens'. I have argued for a perspective which acknowledges a 'changing same' (Gilroy 1993). Within such a perspective we all 'voice' and 'hear' differently; nuances exist both within and between cultures. I am no more able to 'hear' individuals from my own culture if there is not the deeper intuitive bond of 'recognition' than I am able to 'hear' Saeeda Shah or Maria Hanifa. We need to take the **risk** of making these limitations explicit. This stance allows for the legitimacy of my 'voice'. Above all it allows for a multiplicity of 'voices' in any research area who differ in age, ethnic background, religious faith, physical ability, sexuality and class. It allows for people to do their own washing, to hang an array of garments on the line. It is about critically reworking these perspectives so that theory and action can develop and **spaces** for exploration can be created. It is **not** about exploration aimed at colonization. It is about exploration to bring about a clearer understanding of our world.

Notes

1 The question of caste among Muslims from the Indian subcontinent is a contentious one. Some will deny caste exists because of equality of status imposed on all Muslims by their religion. Whether or not it is considered that caste exists, or how caste is defined, are questions beyond the scope of this book, but I know from my visit to Pakistan that Muslim communities are divided into groups which bear caste, clan, family, *bradari* (extended kinship group) names. The terminology used depends on the view of the user.
2 I'm referring here to 'Religion Rasalah' which Mernissi (1993) differentiates from 'Religion Political' – 'high religion' and which is further distinguished from 'folk' religion. It derives from the Qur'an, where the interpretations are least controversial and command the highest level of consensus ideologically.
3 Although there is plenty of evidence to show how immigration was encouraged by the British Government to meet the demands for cheap labour in the post-Second World War era.
4 Pakistanis have quite strong community links which are not easily affected by spatial or temporal distances (see also Anwar 1979), and which can be one of the deterrents to the adaptation process.
5 See Griffiths (1995a) for an argued discussion of this point.
6 GCSEs are General Certificates of Secondary Education taken in both core and optional subjects at the end of Year 11. A Levels are Advanced Level exams taken at the end of Year 13.

2   Flash-backs-and-forth: re-searching the roots

Saeeda Shah

Introduction

The research carried out by Kaye Haw focused on issues relating to the education of Muslim girls in Britain. As it turned out, perhaps due to research pragmatics and practicalities, the research participants happened to be Asian Muslims, and predominantly Pakistanis. In my view, it is important in this context to explore the construction of the participants as a group or community in order to understand the dominant patterns of attitudes and behaviour, and to appreciate the variations. Education cannot be separated from other social processes. The educational needs of a people can only be understood and realized in the wider social context, in interaction with complex multiple factors active therein (Ball 1990). As this research focuses on a group, although loosely defined, its educational needs and other related issues need to be explored in the group context, while conceding full recognition to individual variations. Therefore, the discussion of the term 'Pakistani community' is perceived by me as pivotal to any work which focuses on the educational experiences of Muslim girls in this country.

This chapter has four sections. The first section explains the collective identity of the Muslim *Ummah*, in the broadest terms. As a religion laying claims to universality and perpetuity, Islam teaches and acknowledges diversity and plurality within an overarching unity. The second section discusses the concept of a Muslim, Pakistani, immigrant community in Britain and explores the factors and processes contributing to its constructions. As this is an immigrant group, the third section looks into the Islamic concept of emigration, and details the immigration contexts of the focused community in relation to its particular educational issues. The fourth and concluding section briefly explains the Islamic concept of education/knowledge for all, with specific reference to female education and sex segregation. This final section also provides an insight into the issue of single-sex schooling for immigrant, Pakistani Muslim girls by placing it in a wider religious, historico-political and socio-economic perspective.

Islam and the Muslim *Ummah*

A dominant majority of the Pakistani immigrants in Britain are Muslims. Islam, in essence, and irrespective of all cultural and local variations, stresses the importance of family and community. It presents these as basic requirements in the establishment of an Islamic social structure. The term 'community' ultimately embraces all the believers, regardless of their gender, colour, nationality or any other such variation. In the first chapter of *Ummah or Nation* Dr Al-Ahsan (1992) discusses the Qur'anic concept of *Ummah*, referring to the 64 occurrences of the term in the Qur'an. According to the author, the standard meaning of the term is community, and its root word is '*umm*' which means 'mother' in Arabic. Commonly this term is used among Muslims to convey the fact that all Muslims the world over constitute one *Ummah* or community.

The essential structure of the Islamic way of life is family based and community oriented; the patterns of *abadah* further emphasize the value of group. The five pillars, *Salat, Saum, Haj, Zakat* and *Jihad*, broadly speaking are community related in spirit and practice:

- *Salat* (prayers) is compulsory for every Muslim above the age of nine years, five times a day. After ablutions it can be performed at a *tahir* (clean) spot anywhere and also alone. However, its rewards multiply if offered in the mosque along with other Muslims, where social contacts can facilitate diverse and multiple activities of common welfare;
- *Saum* (fasting) is another individual activity, demanding not just complete abstinence from all foods and intercourse (or any sex-related physical relationship), from *fajar* to *mughrab*, in the month of *Ramazan*, but with equal stress placed on a complete observance of the moral and social codes. Also, fixing a specific month for its observance builds this personal action into a community activity. Further, *Saum* gains a much higher value when other Muslims are invited/facilitated/supported to observe it;
- *Haj* (annual pilgrimage to Mecca) is the annual gathering of all Muslims from all over the world in Mecca, in the month of *Haj*. It is recommended for all Muslims, once in a lifetime, provided they can afford it. It has multiple religious, social and economic implications;
- *Zakat* (alms-giving) is the annual compulsory 2.5 per cent alms-giving by a *sahib-e-nisab* Muslim from personal savings and possessions, including the value of gold and silver. It is given to other Muslims only, and those specified in Islam. Its aim is to help the needy and work for the general welfare of the *Ummah*;

- *Jihad* (struggle) is again another individual as well as group activity, performed for God and aiming at the expansion and protection of Islam. Seeking knowledge, earning *rizak-e-halal* for the family, protecting the weak, helping the poor, fighting social evils or spreading Islam and defending it, are all different forms of *Jihad*, equally valued and promised reward. The notion here is placing priority upon community interests.

All these *abadah* aim at the development of an individual in an Islamic context, besides creating an awareness of the specific rights, duties and obligations within the community, which in its widest sense includes all those who believe in God and His biddings. The basic requirements of *Imaan* are a belief that God is one, and Mohammed his *abad* and prophet, with added belief in all His prophets, the 'holy books', the angels, the 'day of judgement' and the life after death. Those who submit to God and His commands are one *Ummah*, and every compulsory *abadah* (mentioned earlier) and other related socio-religious activities (*Eids, Daras, Khatam-al-Qur'an, Milad* and ceremonies for births, deaths and marriages), in essence and practice, aim at reinforcing and strengthening this bond. In the case of the immigrant Muslim Pakistani community, Anwar affirms that 'patterns of religious activities constituted a separate Pakistani cultural existence' (1979: 168).

Ummah: the concept and inceptions from subcultures

Mutual obligations within the *Ummah* receive further stress as other variables and strengthen the community bonds. The strongest emphasis is placed on family, kinship and neighbours. In today's Muslim societies, Islam may 'not [be] strictly practised but is still a binding force' (Hill 1970: 145). Certain aspects of these pivotal teachings of Islam receive particular emphasis in interplay with different regional subcultures. In that part of Asia known as the Indian subcontinent, Islamic teachings and injunctions regarding the immediate and extended family and neighbours and other Muslims, are reinforced by the local patterns of behaviour concerning family and *bradari*/tribe. Overriding 'family obligations of social and financial commitments' and the primary importance of 'earning money for the family' (Shaw 1988: 165, 160) and/or extended family, which many cultures have difficulty in apprehending (p. 158), are in accordance with the teachings of Islam and also a traditional social obligation in Pakistani local cultures, in general. It becomes a doubly emphasized phenomenon, deeply embedded in ideology and culture, creating a network of relationships that is complex but extended, fluid and encompassing. Their 'disregard of the British way of life and old people's homes' (Banton 1972: 128) and scorn for the 'decadent Western standards' (Hill 1970: 98) and 'morally decadent society' (Banton 1972: 160–1), reflect reverence for their own social traditions and an inability to appreciate practices common in more individualistic cultures.

'Retention of links' with the area of origin, and 'remittance patterns' among immigrant Asians, mentioned by Saifullah Khan (1977), all reflect an adherence to cultural traditions, strengthened by religious obligations. In these subcultures, land and family/*bradari*/tribe play a major role in the formulation of personal identity, and the practice of sending the dead bodies back to be burned in the 'homeland' is another aspect of stressing cultural identity. It is the replay of the 'rhetoric of return', if not in life then in death, by these 'satellites in Britain, out-posts from the base camp' (Jeffery 1976: 144). Sending money back to the extended family in the parent country by cutting down on their own needs also reflects a consciousness of a collective bond and responsibility. It may not always be inspired by love. Often it is a religiously motivated obligation, or 'fear of *bradari*' and social imputation. It is perhaps more likely to be the second than the first. The constant threat is 'what the *bradari* would say', and this leads to positive and negative acts in the respective contexts. This same fear of *bradari* is another reason for not sending their daughters to school, and the prime source of female suppression and oppression among the immigrant community as well as in the parent context.

Community/communities

At the end of British colonial rule in different parts of the world, the number of immigrants from ex-colonies increased. The British/non-British divide increasingly caused ambiguity as non-British groups grew larger in number, size and complexity. For pragmatic purposes these groups became defined with reference to region, religion or colour. The freedom movements of the mid-nineteenth century, inspired by nationalism, further contributed to the group formulations around territorial and ideological bases.

Various elements and concepts like physical security, family/*bradari*, marriage, religion, area/country of origin, played a part in setting the very fluid dimensions of community boundaries and conversely strengthened the bond of community leading to 'encapsulation' (Anwar 1979, Chapter 3). Hill also mentions this 'concentration from particular villages', suggesting that 'many of the Asian immigrants will be oriented towards home communities' (1970: 131). Desai makes the observation that the clustering of immigrants in streets in some areas points to the tendency to gravitate towards shared culture (Desai 1963: 22). He also mentions the case of a part-time Bengali student who was refused entry to a dance hall with his white landlady as an extension of colonialism, where the subjects of ex-colonies are viewed in a negative force play in the active formulation of a situated and flexible concept of slave/master relationship and not as equals (p. 125). These interacting positive and negative force plays act within and between communities, so that variables constantly cut across boundaries to renegotiate and reinterpret meanings and notion.

Stuart Hall argues strongly that formulation of an ethnic identity 'is essentially a politically and culturally *constructed* category' (Hall 1992: 259), and draws attention to the 'issues of 'representation' and 'ambivalence of identification and desire' (p. 255) in his discussion of 'new ethnicities'. A debate about the nature of Pakistani ethnicity in the British context was initiated by Verity Saifullah Khan (1977), raising the question about the 'legitimacy' of such a construct as 'Pakistani community'. She points to 'the internal differentiation of the Pakistani community' (1977: 228), which mostly arises from the political, ideological or sectional (religion-related) differences. She claims that Pakistanis do not 'perceive the population of their fellow naturals as a community', which in her view means: 'a group of people with common identification, values and perceptions who interact with each other and have common association and leaders' (p. 227). These fixed definitions contradict the political, ideological, symbolic and socially fluid interpretations of the term, where meanings and implications are negotiated and renegotiated at different levels in different contexts: 'The issue is not how *natural* differences determine and justify group definitions and interactions, but how racial logics and racial frames of reference are articulated and deployed, and with what consequences' (Donald and Rattansi: 1992: 1).

The British Pakistani community

Is there a 'Pakistani community', or any other community with fixed definitions and permanent boundaries? Most sociological analysis would disagree, pointing to the differences that cut across solidarities. The issue is categorization and the processes leading to it, and the two important dimensions are: how community is defined, and who defines it.

This section explores both aspects and finally discusses 'Pakistani community' and its construction with reference to the British context, and why an understanding of this is necessary to an understanding of the educational concerns of British Pakistani Muslim communities.

Avtar Brah emphasizes that:

> the usage of 'black', Indian or Asian is determined not so much by the nature of its referent as by its semiotic function within different discourses. These various meanings signal differing political strategies and outcomes. They mobilise different sets of cultural or political identities, and set limits to where the boundaries of a 'community' are established.
>
> (Brah 1992: 131)

In his study of the Bangladeshi community John Eade claims that: 'communities and classes were constituted in political institutions and practices . . . expressed through various ideological constituencies, as both community workers and political activists sought to articulate the needs of the other' (1991: 85).

At the intersection of cultural and political contestations a discourse is created 'that urges to take care of its own problems, and assumes the major burden of managing its own public affairs' (Gilroy 1992: 49). It is a political stance to contend assimilation and defend identity and interests – 'a new cultural politics which engages rather than suppresses differences . . . a difference which is positional, conditional and conjunctural' (Hall 1992: 257).

Gilroy analyses the processes involved in the formulation of a 'community' in the context of a social movement. He suggests that 'a political language premised on notions of community' provides a context for spontaneous orientation of 'demands' and:

> its use evokes a rich complex of symbols surrounded by a wider cluster of meanings . . . community, therefore, signifies not just a distinctive political ideology but a particular set of values and norms in everyday life: mutuality, co-operation, identification and symbiosis . . . The social bond implied by the use of the term 'community' is created in the practice of collective resistance to the encroachments of reifications, 'racial' or otherwise.
>
> (Gilroy 1987: 234–5)

These solidarities are constituted and become manifest through their situatedness (Brah 1992: 143). However, it does not imply any denial of internal conflicts, divisions or ideological oppositions. In fact: ' "conflicts" of this type cut across the intraethnic solidarities of "homeboys" or "landmann" which are usually based on regional associations and which themselves divide ethnic groups internally' (Eade 1991: 89).

Simon Taylor's (1993) interesting study of Jewish and Caribbean immigrant communities in England reflects the conflict between the Anglo-Jewish community, the early settlers and the Eastern European Jews who emigrated following a general exodus in the early 1880s. He also points to the class conflict among Caribbeans who arrived to settle mainly in Birmingham and London at the end of the Second World War.

I disagree with Saifullah Khan's caveat that the existence of conflicts/disagreements, mainly ideological (political or religious), serves as a negation of the very concept of community. There is no perfectly homogenous community. More convincing is Gilroy's (1987) conception of community as 'as much about differences as it is about similarity and identity'. It expresses the member's commitment to the continuity and perpetuation of the group, working at the level where conflicts and oppositions do not emerge as active barriers. 'Divisiveness at one level thus implies a transcendant unity at another level' (Werbner 1991: 20). When the threat is to the group's 'values', group members join and mobilize forces, rising above their internal conflicts and contradictions (this was evidenced by the Rushdie affair). Such politically constructed terms work:

with and through difference, which is able to build those forms of solidarity and identification which make common struggle and resistance
possible but without suppressing the real heterogeneity of interests and
identities, and which can effectively draw the political boundary lines
without which political contestation is impossible, without fixing those
boundaries for eternity.

(Hall 1992: 255)

The term thus refers to 'imagined boundary' between one status group and
another, clustered by symbolism, definitions and interpretations. 'It continually transforms the reality of difference into the appearance of similarity
with such efficacy that people can still invest [their] community with ideological integrity. It unites them in their opposition, both to each other and to
those 'outside' (Cohen quoted in Gilroy 1987: 236).

Internal constructions

Proceeding from this assumption that community is a political and cultural
construction constituted in articulation with complex and diverse internal
and external forces active in a context, this section explores these with reference to the British situation. Internal definition refers to the self-perception(s)
of a group of people as a unit. In the case of immigrant communities – Jews,
Poles, African-Caribbeans, Asian-Pakistanis, Indians, Bangladeshis – three
major phases of their experience seem to have influenced their 'self-construc-
tion' as communities: the context of origin; the context of immigration; the
process of settlement.

These interact with situational elements to formulate their group identities in different ways over different lengths of time. In Werbner's opinion,
internally a community is constituted by its 'close-knit network and intense,
ethnic specific sociability' (Werbner 1991: 12). It is an expression of the
desire to defend their sociocultural form and a refusal to surrender their
ethnic identity, which they might feel is threatened in the new context.

In their perplexity at the unknown, new groups hold on to the known old
identity, drawn from the context of origin at the time they moved out of that
context. While they hold on to the known old identity, the original parent
community shifts and changes. The immigrant community develops its identity as a symbol of defence and defiance, to make its members be seen as they
politically want to be seen, and to veil all that they don't wish to be seen, by
those outside. Group identities are further reinvented by ethnic leaders with
their personal, political and religious aims, who foster specific ideologies,
instructions and values. It is a highly charged terrain of contending ideologies
and interests, each laying claim to power of 'discourse formation and dissemination' (Foucault 1980a), and it was perhaps these currents of tension
and conflict within and across communities which influenced Verity Saifullah

Khan to doubt the very legitimacy of the term 'community' for the Pakistani immigrants. Anwar strongly stresses that Pakistanis should be regarded as a community 'because they share a common background, have [some] common interests, some form of social structure, hold a common religious belief and a value system' (1979: 12), arguing that an ethnic community may have social rather than distinctly territorial boundaries. For me, this self-definition as a 'Pakistani community' has a value and a meaning as long as the concerned people respond to the constructed symbol in relevant contexts.

External constructions

Immigrants, or immigrant groups externally, are defined by different elements in the host context which can be put into two broad groups: the masses and the media; and the state, its administrative machinery and public services departments.

Literature abounds with records of racist behaviour meted out to immigrants which reflects the popular construction of these people and groups. 'Racism, of course, operates by constructing impassable symbolic boundaries between racially constructed categories' (Hall 1992: 255) and attempts to naturalize and perpetuate them (Brah 1992: 143), leading to the formulation and dissemination of a discourse reflecting complex and multiple historical, political, ideological and cultural contestations and implications. Generalizations from individual examples to wider populations lead to misunderstandings, ambiguities and hostilities. The media, in its own interests and traditions, plays a strong role in spreading and perpetuating this atmosphere of mistrust and resentment (Said 1981; Ahmed 1992; Hall 1997).

After the Nottingham riots of 1953, the media played an active role in constructing negative images of the non-white immigrants and 'during the 1960s onwards white hostility towards coloured immigrants seems to have grown, and certainly become much more open' (Banton 1972: 172). They were invented by the media as deviants 'from the accepted cultural norms of the host society' (Hill 1970: 115). In his study of Jewish immigrants Simon Taylor argues that 'for most first generation immigrants the outside world tended to be regarded with hostility and suspicion' (1993: 61) because of differences of religion, customs and cultures, and this holds true with many similar cases. These differences have often been exploited by the media, perpetuating hostility and suspicion rather than diminishing it, conveying a strong message of rejection and exclusion. As a reaction to it an equally strong tendency developed to gravitate towards a concept of 'community', perhaps as a sheer defence strategy and for the purposes of physical security. Jeffery stresses the role of this element in the formulation of the 'community' by referring to studies that suggest and support the idea that 'conscious re-assertion of Pakistani-ness is a probable response to such rejection' by the indigenous population (1976: 182). 'External' definitions formulated and disseminated by the masses and the media played a strong role in smoothing over the 'internal differentiation' of the Pakistani community (see also Hall and de Gay (eds) 1996).

Immigrant communities are imagined and created by the state and administration for the pragmatic purposes of 'managing' them and other related issues. Political, social, economic and administrative implications are all involved in a tense, complicated context where relations between immigrant groups and the state are played out, and which subsequently define the communities and their boundaries, from their own particular positionings. Werbner's argument is that these administrative measures tend to resolve 'the divisions within the community surface . . . for the sake of administrative efficacy' (1991: 116), appropriating terms for the convenience of policy formation and resource allocation and further perpetuating the symbolic image.

Members of the local public services such as health, education and social services also contribute towards the creation of particular images on the basis of their situated dealings and interactions. Across ambiguities, misunderstandings and misconceptions, images are constructed which highlight the differences and increase the distances. The atmosphere of uncertainty, coupled with exclusion, leads to the 'encapsulation' of immigrant groups, and subsequently develops and strengthens the sense of group belongingness round a concept of community which can be at times politically useful and psychologically satisfying.

Besides these 'reactive' elements contributing to the development of the Pakistani community in Britain, some 'active forces' also played an effective role towards this end. The sources can be traced back to the specific culture and religion of their area of origin.

Immigration: the concepts and constructions

The term 'immigrant' requires some deliberation in the context of this discussion of community. Muslims have a tradition and history of emigration as far back as the emigration of the Prophet, which occurred in the second year of Islam, first to Taif (a city in Yemen) and later to Medina. *Hijra* (migration) is a special concept within Islam. Almost every Muslim, even with very limited knowledge of Islam, has some knowledge of the Prophet's emigration from Mecca to Medina, and understands that it was undertaken in accordance with God's biddings, because life for the Muslims had been made too difficult in their homeland, Mecca. It has connotations with a better life and is perceived as an act favoured by God.

The Qur'an and *Hadith* encourage travelling and emigration for different purposes such as to spread God's message; to seek knowledge; to study God's universe; to earn a better living (Qur'an 97: 107).

The Qur'anic injunction that 'the land belongs to Allah' is not simply a negation of people's sweeping ownership, but a command to ward off territorial affiliations from growing so strong as to disregard the Almighty's pleasure. The Qur'an plainly suggests that if it becomes hard to live in one place, one should seek God's favour in another place.

Hijra is perceived as a form of *Jihad* as well,[1] if it is undertaken in accordance with the Qur'anic teachings. It also acquires the status of *Jihad* if it signifies an effort to earn *Rizak-e halal* (the pure and rightful income; see also Muslims in Western Europe, Saifullah Khan, 1992).

I am not implying or assuming that all Muslim emigrants are or have been aware of these multiple layers of meaning and implication. The point that I wish to make is that the notion of *Hijra*, particularly because of its association with the Prophet, is socially encouraged and appreciated in Islam, particularly if it is undertaken for the sake of God, religion, family and/ or community. Any Muslim person or family choosing to emigrate, would not have any religious barriers or inhibitions adding to the issues that are more personal, emotional, social or pragmatic. The underlying postulate is that wherever a Muslim lives or chooses to live, s/he remains an equal member of the Muslim *Ummah*, irrespective of caste, colour, culture or country. Muslim history is replete with examples of emigrations for various purposes: religious, social, economic or political.

Another dominant pattern that emerges from the study of this process in Muslim history is that, at its initial stages, it has always been the male members of the *Ummah* who choose to emigrate, and women, children, the sick and old joined later. Women usually did not join in the tentative explorations of the possibilities of settlement in a new land until it was considered to be safe and comfortable enough to do so. This can be interpreted as a code of behaviour in patriarchal traditions, or a commitment to family welfare in a Muslim context, or simply a protective attitude towards the family. This same pattern has been active during the migration processes of Asian Muslims to Britain as well.

However, this is not ordained by the Qur'an and, also, there are examples in Muslim history of women joining in the emigration at the very start, even when it was clearly foreseen as dangerous in the circumstances.[2] Perhaps in keeping with this dominant Muslim tradition, there were only 15 per cent of women among the first Pakistani immigrants in Britain according to the 1961 census. Among this 15 per cent of women there were a very small number of children, especially school-age girls, who remained almost invisible in the British education system even when they were sent to schools, which was not very often the case. This brings us to the next section of this chapter, which aims to analyse the complex constructions of Pakistani Muslim communities in Britain and their peculiar patterns of emigration.

From Pakistan to Britain: patterns of immigration

The Asian Muslims who started trickling into Britain at the beginning of this century belonged to two broadly different backgrounds. One was the moneyed class who had ultimately decided to educate their children in western institutions. It was a 'status marker', but for some it was also a guaranteed entry into the ICS (Indian Civil Services, socially and politically the most prestigious jobs in late-colonial India), law, and higher education. This group was usually comprised of men, with only an occasional woman among them (Nielsen 1992).

The second group mainly consisted of working-class men who either came as personal attendants to their British employers, or were Asian soldiers/sailors in the British Navy, Merchant Navy and Army who decided in the post-war, modern period to find work in British factories rather than face unemployment and poverty back home.

The creation of India and Pakistan in 1947 added another dimension to this phenomenon. Large scale emigrations of different social and religious communities across the newly created borders destroyed the settled patterns of sociocultural existence. For many it became a 'grab and hold' situation, where many poor became rich overnight. These rich-poor were understandably bewildered by their new situations. Previously established class divisions and distinctions of the pre-partition society became muddled by these context-compulsive mob migrations and were replaced by an emerging trend, among the peasant/working classes in particular, to challenge the traditional social patterns. The two options for maintaining or obtaining status in that specific sociocultural context appeared as: to have an education and high status job/position; or to have money.

Stories and examples of sailors and soldiers, uneducated and from poor backgrounds, returning with apparently plenty of money from abroad, provided impetus for other individuals to improve their own economic conditions. It also brought an awareness that making money was not necessarily linked to having an education or a traditionally rich background. For the uneducated, resourceless people of a socially and politically disturbed region the simplest and easiest choice was to go to *Waliaat* (England) and become *waliaati*, which had connotations with money. The absence of restrictions on travelling within Commonwealth countries facilitated the choice and process. This flow towards industrialized Britain was not merely a way out of poverty but, in fact, was becoming a means towards acquiring status and position in their home society as well, offering a promise of emancipation from the traditional class structures.

The mass exodus following the creation of India and Pakistan contributed towards the weakening of more localized bonds of land and community. For those who had experienced emigration first-hand, moving from place to place looking for a suitable locality in which to settle, it became a part of the process for survival. In many cases immediate socio-economic pressures took precedence over ideological/political preferences. Multiple contextual factors rendered it unimportant whether to continue living in Pakistan – the Muslim land of dreams – or to move to England (a non-Muslim society) for more practical reasons. It became a temptation for all those who were unemployed, or who wanted to improve their living conditions, and who additionally had someone to sponsor their migration and subsequent settlement, to try and earn money in England.

A flow of Asian immigrants to Britain began in the 1950s, with the bulk arriving from 1960 onwards (Saifullah Khan 1977; Anwar 1979; Werbner 1991). To explain the emigration phenomenon as resulting from economic factors would be too simplistic and misleading. Economic factors may be one of the strong reasons in the majority of cases, but there is a complex interplay of causes which can be analysed by situating it in the wider socio-historical context underpinned by the Islamic concept of *Hijra* discussed earlier. The catalytic destruction of rigid class boundaries during the politically induced and ideologically guided freedom-cum-partition movement in the Indian subcontinent led to the renegotiation and re-interpretation of many fixed structures. Money gradually became the central issue in the emerging social structures, signalling a short cut to status, and migrating abroad appeared to be the means of attaining it.

Meanwhile another phenomenon acquired important dimensions. The construction of what was at the time the world's largest dam in Pakistan in the late 1950s, was a multinational venture. The dam site was in the district of Mirpur, where about 200 villages with approximately 100,000 inhabitants needed to be evacuated. Early small-scale evacuations for initial planning and construction purposes began in 1963, which again set people thinking about the future of their families.[3] It would again be simplistic to assume that the 'large number of Mirpuris in Britain are a direct result of displacement by the Mangla Dam' (Saifullah Khan 1977: 67), but it can be argued that in the social and emotional turmoils caused by the impending and accomplished evacuations, people chose to re-unite their families/extended families in Britain rather than face the uncertainties of settling in new places, especially as this was more than likely to be in the absence of the male members of their families. In a new social subculture they needed males to settle satisfactorily. Both options, moving to another place in the home country or joining the split family in England, involved severing existing bonds, but in the case of Britain the reunion would perhaps ease the economic strains of maintaining families in two different countries.

An interesting fact is that, in the beginning, these Asian Muslim emigrants were mostly men under the age of 40. They were the young, strong and healthy who could fulfil the demand for hard and cheap labour in post-war industrialized Britain. It was an interplay of supply and demand, in a particular context, in which women and children had no role to play. Perhaps a wrench like the Mangla Dam project and a jolt like the Immigration Act of 1962 were needed to introduce changes in immigration patterns. The 15 per cent of women of the 1961 census increased to almost 50 per cent in the 1981 census (Werbner 1991). It was not just a response to the 1962 Act, but an interplay of diverse and complex socio-economic and political elements in both the host and the home contexts, as well as perhaps the influence of traditional patterns.

The beginning of debates around the 1962 Immigration Act, in and outside of Parliament from 1961 onwards, was certainly a major watershed, as Asian labourers in Britain suddenly became aware that contrary to their wishes and plans, their sons back home in Pakistan would not have a natural right of entry into Britain when they were old enough to work. Many who had returned to Pakistan after a few years' work also realized within months that the money they had been able to save had been used up by gifts for the 'family/*bradari*' and improvements in living standards at home, requiring a return to work to maintain the family. The majority of these returning immigrants lacked practical knowledge, relevant information and the necessary resources to invest their savings safely into ventures in Pakistan which would generate a regular source of income and a return on their investment. Neither did the home government in Pakistan offer such services to these returning immigrants. Gradually, there was a realization that the split family arrangements did not offer any bright hopes for the future, at least not those which were originally envisaged. Further, in Britain the discontinuation of the tax rebate to those workers whose dependents lived in Pakistan resulted in income cuts, decreasing the amount of money to be sent home, where the demand was also steadily increasing.

The young sons, sons-in-law and nephews joined the earlier emigrants in response to these increasing demands and came to Britain. At this point getting their sons into Britain to work meant bringing their wives as well and subsequently, the daughters – at least those not of marriageable age even by the home standards (the young girls were not to be morally besmirched through exposure to the non-Muslim British society). Indefinite periods of separation from the family might also have contributed towards this shift. By now many families had been living apart for years, some for up to a decade. Another encouraging factor was that through sheer hard work and community support, those who had migrated to Britain had improved both their living conditions and their standards of living and could afford to keep their families with them even when the women did not work to bring additional money into the household.

Another interesting development occurred with the realization that according to the now effective British law, their daughters could secure permanent entry to Britain for their fiancees/prospective spouses. In view of the traditional marriage patterns within the extended family or *bradari*, girls were encouraged to emigrate so that visas for future sons-in-law could be secured. The number of school-age girls therefore increased among the Asian immigrants, leading to issues of their education in the British compulsory school education context, particularly in view of the specific sociocultural and economic background of the immigrants in the parent context.

After the arrival of their families, the immigrants were faced with the issue of sending the children to schools. It became acceptable to send the boys to schools because they would need English and basic education skills to survive in the adopted country and to perform their role of family breadwinners in an Islamic context. Although there was, and is, a constant fear of reinterpretation of the parent-child relationship appreciated by Islam and reinforced by the parent culture, through exposure to the values and structures in the host culture, the options had to be exercised in the given context. For Muslims, Islam is an oasis of stability within a surrounding wilderness of confusion, but an understanding of some rules of the game in the wilderness is essential to maintain and protect the 'oasis'. Given the gendered role of 'boys' in Muslim patriarchy, the rules of the game were ones which had to be learned by the boys through participation in the 'host' context. This did not apply to the stereotyped daughter. Therefore, to send the girls to schools, more so if it was a mixed-sex institution, was problematic. There were linguistic, cultural, social, religious and racial barriers which became acute in interaction with these added gender dimensions.

Further, education was not a part of the family traditions in the case of the majority of these immigrants, who came from a working-class background. It was more strongly not so in the case of girls, which added to the situational complications. The concentration of communities in particular locales and 'clustering' (Anwar 1979) of *bradari* in streets increased the fear of *bradari* gaze which could expose them as deviants. Moreover, *bradari* pressure and opinion carries a great deal of weight in the absence of control over sources of authentic knowledge.

Islamic concept of knowledge and the gender issue

In Islam knowledge is highly prized, and the explicit promise in the Qur'an is that 'God will raise in rank those of you who believe, as well as those who are given knowledge' (Qur'an, 49: 11). The Prophet's favourite supplication was a verse from the Qur'an (20: 114): 'O my Lord, increase me in knowledge.' In the Qur'an, knowledge is presented as the 'legacy of prophets', propounding that 'whoever has been given knowledge has been given abundant good' (2: 269). Knowledge is the quality of God, the *Aleem*, who is the source of ultimate, absolute knowledge. Man has been given some knowledge, 'taught man that which he knew not' (Alaq: 5), to raise him above other creations. Man partakes in many Godly qualities, among which knowledge has a unique position. It is repeated in many places in the Qur'an that none can grasp the message of revelation except men of understanding and those firmly grounded in knowledge (*Suras*: 2,3,6 and many others).

In Islam the concept of knowledge develops and is classified into two major categories: the revealed knowledge and the acquired knowledge.

The revealed knowledge is part of the absolute knowledge, that is, God Himself. It is granted to only a few chosen for specific purposes. In theological annals, almost all the recipients of revealed knowledge were men, with the exception of a few women like Mariam who were partially blessed with it. It has been commonly delivered to the prophets, who all happened to be men, leading to gendered associations and interpretations of knowledge. These interpretations just ignore the influences of patriarchal societies in which the religion operates. Ideally, the Qur'an and the *Sunnah* enjoin upon Muslim women and men to acquire knowledge, and to seek God through knowledge which is the ultimate aim of education in Islam.

The First World Conference on Muslim Education in Mecca (1977) defined 'acquired knowledge' as 'including social, natural and applied science susceptible to quantitative growth and multiplication, limited variations and cross-cultural borrowings as long as consistency with the *Shari'ah* as the source of values is maintained'. The acquired knowledge, or the functional knowledge is explained by Choudury as 'an evolutionary process embracing interactive intelligence and experience gained in all sub-systems of the universe' (1993: 60). In the Qur'an the commands to seek knowledge are directed at both men and women, without reserving any knowledge(s) for men. The *Hadiths* abound in the Prophet's insistence to pursue knowledge wherever they find it 'even to the borders of China' (Muslim Educational Quarterly Vol 12, 3, 1995: 13), without any gendered discriminations. The Prophet taught men and women in the mosque in Medina, and when the women of Medina once complained that the specific teaching time did not suit them because of the nature of their work, the Prophet immediately conceded and made the required alterations (Mernissi 1991).

Knowledge is a major contributing factor to the 'process of moment-to-moment becoming of the Islamic personality' (Choudury 1993: 6) incumbent upon all Muslims regardless of their gender, race, colour or country. However, Islamic societies have been predominantly patriarchal, like many others in the world. The spaces for interpretation have been traditionally occupied by men, with control over the formulation and dissemination of knowledge(s). Power plays of politics and priorities in the socio-economic contexts decentred women and relegated them to 'otherness', an approach refuted by Islam, a religion which commends plurality, diversity and equality. Educating the boys or giving them priority is not in conformity with the Islamic teachings but a complex interplay of multiple socio-economic factors in the patriarchal structures where lack of resources may lead to denying the 'right to education' to women (Shah 1989; Weiss 1994). This right can be denied because: women are unpaid workers in the house; there is an unwillingness to send them to mixed-sex schools, if and where single-sex schools are not available; the family will not benefit from spending money on them, as they leave the house after marriage; in certain sub-groups it may be difficult to find a spouse for the educated daughter, and an unmarried daughter can be a social stigma. This right to education is also denied because it is men who are breadwinners; they will stay and look after the extended family, and social and economic status is associated with educated males.

Control over the interpretation and dissemination of religious knowledge, sociocultural traditions in the patriarchal systems and economic pressures, all contribute in a complex situational interplay to condemn women to deprivations, which are further validated through manipulated interpretations of religion.

The First World Conference on Muslim Education (Mecca, 1977) concluded that: 'Education should therefore cater for the growth of man in all its aspects: spiritual, intellectual, imaginative, physical, scientific, linguistic, both individually and collectively and motivate all these aspects towards goodness and the attainment of perfection' (Al-Attas 1979: 158); and the Qur'an claims that 'only those who have knowledge really fear God and tread the path of righteousness' (35: 28). Within the religious discourse, if knowledge is the prerequisite to 'tread the path of righteousness', denying access to knowledge is equivalent to denying access to 'the path of righteousness'; and denying it to women implies marginalizing them not only in this life, but in the life after death as well,[4] which would be in opposition to Islamic principles of justice and equality. Further, the term Man in the Qur'an has been interpreted as non-gendered, referring to both men and women when used collectively. The focus of my argument is that an Islamic concept of education is based on 'knowledge for all', with complete disregard for all types of discrimination.

Single-sex schooling

Another issue in the context of Muslim female education is sex segregation. This debate concerns the conditions surrounding the processes of teaching/learning in relation to gender dimensions. The following discussion regarding sex segregation in the present context does not concern itself with its advantages to women in patriarchal societies; nor with social appropriateness in certain subcultures; nor with economic feasibility/pragmatics; nor with patterns of cultural traditions.

These and many others are situational variants and are considered from different perspectives in later chapters, but for now they are treated as overarching axioms, manipulated for gender exploitations. Although the Qur'an recommends preferred demeanours for men and women,[5] it does not command sex segregation, and particularly not with reference to teaching/learning situations. The preferences for appropriate dress and behaviour codes, specifically for mixed contexts, are made explicit for both men and women in the Qur'an.

Seeking knowledge is *faraz* (obligatory) in Islam, for both men and women. The Prophet himself taught men and women, together at times, in the mosque of Medina (Al-Hibri 1982; Mernissi 1991, 1993). His wife Ayesha continued to teach men and women in the same mosque. As the Prophet himself and his wife taught mixed-sex groups, it follows that sex segregated institutions could not be mandatory in Islam or otherwise the assumption (God may forbid it) would be that the Prophet acted against the Islamic injunctions, even if occasionally.

The colonial period: Muslims and education

The immigration process gained momentum soon after the end of colonial rule in the subcontinent. Two hundred years of colonial imperialism were greatly deleterious for the indigenous Muslims, in every field of activity – social, political, economic – but more so in education. This had two major causes: the colonial approach towards education for the indigenous people; and the Muslims' response to the offered educational system.

The colonial agenda was commercial in its orientation, so that education for the indigenous population claimed very low priority: 'Colonial administrators were not very committed to education since the reason for colonialism was exploitation and not the uplift of indigenous populations. Schools were established slowly by colonial governments, and even strong local pressure for education did not ensure a large system' (Altbach 1982). The education that was provided focused on higher education, aiming to prepare a group of loyal and efficient natives to facilitate the day-to-day administration, and people who could furthermore serve as a vital link to, as well as barriers between, the rulers and the ruled. Lord Macauley's famous minutes (see Curtain 1971) make this agenda quite clear.

The beginning of colonial rule in the Indian subcontinent was the end of 1000 years of Muslim supremacy in the region. Muslims were intentionally repressed by the rulers for political reasons – their potential threat to imperialism. Their education system was strangled through the confiscation of its sources of funding, as well as by devaluing it politically. The Muslims, overwhelmed and bewildered, reacted by boycotting the system which was imposed on them. They opted to stay out of it. This expression of resentment and anger initiated a prolonged period of deprivations – political, economic, social and educational – for the Muslims in the region. A partial reparation to education was achieved by people like Sir Syed, Hali and later Iqbal from the mid-nineteenth century onwards, all of whom tried to shake Muslims out of their apathy. However, it remained a slow process because of diverse and complex political, social and economic reasons.

The intention of this quick flashback was to bring the wider pre-immigration context into focus which, to a small extent, accounts for the educational background of the twentieth-century Muslim Pakistani immigrant community in Britain. An interplay of more localized, multiple socio-economic features further influenced its formulation.

Sociocultural dimensions

Pakistan is anatomically an agricultural country. The ownership of land has been invested in a small group of families, especially prior to land reforms. In that feudal society, peasants and even small farmers were traditionally victimized by their feudal lords. Living under financial constraints, subsistence rather than education is a priority. Further, the feudal lords and other people in positions of power did not desire the mass of people to have access to education because they foresaw that education would bring about discontent, which would ultimately lead to a weakening of their hold. People were brainwashed into believing that the knowledge of the Qur'an and other religious areas was the reserve of the *ulema*, and education for the common man in Islam implied learning to read the Qur'an. In the case of female education, it received added reinforcement from manipulated religious discourses. The gender differences acknowledged and celebrated in the religion were interpreted as 'difference in the sameness', with negative implications, rather than as intended 'difference in equality'. This dichotomy relegated women to spaces of 'otherness', making them invisible, behind veils and walls (*chadar* and *chardewari*). They were not to be seen or heard, even when they did all the work in the homes and the labour in the fields, as was the case for the majority of women. The symbolic veils and walls (*chadar* and *chardewari*) operated beyond physicality. Allowing women the (Islamic) right to education was deemed to be violating the assumed sanctity of veils and walls and, again, there was the realization that this could be increasingly problematic to those enjoying positions of power.

If educating girls were just a pragmatic/economic issue it should not have been a barrier in the case of the British immigrant, for whom there is ten years' free schooling in state schools. Moreover, some Pakistani immigrant parents have spent and are spending money which they can ill afford on the schooling of their daughters in private schools for Muslim girls (Haw 1995a). The reluctance on the part of Pakistani immigrant parents to send their daughters to state schools, especially to mixed-sex schools, reflects the dichotomy between the private/public spheres leading to the confinement of women within four walls (*chardewari*), away from the man's world. It is a common mode in patriarchal feudal societies and may likewise be a preferred practice in Muslim societies; but it is not mandatory in the Qur'an or Islam as such.

Conclusion

The issue of single-sex schools for Muslims has complex sociocultural dimensions. Even when a particular family or parents may not have any preference for single-sex schooling, they would opt for the single-sex option in submission to pressures from the extended family, *bradari*, tribe or community, 'family obligations of arranged marriages, social and financial commitments' (Shaw 1988: 65), 'respect for traditions' (Hill 1970: 98), 'claims of kin in marriage' (Jeffery 1976: 134), the concept of *izzat* (honour) regarding women, and a whole web of socio-economic elements which render people helpless to make any independent decisions, even when they desire to do so.

For a Muslim woman and her family, being a spinster and being divorced carry equal stigmas. The authority lies with those who have power over relationships, and even parents who are in agreement with mixed-sex education have difficulty in questioning this authority. Whether men are hiding their shame or protesting their honour, the outcome is confinement for the women. Many young girls, British born Muslims of Pakistani origin, have told me that they cannot continue their post-school education because of *bradari* pressures even though their parents are willing for them to do so (see also Basit 1995). I know young women among immigrant Pakistani Muslims who have continued their studies after marriage (with the support of their husbands, otherwise there is the threat of divorce), for then, studying in a mixed-sex institution is no longer seen as jeopardizing their chances of marriage (see also p. 118, Chapter 6 and Riffat's story, Chapter 6).

It would be simplistic to link the demand for single-sex schools to any one factor or even a few factors as mentioned above. In the collective cultures of Muslim societies, independent decisions and decision-making processes are not practically possible because the fear of social boycott is not just an inconvenience, it is an insult. Submission to the collective subculture is essential to survival within that group and essential to the preservation of the cherished identity.

Notes

1 *Jihad*, broadly speaking, is a commitment to live like a true Muslim and to contribute towards the 'spread of Islam'. There are two major terms associated with it: *Jihad bil-Ilm*, which means effort through knowledge; and *Jihad bil-Saif* which signifies the 'defence of Islam', where *saif* literally means 'sword'. *Jihad* in all its forms symbolizes a struggle higher and more valuable than one's own life, and carries promises of highest reward. See also Christie 1991; Nielsen 1992.

2 An outstanding example is the *Hijra* of Hussain, the Prophet's grandson, in 13 Hijra, from Medina to Mecca and later to Karbala (a place in Iraq), accompanied by the women and children of his family. However, after the martyrdom of all the

male members of the family, with the exception of one sick son in Karbala, the sufferings of his *Ahle-baait* (the extended family) indirectly strengthened the tradition.
3 My family village was one of the affected 200 villages, and I witnessed and experienced the procedures and processes, continuing up until 1968, during my secondary and higher secondary years of schooling.
4 Life after death is a part of *Imaan* in Islam.
5 The detailed instructions in this regard are made explicit in the fourth *Sura* of the Qur'an named *al-Nisa* (woman).

3 Schooling for Muslim students in contemporary Britain

Kaye Haw with a contribution from Maria Hanifa

Introduction

Muslim communities are not unitary and do not speak with a single voice. There are not just class and gender differences but a number of political and religious differences as well. These communities are also multiracial, multicultural and multilingual and comprise the largest religious minority in Britain today (Ashraf 1986). It is this religious dimension which provides a uniting factor.

Since Muslim immigrants first began arriving in this country from the Indian subcontinent and parts of Africa in the 1950s, '60s and '70s, they have negotiated long and hard with local education authorities and other appropriate bodies for schools to accommodate the religious and cultural needs of their children (Nielsen 1986; Midgely 1989). The response to these efforts has been both 'ad hoc' and pragmatic.

Consideration of the demands from some sections of the Muslim community in Britain for an education which incorporates the precepts of Islam and Islamic culture necessitates the unpacking of some complex issues. In the British context one strand of the debate is grounded historically and concerns the involvement of both Church and State in the education system of Britain. Another strand of the debate concerns the aims of Islamic education, because this provides the perspective from which to explore reasons for the establishment of private Muslim schools and their bid to gain voluntary aided status alongside Roman Catholic, Church of England and Jewish schools.

State schools in Britain have attempted to adopt measures to accommodate the needs of their Muslim pupils, and this has usually been achieved under the auspices of equal opportunity initiatives adopted by individual local authorities and schools. However, accommodation of these needs revolves around issues such as cultural diversity, social cohesion, and the extent of minority rights in a democracy. This is the focus for this chapter.

The chapter is divided into three sections. The first section gives a general review of the issues which arise in the education of British Muslims in the state schooling system. This provides the framework for the second section of the chapter, which explores the debates concerning Muslim schools in the context of British multicultural/antiracist initiatives and moves to obtain voluntary aided status. The concluding part of this chapter features Maria Hanifa, a manager of a Muslim school. She gives an account of how and why her school was established and ends the section with a more general discussion of educational opportunities for Muslim girls in Britain.

Muslims and the British state school system

Education has been, and continues to be, a central concern of established Muslim communities in Britain. It is also argued that schools are places where certain 'truths' have constantly to be proved; they are a key site of the production of culture, a place where dominant cultures are transmitted and where cultural meanings are resisted and contested. Schools are therefore key sites of production of a changing culture in their own right (Willis 1977; Giroux 1983; Walkerdine 1990).

The great majority of Muslim pupils first entered British schools in the early 1970s and presented what were referred to as 'some problem areas for Local Education Authorities' (Townsend and Brittan 1972). These problem areas were school meals, school dress, religious and physical education, and co-education. Building on this, what follows is not an exhaustive review, but it is sufficient to signal the concerns that Muslim parents articulate when faced with the British state education system[1] up to the present day. These concerns can usefully be grouped into four major areas, namely:

1 the failure of the state system to adequately provide an Islamic education;
2 the issue of how a minority maintains the integrity of its cultural identity;
3 the issue of parental involvement;
4 everyday, practical cultural issues.

The failure of the state system to adequately provide an Islamic education

The need for Muslim teachers and authentic Muslim materials is stressed time and again by Muslim parents and Muslim communities (Union of Muslim Organisations 1989; Sarwar 1991). These concerns have largely not been met by any initiatives for multicultural developments in education in Britain and in fact have arisen mainly because of the failure of the multifaith approach to religious education adopted under the auspices of multicultural education.

The issue of how a minority maintains the integrity of its cultural identity

Sarwar 1991 places great emphasis on this, believing that the loss of such an identity threatens the very basis of the Muslim community, and pointing to the difficulty that Muslim children experience living within two cultures. The influence of Christianity in assemblies and religious education (emphasized in the 1988 Education Reform Act), together with other aspects of the curriculum, is seen to undermine and potentially contradict Islamic views of education. These are intractable issues which are not solved by simple solutions within British state schools. The question of how, or even whether, a minority can maintain its distinctiveness in a larger society is central to the issue of multiculturalism. It is an area where there is a vast amount of literature but little consensus of opinion. In British state schools cultural pluralism/multiculturalism is accompanied by a multiplicity of interpretations. For some it can mean a policy of total cultural segregation; for others it can mean a policy of revised integration based upon a more equitable distribution of power; and yet again for others it can be used to justify more educational development, curricular expansion and educational sensitivity. In this way multiculturalism in Britain has been developed as multi-ethnic and multiracial education, although these terms have not been taken as synonymous by their exponents. Educational initiatives under these headings have varied from the use of diversity of backgrounds in primary school settings to the complete redrafting of the curriculum and teaching methods to eliminate ethnocentrism and racism.

Responses to multiculturalism have also varied widely. At its worst it has been accused of presenting children with caricatures of their own cultures (the saris, samosas, steel bands approach: Troyna and Carrington 1987). During the 1980s a variety of texts reflecting on multiculturalism were published which dealt with the intractable difficulties which arise between individuals and groups in every society (Walkling 1980; Little and Willey 1981; Craft and Bardell 1984; Tomlinson 1984; Rex 1989; Verma 1989). In the nineties Modood (1992), reflecting on the reactions of British Muslims to the Salman Rushdie affair, usefully summed up the complexities of cultural identity and reflected as follows:

> Our concepts of racial equality need to be tuned not just to guaranteeing that individuals of different hues are treated alike but also to the fact that Britain now encompasses communities with different norms, cultures and religions . . . Once again dialogue, learning from a variety of traditions, is the way forward, for Muslim views of pluralism are not as they stand adequate either . . . the Rushdie Affair is not about the life of Salman Rushdie nor freedom of expression, let alone Islamic

fundamentalism or book-burning or Iranian interference in British affairs. The issue is of the rights of non-European religious and cultural minorities in the context of a secular hegemony.

(Modood 1992: 273–4)

This is the dilemma, and one which remains to date.

The issue of parental involvement

Most parents face bewilderment when faced with the British school system, especially when their children reach secondary school age where the schools are larger and the staff less accessible. This is often magnified many times for Muslim parents, who find such schools large, unfriendly and intimidating (Haw 1990; Bhatti 1995). Parents face further bewilderment at the point of making choices in school which will affect their children's future career options.

Everyday, practical cultural issues

Everyday, practical cultural issues such as clothing (especially for physical education and swimming), provision of halal food, music, art and sex education, teaching of mother tongue and prayer times and facilities, continue to be of concern to parents and children (Griffiths and Haw 1996). These issues are more readily accommodated by the state school system than the others. Moreover, in some local education authorities such issues are no longer likely to emerge as problems. Indeed most of these concerns have been the target of the main thrust of multiculturalism. However, knowledge of culture varies between teachers and between schools. So does the understanding of the workings of direct, indirect and institutional racism which takes cultural difference as its springboard. Recent research has highlighted the adverse effects of superficial knowledge, even in classrooms and schools with good records of antiracist activity (Connolly 1995; Nehaul 1995).

The evidence from small-scale studies conducted in these areas is complex. This makes it difficult to provide an overall picture of the issues which will do justice to the range and diversity of opinion both in schools and amongst Muslim parents and their children. However, it would seem that in Britain state schools have made, and continue to make, genuine attempts to have their Muslim students recognized within their school community. To achieve the aim of making their Muslim students feel comfortable about being Muslims within British state schools, the approach has been to initiate a series of structural/policy initiatives arrived at through some consultation with parents and community representatives concerning the issues outlined in the four analytical categories at the beginning of this section. In this sense much has been achieved in terms of ensuring that informal exclusion from the curriculum and the more general areas of school life have been addressed. Such initiatives implemented by schools throughout Britain include or have included some or all of the following:

Formal curriculum
   Curriculum materials which include resource material about Muslims
   Particular emphasis placed on language support
   Consultation over religious education and personal and social education
   Islamic Studies at GCSE and A level
   Adaptation of physical education facilities and showering arrangements
      within the physical limitations of school facilities
   Consultation and sensitivity over swimming arrangements

Informal curriculum
   Prayer facilities
   Dietary accommodation
   Establishment of an Islamic society
   Respect shown to other languages by use of dual language signs and
      interpreters
   Adapted school uniform
   Recognition of holidays/festivals and visits to Pakistan
   Arrangements of events which are culturally based, with the help of par-
      ents on the organizing committee

Community and parental links with school
   Mother tongue speakers in school and at all parents' evenings
   The appointment of Muslim governors/active Muslim parents
   The appointment of Muslim staff
   Regular consultation with the local mosque and community representa-
      tives
   Recognition of, and consultation with, different groups of Muslims (for
      example attending different mosques; holding different degrees of
      religious orthodoxy).

Generally, Muslim parents view these initiatives and consultation exercises as positive moves on behalf of state schools to accommodate their cultural and religious needs. Where there is and has been such negotiation, where channels of communication between schools and their Muslim parents are facilitated, these parents seem also to be happy to make appropriate concessions over these same issues.

   However, the implementation of such structural initiatives can mean a reification of culturally held stereotypes formulated within historical, spatial and political contexts which do not allow for diversity of opinion, complexity and change. Such structural initiatives also mask the deeper issue of what it actually means to be a British Muslim in a state school and in a plural society which is fluid, fractured and shifting. Already and increasingly state schools will be responsible for educating the children of Muslim parents who have themselves been entirely educated in the British school system. They will have concerns which may well be different from their parents who migrated to this country. This is a focus of the book, and crucial to an exploration of these issues is a discussion which focuses on the religious and cultural dimensions to this debate. Such a discussion also needs to be situated within the context of the establishment of Muslim schools. This is the theme of the next section of this chapter.

Muslim schools and voluntary-aided status

The aim of the first part of this section is to pinpoint where the aims of an Islamic education may differ from those of the existing state school system in Britain, and to show where the educational aims of the two cultures converge and diverge. This, together with the following historical overview of the involvement of the Church in the education system of Britain, provides the context for a discussion of Muslim schools and voluntary-aided status.

Aims of Islamic education

The ensuing discussion reflects **my** perspective as a non-Muslim woman approaching mainly Islamic literature concerning the aims of Islamic education in an academic sense. Initially I was struck by the way that Muslim religious traditions were produced as fixed, so that what follows reflects that fixedness although the rest of the book tries to move away from such notions.

According to Islam we are born in a state of *fitrah*, that is with the innate inclination to believe in and submit to God (Mohamed 1991). Mohamed explains that it is the responsibility of humans to realize the essential spiritual nature of the human being; in this realization lies the knowledge of God. Thus we are not only physical and psychological beings but also spiritual beings.

Guidance for an Islamic way of life is expressed in its perfect form in the Qur'anic revelation and, according to this, God has endowed human beings with the faculties of heart ('*qalb*) and intellect ('*aql*), by means of which we may be able to understand divine revelation or recognize the Creator. In contrast to western secular education, which recognizes our capacity for sensory and intellectual perception only, Islamic education recognizes that we have the faculties for a third level of perception, spiritual perception, which is the highest level of perception in the hierarchy of human cognition.

The purpose of human beings is to submit to the divine will, which accords with our essential nature (Qur'an, 30: 30). Islam, which means submission, is therefore in harmony with the nature of the human being and our purpose is to obey God, that is, to worship (*abadah*) God (Qur'an, 51:36). God, having equipped people with the faculty to distinguish right from wrong, has made us accountable to Him, and as we have this potential we are meant to be the *Khalifah* (vice-gerent) of God on Earth (Qur'an, 2: 30), and as such the heavy burden of trust (*amanah*) is placed on us.

Therefore we have the responsibility of divine will on Earth. This does not imply justice in the socio-political sense only, but more fundamentally rule of the higher self (*Ruh*) over the lower self (*nafs*) (Mohamed 1991). If we permit the lower self to predominate we are committing injustice, transgressing divine law and going against our own nature (*fitrah*). When we control the lower self (*nafs*) the essential spiritual nature is asserted and we are able to reaffirm the Covenant with God within our total self so that we may express affirmation in action (*'amal*) in obedience to God's Law (*Shari'ah*). When the lower self is transformed into the highest level of spiritual development (*al-nafs al-mutmainnah*) through obedience to God, then we do justice to the role of *Khalifah* on Earth.

We are therefore the locus through which Islam is expressed, through which total and willing submission to the one true God is realized. This also becomes the aim of Islamic education, which is to teach us how to worship God and so fulfil the task of *Khalifah* on Earth.

From this explanation it can clearly be seen that a central tenet of Islam is that we are spiritual and moral beings provided with spiritual and intellectual aspects of ourselves through which the full potential of *fitrah* can be realized with the guidance of prophets and divine revelation. From the belief that Islam is in consonance with human nature it follows that it becomes the means by which the full potential of our nature, spiritual as well as material, may be realized. It is within the context of this perspective that the aims and objectives of Islamic education have to be examined.

The basic aim of Islamic education is the actualization of *fitrah* in all its dimensions within a social context and it is therefore concerned with the development of the whole person – body (*jism*), mind (*nafs*), and spirit (*Ruh*) – in and for society (Mohamed 1991). Consequently Islamic education is rooted in definite *a priori* principles which also provide criteria for critically evaluating society and the individual.

The primary purpose of Islamic education is to produce a good person and, since it is the spiritual self that forms the most direct link with God, it is important that all aspects of a person's personality should come under its control. In Islam the individual's spiritual growth (*tariqa*) takes place only within the *Shari'ah* (the divine law; Halstead 1986). The *Ummah* (community of believers) walk together along the broad highway of the divine law, which sets out God's will for people in both their private and their social life, and by means of which an individual is enabled to live a harmonious life in this world and prepared for the life to come.

Religion for the Muslim is essentially a matter of following the divine law, which contains not only universal moral principles (such as justice and charity) but also detailed instructions relating to every aspect of human life. Thus the *Shari'ah* integrates political, social and economic life as well as individual life into a single religious world view (Halstead 1986).

Further, in Islam there is no question of an individual working out for themselves their own religious faith, or subjecting it to rational objective investigation, for the divine revelation in the *Shari'ah* provides all the requisite knowledge of truth and falsehood, right and wrong. The task of each individual is to come to understand this knowledge and to exercise free will, by either accepting or rejecting it. The Islamic notion of free will thus contrasts with the notion of personal autonomy that is widely considered to be crucial to the concept of liberal democracy. Education in Islam therefore aims at 'the balanced growth of the total personality of man through the training of man's spirit, intellect, rational self, feelings and bodily senses.' (Al-Attas 1979: 158).

In this way an individual may develop faith in God and recognize their obligations as *khalifa-tallah* (God's vice-gerent on Earth), and learn to 'treat the world as a great trust which must not be abused' (Husain and Ashraf 1979: 41). Thus Ashraf defines the aim of education as 'the means or the process of helping the child to grow and become a "Man"' (Ashraf 1992: 13).

Ashraf emphasizes that there are two classes or categories of notion concerning the person: the scientific-secularist idea of a person and the philosophical-religious one. The former model is the one which predominates in British state schools, while it is the latter which is prescribed by Islam. It is the wholeness of a person which Islam seeks to achieve; thus the aim of education should therefore be:

> . . . to guide a child so that he shapes himself as a whole being and not a fragmented creature. He should have knowledge of his relationship with God, Man and Nature. His will should be trained so that he acts for the sake of God, selflessly, objectively and willingly with the highest norms of truth, justice, honesty, righteousness, love and beauty in his mind.
>
> (Ashraf, July 1992 Islamia: 13)

This consideration of 'knowledge' defines a fracturing between Islamic and western concepts of education. The difference in perception rests on the fact that whereas western philosophy allows religious knowledge as a distinct form of knowledge in isolation, Islam only acknowledges a holistic approach where the validity of the true faith is paramount and one which confines all knowledge to within the parameters of the Qur'an and the *Hadith*: one system seeks individual autonomy by which the educational process invites young people to think and act for themselves within society, whilst the other attempts to maintain a strong sense of community and family solidarity within a religious framework. These issues are of considerable importance to any discussion concerning the education of Muslim children either within the state system or in private Muslim schools, but first the involvement of the Church in the education system of Britain needs some consideration.

The duality of Church and State

In nineteenth-century Britain elementary schools for the instruction of children of the poor were established by the Church of England and other religious organizations. So widespread were the foundations of the Established Church (and to a lesser extent of other denominations) that when the State intervened in education it was impracticable to alleviate the Church of all responsibility in this field. The Elementary Education Act of 1870 was a piece of compromise legislation in this respect (Lawson and Silver 1973). It did not introduce free or compulsory education, but made both possible; neither did it supersede the voluntary schools. It brought the State into education as never before and it created the school boards (precursors of local education authorities) as democratic organs of local administration.

After 1870 Church schools suffered greatly from lack of funds and became generally inferior to the more prosperous Board Schools. From this period there followed a battle between Church and State over the control of education (Cruikshank 1963; Lawson and Silver 1973). The 1902 and 1906 Education Acts established the principle of voluntary maintained denominational schools alongside those run by the local school boards. The 1902 Act effectively rescued Church schools from their decline and brought them under the umbrella of local authority financing. To qualify for such finance they had to accept certain conditions (Clause 7(1)(c) and (6)) but they kept their distinctive style as Church schools (Cruickshank 1963). Managers were to include representatives (usually one-third) appointed by the local education authority (Clause 7(1)(d)), and these were to appoint teachers subject to the consent of the local education authority, and to control religious instruction.

Following the 1944 Education Act, three types of voluntary school were created – aided, controlled and special agreement (CRE 1990). This Act defined as 'voluntary' all schools maintained through the rates but which had not been established by a local education authority or a former authority (Section 9(2)), and set out a procedure for the establishment of new voluntary schools in Section 13.

These voluntary schools are differentiated according to degree of public control, local authority funding and funding from the Department for Education. The detailed procedure and the exact requirements varied according to whether the school in question was to be 'voluntary controlled' or 'voluntary aided'. Those which could not afford to modernize their buildings to the required standards became 'voluntary controlled'. The local education authority then financed the modernization and the Church (or other voluntary group) retained only nominal control over the running of the school.[2] To acquire 'voluntary-aided' status the school had to meet half the costs of modernization, whereupon they retained control over appointment of staff, religious instruction and the secular curriculum. This last autonomy is currently very much constrained by the need to conform to the National Curriculum.

The 1944 Act does not stipulate that only Christian churches or groups in Britain may apply for voluntary-aided status for their schools. In fact Jewish schools have been established through this procedure and it is through this legislation that Muslim (and to a lesser extent Sikh and Hindu) groups are seeking state funding for their schools. The financial benefits are considerable; the Department for Education may make discretionary grants of up to 85 per cent of the cost of the original purchase and extension of the buildings and must pay 85 per cent of subsequent external repairs and alterations. Staff are paid by the local education authority.

There are more 'aggressively' secular systems of schooling in other parts of the world such as the USA and France. In the USA religious groups can and do influence the curriculum (for example over the issue of evolution) but all the props of religion are absent by law. On the other hand in Britain there is the continuing danger that the role of the Church and the role of religion in our schools will be determined more by accident than design. For much of this century the role of the Church in schooling has been given little attention; however, the clear intention of the 1988 Education Reform Act is to reinforce the specifically Christian roots of the education system. This has repercussions for the British Muslim community.

Muslim schools

The discourses of multiculturalism and antiracism are major influences in any debate about effective education for Muslim students in the British context and need some basic exploration at this point. An analysis of multi-cultural/antiracist initiatives to date can usefully be categorized in several distinct phases, all of which have been extensively written about. These phases are:

1 the assimilationist phase of the 1960s (Coard 1971; Townsend and Brittan 1973; Verma and Bagley 1975; Mullard 1985; Halstead 1988);
2 the integrationist model of the 1970s which attempted to shift the emphasis of thought and policy away from cultural imperatives and towards political integration from a position of expected equality (Mullard 1985);
3 the refined version of this integrationist model which came to be known in the late 1980s as cultural pluralism/multiculturalism.

By the end of the 1980s the efficacy of multicultural education was being challenged from many perspectives (Walkling 1980; Little and Willey 1981; Craft and Bardell 1984; Tomlinson 1984; Troyna and Carrington 1987; Rex 1989; Verma 1989). The antiracist argument for a 'stronger' version of multiculturalism went beyond its focus on self-identity, ethnic culture and family background to the roots of racism by examining the operation of unequal power relations and the role of institutions. Students were encouraged to understand the historical processes of colonialism and immigration as a means of understanding contemporary British 'multicultural' society, and antiracist policies were developed by some local authorities, such as the now disbanded Inner London Education Authority (ILEA). Such policies were implemented against the backdrop of a progressive centralization of power and subversion of local democracy culminating in the abolition of the Greater London Council by central government in 1986 (Kavanagh 1987) and the abolition of the Inner London Education Authority in 1988 as well as other metropolitan authorities. This also coincided with a backlash to antiracism which focused on the discourse of citizenship, fuelled by the New Right, the New Left and disquiet from parents.

The 1980s in Britain also saw the publication of several major reports such as the *Rampton Report* on underachievement (1981) and the *Swann Report* on the education of children from minority groups (1985). Four years later came the *Macdonald Report, Murder in the Playground* (1989) resulting from the inquiry into the murder of Ahmed Iqbal Ullah by a white boy in the playground of Burnage High School, Manchester. Between these reports there were incidents such as the Dewsbury affair when 22 parents refused to send their children to the school selected by their local authority because it was predominantly attended by Asian children. A year of legal actions led the authority to conclude that it had not correctly followed certain statutory requirements, and the children were admitted to the predominantly white school of their parents' choice. These reports and incidents attracted a great deal of media attention (Rattansi 1992), some of which was directed at 'loony left councils'. The Conservative government of the time used this as sufficient justification for a series of moves to centralize power through the Education Reform Act and the National Curriculum and the abolition of larger metropolitan local education authorities including the Inner London Education Authority. These policies were implemented at precisely the time when local powers to implement such policies were being undermined by the assault on antiracism, legitimated and partly fuelled by the media offensive initiated by the New Right.

While the multicultural/antiracist debate has been subjected to continuous reappraisal, particularly since the implementation of the 1988 Education Reform Act, to some Muslims it has meant that their religious/cultural requirements have not been adequately met in British state schools. For this reason an increasing number of Muslim schools have been established. The establishment of these schools and the debate about them is strongly influenced by the history of multicultural and antiracist education briefly considered above.

In summary, the failure of the state system to provide an Islamic education is seen by Muslims to arise largely because of the multifaith approach to religous education and other curricular areas adopted under the auspices of multiculturalism. The concern of how a minority group maintains its distinctiveness in a larger society is central to the whole issue of multiculturalism, while the rights of an individual within a group has to be yet another consideration. The debate is further complicated by the implementation of the National Curriculum, which has been interpreted as a rejection of many multicultural initiatives in favour of an implicitly Eurocentric and Christian agenda (Eggleston 1990). Campaigners for Muslim schools have challenged the efficacy of multiculturalism in enabling Muslim children to retain and develop their distinctive identity or to redress racism, highlighting the failure of multicultural initiatives to effectively address the needs of a plural society; criticisms which arguably could not be levelled at the antiracist initiatives.

As early as 1968 it was predicted that demands for 'separate' schools, as they have been dubbed by bodies such as Swann (1985), would increase (Derrick and Goodall 1968).[3] Such demands became more apparent in the late 1970s as the immigrant communities established themselves and gained the confidence to reassert their cultural and religious norms (Saifullah Khan 1977). More recently, incidents already referred to such as the Dewsbury controversy, the row over Salman Rushdie's *fatwas* and the Gulf War have all served to sharpen the community's sense of awareness of its own sense of identity and of the depth of the philosophical chasm separating Muslim culture and Islam from what is viewed as the predominantly secular and libertarian nature of contemporary British society. Such incidents have also heightened the community's sense of isolation and powerlessness. This has resulted in the formation of Muslim pressure groups (most recently the Muslim Parliament, BMMS, 1993) which have become more expert in making their voices heard.[4]

Very often such private schools have been established as local education authorities have closed single-sex schools (Nielsen 1986; Haw 1990). It is thus the issues of gender and religion/culture which have been the main thrust and impetus behind the establishment of these schools in Britain. In 1979 two local education authorities were approached by Muslim communities to establish single-sex schools (Little and Willey 1983). Such representations gathered momentum in the early 1980s with applications made to the local education authorities of Birmingham, Bradford and Kirklees.

In January 1989 it was noted that there were 15 private Muslim schools in Britain and plans to set up another 20 (Midgley 1989). A directory of schools provided by the Muslim Educational Trust in December 1989 listed 21 schools in varying degrees of establishment and permanence (Haw 1990). A further update in July/August 1991 listed 21 full-time Muslim schools or pre-schools in England. Of these 11 were secondary schools for girls. In 1996 *Al-Madaris*, the Newsletter of the Association of Muslim Schools, noted that there were 48 known full-time Muslim schools in Britain, 31 of which are members of the AMS (Association of Muslim Schools). These schools catered for approximately 1200 girls out of an estimated total population of 250,000 Muslim pupils in this country (Weston 1989; Berliner 1993).

Some of the early inspection reports on private Muslim schools revealed poor and inadequate premises, no specialist science or sports facilities, a lack of or inappropriate textbooks, and/or other equipment and staffing problems in terms of both qualifications and permanence (Haw 1995a). It was reported that one school had four head teachers in less than two years (Parkin, 1984). However, it is important to note that it is not only Muslim schools which have received such reports. Similar reports have been published about Jewish schools (see for example the report on Talmud Torah Machzikei Hadass School, Hackney, 20–4 June 1983).[5]

Bradney (1987) notes that inspection reports on these religious schools primarily relate to the suitability of the premises, competence of the teaching staff, and efficiency and suitability of the instruction provided. However, for schools set up to promote the interests of ethnic minorities or religious groups, as important are the difficult questions concerning what constitutes 'efficient and suitable education' because these 'are potentially the most contentious ones' (p. 413), for the purpose of these schools 'is to provide children with an education in a way of life which is avowedly different from the one prevalent in the UK'.

This is a key issue with respect to 'separate' schools, for it raises the complex questions not only of the purpose of education but also of the extent to which it is practical or even desirable to tailor children's education to the philosophical and religious beliefs of the parents.[6] It is also necessary to put this particular debate in the context of the education system, schools, their facilities and resources in Pakistan, for this has a bearing on the expectations Muslim parents bring from the 'parent' community to this country. A further contextual perspective that requires consideration here is the construction of 'community' and the sociocultural/religious dimensions influential in such a construction as discussed in Chapter 2 by Saeeda Shah.

There are Muslims in Britain who feel so strongly about their rights to Islamic schools and state funding that they are willing to vigorously pursue several options. One is to campaign for Muslim voluntary-aided schools. However, the assumption rarely voiced is that Muslim schools are in practice very different from existing Church schools in Britain, taking their religious mission much more seriously and promoting fundamentalism and indoctrination in the classroom. Generally, opposition to these schools is voiced on two grounds:

1 that their establishment encourages a racial and cultural divide which is already worryingly deep for, unlike other denominational schools, Muslim schools cater for a predominantly visible minority;
2 such schools reduce the educational opportunities available to Muslim girls because it is believed that they reflect a cultural tradition which relegates them to an inferior position and gives them a substandard education aimed at a preparation for a life of domesticity and motherhood only.

Consequently some of the questions asked of these schools include: first, are they a reaction to discrimination, conflict and educational failure? and secondly, are they a fundamentalist means of empowerment and strength which will crystallize the racial, cultural and religious issues separating some Muslims from the white indigenous British population?

It is a complex debate not least because the issue of 'race' is inextricably involved in the question of these schools and voluntary-aided status, despite the fact that Muslims themselves wish it were otherwise. It could be suggested that local authorities would be in breach of the Race Relations Act 1976 if they sanctioned voluntary-aided Muslim schools, because this would effectively be segregating on racial lines, as these schools are normally located in areas where a large number of the children are ethnically Pakistani. Section 1(2) of the Act deems this to be unfavourable treatment. Further, it is argued that such schools would militate against the need to 'promote equality of opportunity and good relations between persons of different racial groups'. But within race relations legislation there is also the issue of 'one class of people' being treated less favourably than another, and arguably this is happening to Muslims over the issue of voluntary-aided schools. It has prompted the Commission for Racial Equality to state:

> **In line with the Race Relations Act 1976,** so long as existing arrangements for granting voluntary status are in force, no application from a minority faith school should be given less favourable treatment, either by an education authority or by the Department of Education and Science, than any other application. Any decision or application must be made on non-racial grounds.
>
> (CRE 1990: 22, emphasis added)

The Commission for Racial Equality also cites the 1944 Education Act. This allows for any religious group to establish voluntary-aided schools. Section 76 states: 'The minister and local education authorities shall have regard to the general principle that . . . pupils are to be educated in accordance with the wishes of their parents.' However, this clause does goes on to say that this is to be consistent with efficient expenditure of public monies, and this has been used to justify a failure to respond to parents' wishes.

The Islamia Primary School, Brent, North London won permission in principle to seek voluntary-aided status in June 1986 (Haw 1990). It then took three more years to obtain planning approval for necessary extensions, only for it to be refused such status in May 1990 by the Conservative government of the time (Lodge 1990a,b). The case went to appeal but was finally lost in August 1993 on the grounds of surplus places in the primary schools within a two mile radius of the Islamia school (*British Muslims Monthly Survey*, 1993, Vol. 1, No. 8).

The Muslim Girls' Community School Bradford, now Feversham College, was also unsuccessful in its application for voluntary-aided status in early 1995. There were two reasons given: first, its failure to provide an adequate information technology curriculum, and secondly, that the accommodation on the present site did not meet required standards (*BMMS*, Vol. IV, No.9). In its favour it had and has: the backing of the local authority; suitable premises; a long waiting list; stability; a satisfactory and improving academic reputation; and over-subscription of local schools in certain areas. The school re-applied for voluntary-aided status early in 1997. There are also other Muslim schools which have either applied or are contemplating an application depending on advice from the Association of Muslim Schools,[7] and with regard to these applications there are those who believe that it is only a matter of time before such status is granted to one or more of these schools.

This is the context for the debate about Muslim girls' schools. As already mentioned it is a complex debate and one which has tended to be dominated by academics and the media rather than those who have established or worked in these schools themselves. The last section of this chapter seeks to redress this imbalance through the 'voice' of Maria Hanifa talking about the establishment of the school that participated in the research and her vision for Muslim girls' schools in Britain.

Establishing a Muslim girls' school: the debate from the 'inside' – Maria Hanifa

I was not employed in the school when it was first established but I have talked with the governors about the establishment of the school. It was not in response to one particular event or events, although there were some incidents which perhaps ensured that it would be established. The governing body as a group had been thinking about establishing a school from the mid-1970s and it was eventually brought into being in the early 1980s. It was established in response to a strongly felt need in some sections of the Muslim community in the locality. As with many major events it eventually happened because of one individual. At the time he was part of the Muslim Association in this area and had a secondary school-age daughter. He was told to look for a suitable building. Once such premises had been found, the building was bought by the Association about a year before the school was opened. A lot of work had to be done on the building to make it safe.

We still have two girls' schools in the area, one a state school where I have already worked and the other a Catholic school. The state school is 95 per cent Asian and we have other schools that are virtually 100 per cent Asian. There is the option of persuading such schools to 'opt out' and become more Muslim, but our people are still not familiar with the education system. To some extent they are also afraid of doing it because they feel that they will come under attack straight away. Setting up this school was a risk. Although its establishment cannot be ascribed to any particular events it was set up during a time of tension. There was the Rushdie affair. At the time some of the comments from my colleagues, from the general public, from the press amazed me. The hatred, the tension, all those stereotypes came to the surface.

During 1984 and 1985 there was also another debate about whether five inner city schools should become Muslim schools. The Muslim community was not aware of the implications of this or what was possible. Governing bodies at that time had all the power. They could have easily taken over the mainstream girls' school that I was working in, but somehow even my own community had the perception that with such a change the standard would drop. But education is a three-way process. There need to be good teachers, good students, and encouragement. You can do your best but if there is no encouragement from home, from the parents, there will be a problem. I think with Muslim schools that is one of the hurdles that still has to be overcome.

Once the school was established, parents used to ask about the qualifications of the teaching staff and their background. They wanted non-Muslim teachers; a non-Muslim, white teacher would be better than a Muslim teacher. I am very pleased to say that now this does not matter. We have overcome that. People never ask who the staff members are, but in 1989 parents would ask. They were putting their daughters in your hands and they wanted to make sure that everything was the best. Part of the difference is that now there are more ethnic minority people becoming qualified as teachers.

As a Muslim girls' school we gave Muslim women an opportunity to come into school. I think that was the positive part of Muslim schools. These ladies, who would hesitate to go into mainstream schools, managed to come in; not only to come in, but to complain. They were not always happy. They would come in and question. They were taking an interest and were aware of what was happening in the school. They found the confidence and courage to come into school. There were two reasons for this. First, because they now found an Asian woman as head teacher and it was easier to have a conversation with her, especially if they did not speak English well. Secondly, we adopted a policy that we were not only educating the students but their mothers as well on the importance of education for their daughters. At our first parents' evening I remember six mothers sitting around a teacher asking about their daughters. There was no privacy; that concept of one-to-one consultation had to be developed over time. They felt quite relaxed and easy, sitting around the teacher asking about their daughters. It was something which I enjoyed, it was a lovely family atmosphere. They brought our different cultural values into the school. I think some of the non-Muslim teachers found it difficult. The mothers would go and sit in the staff room, so the staff had no privacy, but they had a right to come in. That was the best part.

There was also the media. They were there because of the Salman Rushdie story and the Gulf War. Being from a Muslim community the spotlight was on us, especially on our school. We made the decision that we would give interviews and I think it helped. People got to know that we existed. It was important. We played a political game. The media were presenting a very stereotypical picture and they were presenting it anyway, so we decided that we should take part in the debate. We were very careful not to take sides in those issues outside of school. Our stand was that we were an educational institution so we would talk about what we did in school but not beyond that. We have people within the community who agree and people within the community who disagree, so we were not going to appear to be taking sides. There were some reports and programmes which were more balanced than others, which did not undermine us as schools. They showed both sides, the problems of the Muslim community, but made no judgements. Other programmes were very negative.

We are now established in this country. Now if we see an opportunity we take it, whereas those people who first migrated here sat back. They did not know the language, they did not know the system. What is happening now is that we are saying, this is our right. We are British citizens. The school was established through the will and determination of the local Muslim community with no outside help or advice. They raised the finance, they bought the building, they maintain it. The fees we charge have never covered our outgoings. The majority of the students come from families where there is unemployment or whose parents are in low status employment.

I also feel that we live in a society which is increasingly secular, moving away from religious values. If you are a believer it can put you in a very difficult situation in explaining to your peer groups the need for prayer and why you are going to do it. It puts an extra strain on Muslim students. Muslim schools are able to give their students a positive image of a faith.

When an ordinary girl from a subcontinental family enters a mainstream school in Britain she moves into an environment that is alien to her. There is a big gap between the system of the home and that of the outside world. It takes a lot of adjustment to understand and adapt to these new surroundings. This inevitably leaves an impression on her mind which puts pressure on her abilities and potential. The first generation who arrived here three decades ago had to struggle physically and intellectually to adjust to this new and strange style of living which was so very different from their cultural traditions and religion. When our parents and grandparents speak of their experiences they show sadness and hurt in their facial expressions; a child of 5 or 6 though cannot explain *their* feelings. They are left with permanent scars and weighty memories in their subconscious which may have profound effects on their future.

We are now in the unfortunate position that a large section of the Muslim community has spent most of its energy in the process of earning basic needs and has not, until relatively recently, thought about or even felt the need to educate their daughters so that they can be equipped for a better future. To facilitate this, not only individual but also collective effort is needed.

These parents were themselves the victims of the system. They have been caught in the current of the stream; many have drowned while only a few have survived to reach the river bank. Most Muslims in Britain, instead of being determined to encourage and praise their daughters for their achievements, instil a strange fear in their minds. From the time of their first tentative steps outside the home these girls are made to feel that the education they will receive is going to harm them, as if there are unknown factors and forces which they will be unable to comprehend. As a result, the girls feel fearful and afraid and thus dread entering the system. This trepidation does not allow the space and freedom for them to develop as strong, appreciative Muslim girls.

The Muslim community in Britain has set up many organizations under political, religious and professional umbrellas. However, there are very few organizations in existence which actually encourage positive thinking and guidance. Mosques and *madrasahs* are set up in terraced houses to give instruction to our youngsters but sadly, due to lack of educational training, few basic resources and a limited knowledge of English (which does not meet with the expectations of children born and brought up in Britain), the teachers' expertise is neither acknowledged nor appreciated by the pupils. The pupils cannot relate to these teachers and surroundings, especially when they are compared with the relatively high standard of the facilities in the state school system. This initiates and catalyses a lack of interest in their Islamic studies; any learning that does take place under the sorry conditions of most *madrasahs* is often short-lived and is either easily forgotten or is put to the back of the mind and regarded as simply not worth remembering. These are the opinions of young teenage girls when they are provided with an informal atmosphere and frank, open and free discussion can take place. They ridicule the *madrasah* system and cannot find anything positive to say about it.

I feel that Muslim parents, no matter which part of the world they come from, need to move away from the third world, third grade mentality. They need to think in a positive, dynamic, missionary way that is truly Islamic. Such parents want to give a good education to their girls using modern methods and tomorrow's technology. They need to provide facilities which are of the highest standard, a pure environment reflecting the Islamic way of life, and teaching staff who are familiar not only with religious knowledge but also with politics and world affairs.

The Muslim *Ummah* should make a new start and, instead of creating new issues for themselves, should expend energy, effort and money in an organized manner to obtain moral support and economic help from society at large. The establishment of a Muslim school on a small scale does not solve the whole problem: from a population of two million Muslims, the fact that a few hundred girls obtain GCSEs or A levels is not a great achievement. Such results (although individually commendable) are a drop in the ocean and do not even begin to address the task in hand.

In the past, many protests and meetings have been held but still, in the whole country, British Muslims have yet to run one girls' school to its full potential so that it can serve as an example to all. The time has come for Muslims to realize the need to educate girls, but the message will take time to sink in: many Muslim parents still only want their daughters to stay at school until the statutory age of 16. However, in the not too distant future even GCSE and A level qualifications will be considered mere stepping stones to good education. Is it not possible for a few Muslims in Britain to come forward and give female education the status of *Jihad* so that the enormous gap existing at the moment can be bridged? This should be an issue discussed by *Imams* in all mosques.

For Muslim girls it is essential to have single-sex schools and, more importantly, Muslim schools providing a stable Islamic ethos if they are to receive a truly good education. Good quality Muslim schools must be established in cities which have a sizeable Muslim community. These schools should match the standard of mainstream education; Muslims and non-Muslims alike should be satisfied that the infrastructure of the Muslim schools makes it possible for them to provide the best for their pupils.

Parents must be convinced that it is a requirement not only of English law to educate girls but also of Islam itself. Our inspiration should be the saying of Prophet Muhammad (peace and blessings be upon him): 'Seeking knowledge is obligatory upon every Muslim.'[8] 'Muslim' in this case refers to both male and female. We need dedication and determination. Without such commitment it is difficult to achieve first class facilities. Let us work towards the future of our nation and invest in our children.

In England most of the Muslim schools (of which there are only a handful, perhaps 44 or so) are in converted accommodation. There are therefore immediate limitations on what they can achieve. Despite such limits, progress has been made. These prototypes give direction and guidance to other schools so that they can expand, develop and improve on the existing model. By building on this foundation we can accomplish our main aim: that is, to provide the best education for our young girls within the guidelines of

Islam. Muslim schools do not offer the dimension of religion alone; they foster strong faith, moral values, a sense of responsibility for the family unit, and confidence in individual girls to participate as full and equal members of society.

In such institutions Muslim girls are encouraged to express their religious convictions without fear and they set a positive example. They have given young girls confidence so that by the time they leave school they are good judges of right and wrong, not only on a superficial level but also with a deeper appreciation of life and its aims. There is within Muslim schools an environment where the extension of knowledge makes them aware, and makes them appreciate the existence, of *Allah*.

Muslim schools encourage academic achievement so that students can gain solid qualifications to enable them to pursue suitable careers. Girls must have the opportunity to study all subject areas in order to broaden their experience. English is important in Muslim schools and is the main language of communication. Students should be encouraged to master the language and study it in depth to examination level. Literature should be taught up to A level standard. Arabic, French and Urdu can also be taught so that students can communicate well and develop qualities of tolerance and acceptance of diversity. Students attending Muslim schools come from diverse cultural backgrounds and are multilingual; this enriches the school and strengthens the bond of sisterhood in Islam.

In spite of all the limitations and hardships, Muslim schools have undoubtedly accomplished much. Their communities praise *Allah, subhanahu wa ta ala*, for giving them the strength to initiate this process. Parental involvement is often 100 per cent, unlike in many state schools. This is because the parents identify with the Islamic ethos of the school and can thus blend into the school environment with ease. They participate in functions to raise funds for the school and other worthy causes. This develops the sense of unity that we must care for others as part of a global society.

Although the state schools provide up-to-date technology, without a sense of belonging and peace of mind, active learning cannot take place. Muslim schools provide such an environment and there are fewer pressures on the girls to conform to different standards of 'normality'. The provision of educational opportunities for Muslim girls is a vitally important issue. I believe that the Muslim *Ummah* has the means and ability to provide such facilities. May *Allah* help us to do so and grant us success.

I have now moved as head teacher to set up a new Muslim girls' school. It is small and is starting out with all the disadvantages of my old school. At the moment we are using the facilities of the local mosque. This is not satisfactory. There are no proper classrooms or desks although we have had the financial support to buy textbooks and other resources. We are in negotiations with the local authority for more suitable premises, and this should mean better physical conditions in the not too distant future. I attend many meetings, the work is exhausting, and I am trying to convince the same types of people of the same things all over again. The local community and the students are committed, enthusiastic and hard-working; the school deserves to succeed because of them.

Conclusion

This last section has focused on one particular Muslim girls' school and the vision of one Muslim teacher for the education of Muslim girls in Britain. Overall the chapter has highlighted four points: first, that the cultural and religious needs of Muslim children are approached in an *ad hoc* and pragmatic way. Those needs of Muslim children which are accommodated in state schools in Britain are seen as 'goodwill' gestures in a balancing act which aims to offset and deflect the accommodation of those needs which equal opportunities initiatives have failed to address. Second, the aims of Islamic education fit clearly into the religious category legislated for by the 1944 Education Act. Third, it highlights the extent to which Islamic education conflicts with contemporary British educational practices and objectives. Fourth, the discourses of multiculturalism and antiracism are major influences in the debate about effective education for Muslim students in the British context.

The problem for western society is, as Walkling and Brannigan point out: 'Sexism can be, in theory, rooted in beliefs which are among the most strongly held and which are crucial to cultural identity. That is, they can be the very sort of belief which those of us who value a multi-cultural society think that minorities have a right to preserve' (Walkling and Brannigan 1986: 22). This pinpoints the apparently conflicting ideals between antisexist and multicultural education in the demand for an education which satisfies the requirement for equal opportunities for women but which gives due recognition to the special status accorded to the moral education of women in some cultures. Specifically, it argues that antiracists, by accepting demands from some sections of the Muslim community for single-sex and denominational schools, could be seen as inhibiting the emancipation of Muslim girls.

Antiracists argue that the cultural focus of multiculturalism necessarily brings about this contradiction. For Troyna and Carrington (1987) the central issue is the need to discover what factors have promoted a growth in the demand, by various black minority groups, for educational provision outside the mainstream of state education. In their opinion, addressing this problem entails a concern with the prevalence of racial harassment in maintained schools and the failure to institutionalize antiracist and antisexist education in those settings. They ask the question: 'Is it surprising that some Muslim parents espouse the rhetoric of separatism when multicultural/antiracist, and it would seem anti-sexist education policies, are not worth the paper they are written on?' (Troyna and Carrington 1987: 64).

The argument here is that antiracism's focus on 'power' (economic, political, structural, institutional) through a sophisticated theoretical approach to 'race', class and gender potentially offers a route out of the dilemma of multiculturalism's cultural relativism.

Parental choice based on the desire to maintain a religious or cultural tradition is not illegal, but opinions are sharply divided on its acceptability. The Muslim case for separate schools rests on the argument that multiculturalism presents all cultures in a superficial way and that this is particularly objectionable when the culture is seen to be an expression of its religion. Some Muslims regard 'separate' schools as essential not only for the religious instruction of their children but indeed for their cultural survival.

In this debate over Muslims in British state schools and Muslim schools and voluntary-aided status, three things are very clear: first, the importance of maintaining a religious and cultural identity; second, the importance of an understanding of the concept of a Muslim, Pakistani immigrant community in Britain through an understanding of the factors and processes contributing to its constructions and how this affects attitudes to education in Britain; third, the preference for single-sex schooling for their daughters as a priority (Anwar 1982; Iqra Trust 1991; Mabud 1992). It is this last issue, that of single-sex schooling in the contemporary British context, which is the subject of the next chapter.

Notes

1 For more detailed discussions in this area see Haw 1994, 1995a.
2 It is important to note that not all voluntary schools are denominational.
3 It should be noted here that the term is one that is much objected to by some Muslims because of its connotations of separation and isolation (The Islamic Academy 1985).
4 For an example of a meeting of the Muslim Parliament see *British Muslim Monthly Survey*, Vol. II, No. 11, December 1994.
5 The irony of this is that while there are still no Muslim voluntary aided schools there are Jewish voluntary aided schools. The last Jewish school to be granted voluntary aided status was the Hasmonean Jewish school in Barnet which was granted this status in March 1993. The Islamia school in Brent was refused such status in August 1993 on the grounds that were too many surplus places in neighbouring schools (*BMMS*, August 1994, Vol. II, No. 7). It is also reported that two more Jewish schools in Barnet have been given backing by the local authority to apply for voluntary aided status (*Jewish Chronicle*, 8 July 1994).
6 Britain is a signatory to international and European treaties concerning the wishes of parents and the education of their children which are not incorporated into British domestic law. However, there is an implication that British legislation is consistent with these undertakings (Jacobs 1975; Beddard 1980; Robertson 1982). For a further discussion of these legal aspects see Haw 1994; 1995a.
7 This information was provided by replies to my postal survey which promised confidentiality. I am therefore unable to name particular schools.
8 *Sunan Ibn Majah* and *Mishkat Al-Masabih*.

4 Gender, Islam and single-sex schooling

Kaye Haw

Introduction

Feminists have questioned whether girls benefit from co-education and whether more serious consideration should be given to the single-sex alternative (see Deem 1984; Burgess 1990; Faulkner 1991). Single-sex schooling has also become one of the most persistent demands of Muslims in this country ever since they became numerous enough to make their voices heard (see Anwar 1981; Nielsen 1986). The purpose of this chapter is to provide a review of Muslim and feminist responses to education generally and to single-sex education in particular, for it is in this area that this research is specifically located.

The question is in effect a complex one revolving around the ethos and philosophies guiding the educational practices in both Muslim girls' schools and state maintained girls' schools; who teaches in such schools; and what is being taught. The chapter deals with three themes. The first theme explores differing feminisms and how they locate themselves in the wider and general context of education. The second theme examines feminisms and Islam; and the third theme concludes the section with a consideration of Muslim and feminist responses to the debate over co-education versus single-sex schooling.

Feminisms and education

Feminism has a long history and many different perspectives weave their way through it. The purpose here is to give a brief overview of that history and to concentrate on a particular aspect of feminist theory – that relating to education. It specifically considers how different feminisms relate to differing theories and approaches to the education of girls. This is necessarily an overview because a detailed consideration of the wealth of contemporary international work on feminist epistemology, and current debate, would itself demand a separate book. These debates reflect the broader fundamental feminist concerns of patriarchy, capitalism, power relationships, biology, the body, physical strength and violence, sexuality and sexual violence.

Before highlighting the fragmentations of feminism in relation to education, the commonalities which thread their way through these feminisms are discussed. This relates back to the philosophical considerations discussed in Chapter 1: that there are times when commonalities are more important than differences and vice versa.

First, all feminisms are concerned with women and girls. What unites them is an emphasis on how central gender divisions are to the organization of society and its mode of operation.

Second, Griffiths (1995b) argues that all these feminist epistemologies have a moral/political stance with 'values' and 'power' as organizing concepts, and have been developed in response to the disempowerment of women which forms the basis of other epistemologies. The concern of feminists is that those in positions of power define the knowledge against which all other constructs of knowledge are measured. Further, for all feminists, politics and values must precede epistemology. This is where analysis begins, because feminism is not just about theory, it is about our day-to-day lives and realities. It is of significance:

> . . . because there is a prevailing sexism in and out of formal educational institutions, schools, universities, local authorities, governing bodies, government departments, educational publishing and voluntary pressure groups. It distorts educational practices and educational outcomes. Inevitably it also distorts how we (all of us) understand – i.e. research – them in order to improve them. This is precisely the concern of feminist epistemology: how to improve knowledge and remove sexist distortions.
> (Griffiths 1995b: 219)

This relates to a third uniting factor identified by Griffiths, that of the importance of self or subjectivity. She argues that none of the feminist epistemologies assume that there is an 'objective', 'view from nowhere' or a 'God's eye view', and all assume the self or subjectivity is a starting point in the collective enterprise of formulating a usually feminist perspective. This is evidenced in the work of Irigaray, Code, Haraway, Harding, Seller, Young, hooks and Walkerdine (Griffiths 1995b). These commonalities provide the starting point for charting the development of feminist discourses within and about British education. They correspond to Weiner's three dimensions of feminism, which are:

political – a movement to improve the conditions and life-chances for girls and women;

critical – a sustained intellectual critique of dominant (male) forms of knowing and doing;

praxis-orientated – concerned with the development of more ethical forms of professional and personal practice.

(Weiner 1994: 7–8)

The importance of these similarities needs to be kept in mind while different feminist perspectives on education are considered. These differing feminist discourses are not only theoretically significant but they also affect views about educational outcomes and strategies for change. Measor and Sikes (1992) identify three areas which distinguish different feminist approaches to education. These are: the causes of women's oppression and their concept of patriarchy; strategies for change; the goal for society. Each of these areas has different effects on the study of education.[1]

The following account necessarily reduces and distils different feminist theoretical approaches to education through categorization. This was less problematical in the 1970s and 1980s when Jaggar (1988) identified four different kinds of white, western feminism: liberal, Marxist, radical, and socialist. However, the 1990s have witnessed a merging and multi-positioning of these perspectives in the light of post-structuralist and post-modernist influences so that theorists can often be located as easily at one end of one perspective as at the other end of another perspective, depending on the particular educational issue under consideration. These trends can be clearly traced in academic texts concerned with educational issues, especially if their date of publication is noted. In 1987 Arnot and Weiner identified three feminist perspectives which, they argued, had made the most impact on education: they termed these 'Equal Rights in Education' (liberal feminism), 'Patriarchal Relations' (radical feminism) and 'Class, Race and Gender: Structures and Ideologies' (Marxist/socialist feminism), this last perspective being a merging of Jaggar's categorization. The aims of each of these perspectives differ somewhat in their emphasis, which is directly linked to their differing identification of the cause of gender inequalities or oppression, as highlighted by Measor and Sikes.

In spite of recent developments these feminist discourses remain influential. Liberal feminists deny the importance of both capitalist and patriarchal structures and processes in education. Liberal feminism has also arguably been the most enduring and accepted of all feminisms, being associated with the emergence of liberal individualism and Protestantism at the time of the Enlightenment (at the end of the eighteenth and beginning of the nineteenth centuries) and based on the ideas of natural rights, justice and democracy. The assertion is that individual women should be enabled to determine their social, political and educational roles, and that any laws, traditions or activities that inhibit equal rights and opportunities should be abolished. Access to education is a basic premise of this perspective, as it claims that by providing equal education for both sexes, an environment would be created in which each individual's potential could be developed and encouraged. For liberal feminists equality is achievable by democratic reforms, without the need for revolutionary changes in political, economic or cultural life. Many of the equal opportunity initiatives considered in later chapters of this book are rooted in this liberal, egalitarian position. Methods for realizing these goals include the eradication of institutional sexism through the development of a legal framework to ensure equality of access in educational settings; the development of equal opportunities policies in schools; the encouragement of girls to move into male dominated areas of the curriculum; and the employment of more women in senior educational positions so that they realize their potential at work and in public as well as private life.

The remaining three perspectives that I have highlighted are based on the concept of 'oppression'. Marxist feminism attempts to incorporate ideas about women's oppression and patriarchal relationships into classic Marxism, focusing in particular on the relationship between production and reproduction with reference to the economic, the social and the biological; the interrelationship of capitalism and patriarchy; and the complex interplay between gender, culture and society (see for example Barrett 1980; Davis 1981; Segal 1987). Accordingly, patriarchy has a materialist and historical basis in that capitalism is founded on a patriarchal division of labour. Marxist strategies for change revolve round the liberation of the working class so that capitalism is replaced with a socialist system where the means of production belong to everybody. The oppression of women will then disappear simultaneously. The importance of this perspective in educational terms is the emphasis that it places on class and gender relationships, but its theoretical complexities and its roots in the Marxist analysis of society which is critiqued for being 'gender blind' mean that it has failed to attract large numbers of women to its political position, especially since the demise of other Marxisms in the late 1980s.

Socialist feminists have tried to take account of this criticism while holding on to the basic insights that Marxism offers. They suggest that both patriarchy and capitalism are interwoven, both serving the needs of the other, and that both must be defeated. While acknowledging that we need to know about gender discrimination in school, socialist and Marxist feminists insist that we cannot fully understand the problem without taking account of the whole social context and the class system. As far as education is concerned, research and strategies for change are therefore directed at the interface of gender and class inequality.

Socialist feminists in particular argue that working class girls are disadvantaged at school because they undergo the experience of class inequality and also receive messages about their subordination to men. The division of labour is a crucial factor in socialist feminist theory. They suggest that schools direct a range of messages about appropriate roles and activities to girls and thereby occupy a central place in reproducing the division of labour across generations. In the belief that both working-class girls and boys resist middle-class values imposed in schools, research in this area is directed at deviance (see Hargreaves 1967; Lacey 1970; Willis 1977 for work on boys; and McRobbie and Garber 1976; Llewellyn 1980; Davies 1984 for work on girls).

Radical feminists argue that patriarchy predates capitalism, so that two key ideas in radical feminism are that patriarchy is of overarching importance and also that the personal is political. Sexuality is a crucial issue for radical feminists because they argue that personal and sexual relationships are tainted by an underlying power imbalance and therefore need to be changed. This has led to a re-evaluation of the traditional values of femininity so that women's biology, especially their childbearing capacities, is seen as a potential source of liberation. Initially radical feminists focused on different varieties of male sexual domination (pornography, prostitution, sexual harassment and violence against women) and fought politically against these issues, while more recently the focus has been on the traditional female role (Burris 1973; Daly 1978; Rich 1980; Dworkin 1981; Eisenstein 1984; London Lesbian Offensive Group 1984; Morgan 1984; Bunch 1987; Rowland 1987; Kadar 1988).

The concern of radical feminists is to analyse the way patriarchy is reinforced in schools so it concentrates on the power relationships between girls and boys in school and it seeks to make the educational experiences of women more central to the education of girls. The present curriculum, whether taught by women or not, is therefore a target for change in the need to create a knowledge base that illuminates the experiences of women. Another objective is the establishment of organizations designed to meet the needs of girls, to help them achieve their potential and make full use of their educational achievements while not denigrating the work of their mothers, friends and women in the community.

Radical feminism has attempted to clarify the nature of patriarchal relations in education, looking particularly at the links between male power, sexual violence, masculinity and femininity and sexuality in the context of education. More recently it has been concerned not only to bring out into the open facts about the verbal, physical and sexual harassment experienced by girls in mixed schools, but also to highlight the problem of male sexuality (see Jones and Mahony 1989).

Black feminism in particular has been responsible for causing feminists to re-evaluate their thinking. As far as education is concerned, black feminists have been responsible for highlighting the endemic nature of both racism and sexism by concentrating on exposing the pathologization of black family culture and fracturing the widely held stereotypes of black femininity. This has been achieved through explorations of the actual experiences of black girls in educational establishments (see Amos and Parmar 1984; Mirza 1992), the racism and sexism of teaching staff (Wright 1987) and the construction of black students as problems (Williams 1987). In particular black feminists have been concerned that by distinguishing between 'race' and gender in education and treating them as a duality black girls have been rendered invisible.

In 1992 Measor and Sikes catalogued four main feminist perspectives – liberal, radical, socialist, and psychoanalytic, while in 1988 Tong identified seven – liberal, Marxist, radical, psychoanalytic, socialist, existentialist and postmodernist feminisms. Arnot and Weiner (1987) were rightly criticized for marginalizing black feminism and lesbian feminism so that in 1994 Weiner, now adopting a post-structural analysis of feminisms in education, discusses these as well as Christian feminism, humanist feminism, Muslim feminism and eco-feminism. These have all emerged as feminism has become more fractured. These feminisms are interwoven with, and complementary to, the feminisms that have been highlighted; in particular, liberal and radical feminism, which have permeated and influenced the British school curriculum and educational practices more generally.

At this time other feminisms appear to have had less impact on education, although post-structuralism, principally through the work of Walkerdine, has become influential in Britain. The interest in the way that discourse operates as a 'normalizing' process in which knowledge and power are connected, and the prioritization of the local, it is argued, mean that it is possible to create a 'counter-discourse', thus creating alternative ways to say the 'unsayable'. Strategies for change involve students being encouraged to develop a critical awareness of their positioning in educational discourses. This is a focus of this book. It has been discussed briefly in Chapter 1 and is discussed more fully through the analysis of the data in Chapters 6, 7 and 8. More importantly, it is a thread which weaves its way through this entire work.

I have already pointed out the weaknesses of categorization and its constituent problems, but this analysis outlines how feminism has shifted over the past two decades and how this has impacted with education and educational issues. At the beginning of the section I emphasized the commonality running through these different feminisms, which is the concern to understand what has caused women's subordination. All these theoretical understandings are dependent on ideological and political value positions. Feminism is about resistance to any one dominant discourse, but the distinctions are helpful when examining the positionings of gender and Islam and when assessing the compatibility of Muslim and feminist arguments for single-sex schools, which are the main considerations of the following sections in this chapter.

Feminisms and Islam

All religions are open to political, ideological and symbolic interpretations which are fluid and shifting. This is also true for Islam, a religion and a 'way of life'. Where Muslim women are concerned, racialized discourses articulate with those of gender and religion in their social representation. These change over time so that what was politically and socially expedient for one generation living in and through a particular context is not the same for another. Through these shifts the 'oriental female', especially the Muslim woman, has come to occupy a position of the 'other' in the discursive space surrounding the long history of orientalisms (see Said 1978; Kabbani 1986). Historically she has been and is represented as exoticized and ruthlessly oppressed and in need of liberation; as guardian and guarded; as victim/emblem of religious fundamentalism, as custodian of religious beliefs, even though for centuries it has been men who have been the interpreters of norms, values and practices according to that belief; as reflecting the religious and cultural commitment of the group in her attire and behaviour; as the bearer of 'races' and cultures which are constructed as inherently threatening to western civilizations (Afshar 1994).

Through these constructions of their identity as 'other', Muslim women have needed to negotiate different arrangements with the patriarchal structures within which they have been positioned, because when Muslim communities go through periods of instability it is disempowered groups who have to submit to greater degrees of suppression (Kandiyoti 1991). In Islam this suppression is achieved through claims for the necessity to adhere to absolute laws embedded in the text of the Qur'an.[2] Not all Muslim women are equally affected because there are divisions, as always, along class, cultural, national and traditional lines, with old high status and wealthy families using their position and/or wealth as a means of negotiation with the dominant power. For most Muslim women it is these changing circumstances, this ebb and flow in the fortunes of Muslim communities, that they have had to negotiate and which the young generation of Muslim women growing up in this country are now confronting.

Reflecting its own dilemma as a movement of 'sisterhood' in the 1970s and 1980s, western feminisms have been forced to debate long and hard concerning the position of Muslim women. In the middle 1980s Ramazanoglu neatly summed this up when she stated:

> There is great difficulty in steering interpretation of these arguments between the Scylla of cultural relativism (Muslim women cannot be judged to be oppressed when they are simply celebrating the Muslim way of life – the western concept of autonomy is irrelevant to their culture) and the Charybdis of positive truth (we know Muslim women are oppressed even if they do not, because we possess universal criteria of oppression, external to Islam, which identify veiling, the celebration of motherhood and cliterodectomy as oppressive).
>
> (Ramazanoglu 1986: 259)

Such debates, coupled with the critique of white western feminisms by black feminisms, have meant that the more recent discourses of new ethnicities and feminisms have opened up discursive space for Muslim women. In this space Muslim women have been enabled to explore what it means to be Muslim women, some of whom live as a minority in western societies, and to express the difficulties of finding new ways to negotiate between the unacceptable extremes contained in the above quote.

This has meant that from the mid 1980s there have been a number of works in English or translated into English on the predicament and the possibilities for Muslim women. The consensus of this literature confirms the position of Muslim women as the site of unprecedented struggle within Islam, as well as the considerable resistance to the condemnation by western observers of aspects of Islamic culture such as veiling, female circumcision and family laws.[3] In this respect western scholarship is seen as having little to offer Muslim women either in understanding their situation or in suggesting solutions. Collectively these works assert the rights of Muslim women to search for the causes of women's oppression in Islamic societies while not necessarily accepting that Islam is to blame.

In their historical search for the causes of women's oppression in Islamic societies Muslim feminists have marshalled various theoretical approaches. Ramazanoglu (1986) argues that in an attempt to link the oppression of Muslim women with loosely defined conceptions of feudalism and capitalism, Marxism has been theoretically attractive to some Muslim feminists. This is particularly the case for those who have been seeking to understand historical variations in oppression and the slow transformation of Islam from a system of gender difference to one of gender oppression. The works of Hussain, Fernea, Boudhiba and El Sadaawi draw implicitly on a number of Marxist arguments but have rejected Marxism partly because of the problem of combining gender and class in accounting for women's oppression, but more especially to create a defensive stance against western social theories.

In a similar vein Ramazanoglu argues that while some Muslim feminists see liberalism as a practical means of improving women's access to education, healthcare, employment and legal rights, this view is seen to be oversimplistic on two counts. First, it does not tackle the underlying social problems of poverty, inequality, male honour (*izzat*) and the power relations which maintain female oppression. Second, western emancipation is seen to introduce new evils such as loss of social control, excessive individualism and the destruction of extended family ties, on which women depend for support and their social life and to which the west has found no solution.

Even though there is general agreement that Islam has developed on to cultural systems which are oppressive to Muslim women, there is also agreement that this was not always the case (Mernissi 1975, 1991). For those Muslim feminists who do not espouse religious fundamentalism, who reject the liberal solution as ineffectual, and who reject Marxism as culturally unacceptable, this has meant the necessity of constructing new theories to explain the oppression of Muslim women at different periods and in different societies from within Islam. This has been achieved by demonstrating the cultural and historical variations in oppression within Muslim societies; Hussain (1984), like El Sadaawi (1980), urges women to seek their own salvation within a new Islam so that equality and liberation can be achieved by 'becoming your own woman in your own province', that is, by defining complementary but non-oppressive roles for both men and women.

For some, this has meant disentangling these forms of oppression from an 'authentic' Islam so that this could provide a cultural identity for Muslims without the need to oppress women. The development of a specifically Muslim feminist theology has thus emerged as the foundation for this approach, which some would argue (Risalludin 1996) shows clearly that feminism of a distinctively Islamic nature exists and is carving out a niche for itself. Ahmed (1992), for example, presents the view of Islam as a foundationally non-sexist religion through an historical analysis of the laws and practices of the core Islamic discourses and an analysis of the role of women in early Islamic societies (see also Hassan (1995)).

Adopting a different approach, Kandiyoti argues that such debates concerning the compatibility of Islam and feminism are based on a fallacy. Religious texts, like any other texts, are vulnerable to a multiplicity of interpretations, some more, others less sympathetic to feminist concerns so that the predictable outcome of such debate is one which is based on a dualism:

> . . . we are predictably left, on the one hand, with conservative interpretations which close the door to ijtihad (interpretation) and promote a narrow and literalist understanding of the texts, and those which on the other, open up such possibilities and generate more liberal approaches, a dichotomy which has now been with us for a very long time.
>
> (Kandiyoti 1996: 10)

The way out of this 'either/or debate' is to move Islam, as a source of ideology and of regime legitimacy, from the realm of religion into the area of practical politics so that it then becomes open to inspection through the ordinary criteria used to evaluate any ruling ideology and the practices which emanate from it (Kandiyoti, 1996). Kandiyoti argues that the possibility of pluralistic outcomes for women under Islamic regimes is limited. Her conclusion 'is not derived from the assumption of an implacable fundamentalist logic, nor from the nature of religion per se'. It derives from the recognition that in an increasingly 'globalized' world where compromise and accommodation in nearly all areas of social life are essential to survival, the area of gender relations and women's conduct marks itself out as a zone of struggle for conflicting bids of power and control. For Kandiyoti the only solace is that for women and

Muslim women living under Islamic regimes, the gap between their rights and their contributions is likely to remain a continuing source of tension.

For western feminists these debates have served as a sharp and timely reminder that historical explanations of the causes of gender inequality which treated 'woman' as a universal category of the oppressed are simplistic, and that women's struggles to assert their rights needs to take place without the destruction of cultural identity. There can be no doubt that such perspectives have raised fundamental and critical issues for feminists which focus on whether it is possible to recognize oppression in general and whether it is possible to develop universal political practices to transform different societies if oppression takes culturally specific forms. While Muslim feminists do not deny the significance of sexual politics in the oppression of Muslim women, they argue that Muslim women have always engaged in other conflicts, and that there are political and economic struggles in which they may need to fight alongside Muslim men.

Muslim feminists challenge the level of generalization with which western theorists have generally approached the oppression of Muslim women. By stressing the cultural specificity of their oppression and the different struggles in which they have engaged, they have drawn attention to the significance of colonial history, and the gulf between interests subsequently developed by women of the United States and other colonial powers, and the women of the Arab nations and the wider Muslim world.

The difficulty for Muslim feminists is that faced with a hostile host community, and a patriarchal kin community which is less than supportive of their views, those who resist the ascribed qualities of submission, obedience and propriety run the risk of alienation from their family and community. From her study of Muslim women in West Yorkshire, Afshar (1994) concludes that for many women the conflicts that such views cause are proving destructive in the home and outside it. She argues that it is time that the Muslim community as a whole and its men as a group reconsider the demands that they make of their women and move towards a position that allows Muslim women to choose the combination of identities with which they are comfortable, rather than be forced to adopt imposed identities that have no coherence.

In summary, there cannot be a correct way of viewing the current position of Muslim women. The fragmentations are there, in common with the fracturings to be found in western feminism, so that the views of Muslim feminists are equally divergent, drawing on fundamentalist, liberal, Marxist, socialist, theological and a spectrum of other feminisms. It is also evident from this review that Muslims, both men and women, are united by an Islamic identity and it is this which has relevance to the considerations of the final theme in this section, which looks at Muslim and feminist responses to the issue of single-sex schooling.

Muslim and feminist responses to single-sex schooling

The issue of whether or not single-sex schooling is the answer to equality of educational opportunity for girls is a contentious one. What then are the arguments in support of co-education? The arguments as set out by Dale (1969, 1971, 1974) are analysed by Halstead (1991) as follows:

1 Segregation at any age is artificial and unnatural.
2 Mixed schooling is claimed to result in a healthier attitude to sex and to relations between the sexes.
3 Most students prefer mixed-sex schooling and lessons where both sexes are present because the lessons are more interesting (Dale 1974).
4 Many teachers prefer mixed schooling (cf. Lamb and Pickthorne 1968: 160). The presence of girls in the classroom has a calming effect on boys' behaviour and the consequent effect is more positive attitudes to learning.
5 Mixed-sex schooling involves a commitment to the equality of the sexes in principle and facilitates the equal treatment of the sexes in practice.

Muslims and feminists believe these arguments to be contentious, and it is the reasoning behind their critiques which is of interest here.

Feminists and single-sex schooling

Some feminists argue that there is a great deal of evidence that sex stereo-typing of the rights of women and their role in contemporary society is still a problem (Sharpe 1976; Hakim 1979; Oakley 1982; Kremer and Curry 1986; Crompton and Sanderson 1987; Association of Educational Psychologists 1988). Both sexes still tend to assess themselves and behave in ways compatible with the major stereotype which suggests that intellectual achievement and leadership, competitiveness, independence and effectiveness reflect masculinity, but are basically not consistent with the accepted image of femininity (Broverman *et al.* 1970; Horner 1972).

This means that in an attempt to conform to society's vision of appropriate female behaviour girls and women often display a fear and avoidance of success (Horner 1969, 1972; Balkin 1987). There is evidence to suggest that most women accept this sex stereotyping as the 'ideal' of womanhood, and therefore feel that to achieve or become equal to men in the academic or business sphere, they must lose some of the facets of so-called femininity (Broverman *et al.* 1970; Horner 1972; Spence *et al.* 1973; Sharpe 1976; Byrne 1978; Delamont 1980; Cockburn 1991). Payne (1980) observed that many of the decisions made about the education of girls are largely based on the traditional view of women's role in society. More recent research also indicates that although protected by the implementation of the Sex Discrimination Act (1975), equal opportunities remain for most girls a possibility for the minority rather than a realistic option for the many (Cockburn

1991).[4] Faulkner (1991) also suggests that girls and boys still make different choices within the education system and then leave it to take up sex-stereotyped roles with different life chances. Faulkner concludes that: '. . . girls-only schools by fostering less unfavourable attitudes towards the concept of female achievement and more liberal views of women's rights and their roles in contemporary society, will encourage an ethos within them which is not conducive to the perpetuation of the traditional sex stereotypes of girls and women' (Faulkner 1991: 216).

Debate amongst feminists continues as to whether or not single-sex schooling is the answer to equality of educational opportunity for girls. Echoing the work of Dale (1969, 1971, 1974), which is often considered a definitive work on this subject, Bone (1983), writing for the Equal Opportunities Commission, Steedman (1983) and Marsh (1989) all tend to agree that any findings suggesting possible advantages of single-sex schooling for girls are for the most part inconclusive and contradictory. Kenway and Willis (1986) considered the single-sex school debate and argued that extremist feminist views which consider that any single-sex environment has to be better for girls than any co-educational setting should be dismissed. Nevertheless other educationalists still argue that the mixed-sex system may carry definite disadvantages for the academic and social development of girls (Spender and Sarah 1980; Deem 1984; Mahony 1985; Kremer and Curry 1986; Lee and Bryk 1986; Burgess 1990; Faulkner 1991).

All of these studies have contributed to a developing theory concerning the educational experience and academic attainment of girls in different settings which points to the fact that a single-sex school environment is possibly academically more beneficial to girls and provides an environment which does not reinforce traditional sex stereotyping of girls and women.

Muslims and single-sex schooling

Halstead (1991) outlines the arguments of Muslims for single-sex schooling as follows:

1 Islamic culture does not consider segregation of the sexes to be 'unnatural'. For Muslims this is an argument that implies that 'the extent to which men and women interact socially is biologically determined rather than socially conditioned by cultural, religious, social and economic values, beliefs and practices' (p. 264).

2 Muslims believe that it is the responsibility of parents and the extended family to promote an attitude to sex and a mutual understanding between the sexes set within the context of Islam. There is therefore no wish to see the school taking over this role. In fact within the family framework, it is argued, Muslim girls have more freedom to develop a balanced

understanding, and confidence in the presence of the opposite sex, with less danger of sexual harassment.

3 In common with feminists, Muslims would argue that the presence of boys in the classroom has a distracting influence on the educational achievement of girls: it inhibits girls both socially and academically.

4 Muslims put more emphasis on the relationship between the teacher and student in the classroom than on the interaction of the students, so to adopt a system which is dependent on the use of girls as a civilizing influence is the same argument adopted by the Swann Report (Swann 1985: 510) over the issue of 'separate schools'. In other words, the presence of Muslims in state schools is needed 'to help whites shed their prejudices'. In both cases the group with less power is being used by the educational system to ameliorate a problem that belongs to the group with more. The same argument can also be applied to the 'friendly competition' between the sexes in academic work: Muslims object to the outcome of this (that girls end up second best in the competition for the teacher's time and attention and that boys' academic performance improves while that of girls does not).[5] They also object to the principle behind it on religious grounds.

5 Muslims argue that the principle of equality is not necessarily satisfied by identical treatment. As there is relevant difference between boys and girls in their physical, emotional and mental development, there is injustice in treating them the same when in relevant respects they are different, just as much as there can be in treating them differently when in relevant respects they are the same. 'In Islam the notion of equality has a spiritual basis: Islam proclaims the absolute equality of men and women in terms of the "soul, moral nature, spiritual rights and potential" (Durkee: 1990: 68), but this is not held to be inconsistent with the recognition of physical, emotional or social differences. Differentiated social roles are not a denial of equality in Islam (Iqbal 1975: 12). Women may choose to be "just" wives and mothers or may choose economic or political roles for themselves in addition to these family responsibilities, but in neither case are they considered to be of less worth than men, whatever their roles; men and women will be rewarded equally by God for their labours (Qur'an 3: 195; 33: 35)' (Halstead 1991: 267–8).

Conclusion

In summary, it would seem that Muslims are far more likely than feminists to agree in general over the issue of single-sex schooling, because it is rooted in their religious/cultural beliefs; however, this needs to be understood in the context of the issues raised in Chapter 2 by Saeeda Shah. Further, a comparison of these critiques framed within the context of feminisms and education, considered at the beginning of this chapter, indicates that Muslims and feminists draw on both liberal and radical feminist discourses in their arguments for single-sex schooling. Muslims and liberal feminists support the principle of equal access to all areas of the curriculum and moves towards single-sex groupings in co-educational schools. However, the underlying principles of liberal approaches to schooling for girls are rejected by Muslims. For liberals, equality is based on the principle that it is achievable through the identical treatment of men and women. Muslims, on the other hand, believe that equality is achieved through the recognition of difference, and that differentiated social roles are not a denial of equality (Iqbal 1975). Muslims appear to be more sympathetic to the arguments and approaches of radical feminists with regard to the schooling of girls. Both advocate different kinds of education for girls and emphasize the advantages of women learning with and from each other, and both feel strongly about the sexual harassment of girls in mixed schools.

Notes

1 The term 'patriarchy' is used here to refer to the exploitation of women through the social, economic, political and physical structures identifiable throughout society and which maintain male privileges in a number of ways, articulated by specificities of 'race', class, sexuality, physical ability etc.
2 This is illustrated by the edicts issued by the Taliban in Kabul, Afghanistan, October 1996.
3 For further discussions on these issues see Mernissi 1975, 1991; El Sadaawi 1980; Amos and Parmar 1984; Hussain 1984; Trivedi 1984; UNESCO 1984; Boudhiba 1985; Fernea 1985; Ramazanoglu 1989.
4 Rendel (1992) provides a legal angle to the issue of the right of girls to a non-sexist education. She examines the ways in which the European Convention on Human Rights and its case law could be used to combat sexist education in state or private schools.
5 Recent research argues that the academic performance of boys is being outstripped by girls; see for example Dean (1992), Rafferty (1993).

Part two

RE-SEARCHING THE RESEARCH: DISENTANGLING THE DYNAMICS

5 City State and Old Town High

Kaye Haw

Introduction

Part two, 'Re-searching the research: disentangling the dynamics' has four chapters which are written by me as the researcher, with the exception of Section III of Chapter 7 which is written by Saeeda Shah. The chapters in this part of the book describe the two schools and are concerned with an analysis of the research so that the 'voices' of the staff and students are introduced and given precedence. It is possible to read this part of the book first or on its own. The research as described here is concerned entirely with an analysis of the data which resulted from interviews with the staff and with the pieces of work, informal 'chats' and interviews with students. These chapters are presented as far as possible through the 'voices' of the staff and students themselves: it is **their** perception of their schools, single-sex education, the aims of education for girls and issues of social justice.

The research focuses on a complex and unexplored research context so that the empirical data reflects this complexity. It therefore has the potential to be read and interpreted by people situated in different ways according to their own discursive positionings. For myself there were moments of alienation and empathy which cut across each setting. I came to City State and Old Town High having been educated in a single-sex setting, and having taught in several state schools like City State. These were my perspectives from over here. I came to the Muslim girls' school with some of these understandings, with no religious background but with the freshness and excitement of exploring a different mixture of the familiar and unfamiliar. These were my perspectives from over there. These perspectives have their relational advantages and disadvantages, which are about 'gaze' and focus.

I think I made more assumptions about City State than I did about Old Town High. In the state school my critical readings were blurred by my familiarity and consequent assumptions. **But** at the same time my 'gaze' born out of my familiarity allowed for a certain depth and clarity of focus.

I could implicitly recognize signs, blurrings, distortions, avoidances, barriers which I either pursued or avoided. I had the implicit 'knowledge' to react to their significance through a multiplicity of 'readings' as I shifted my discursive positioning. There were some that were partial readings because of my assumptions. I handled some situations better than others and I made mistakes. Me and my day were significant, the context and who I was, both less and more in focus.

In Old Town High my critical readings were blurred by this lack of implicit 'knowledge' but sharpened by my inability to make assumptions. There were signs, blurrings, distortions, avoidances and barriers that I could not implicitly recognize. **But** the unfamiliarity of my 'gaze', heightened by my difference, meant that I did not avoid them but intuitively and naively explored them because I made no assumptions. I could not so easily 'read' and react to them in their context. I could not so easily shift my positioning, but I achieved a different depth and clarity through another focus brought about by this different 'gaze'. This perspective had its advantages – particularly in a context where *bradari* 'gaze' is so influential. People could talk to me knowing that it would not be filtered back to the community. There were again other partial readings, this time because I did not have the cultural 'knowledge'. In Old Town High I made different mistakes and handled some situations better than others; me and my day were significant, the context and who I was with were both more and less in focus.

I have already argued (p. 42) that the research process should not be about 'safe havens' but about allowing for the legitimacy of a multiplicity of 'voices'. Researchers do differ from the people they are working with in a multiplicity of ways: age, caste, ethnic background, religious faith, physical ability, personality, sexuality and class. There are different moments of alienation and empathy. Whichever they may be, research is about making these limitations explicit and giving legitimacy to the 'voice' of the researcher by placing it in the text. It is about taking the **risk** of opening up any piece of research so that its perspective breaks away from the 'ghettoization' of both research and researchers being constrained to explore the familiar (Haw 1996). Research is about critically reworking all of these perspectives so that theory and action can develop and **spaces** for exploration can be created through holding on to the commonalities while exploring the differences. This involves a recognition that norms exist but that we must be responsible for the 'truths' from which they are constituted, so that through explorations with others we can critically explore our own worlds.

The research was generated from the broader theoretical and autobiographical context made explicit in Chapter 1 and which guided the ensuing analysis. This is just one way of looking at the data. Both the single-sex state school, City State, and the Muslim girls' school, Old Town High, were selected for many different reasons: I already had a relationship with the staff and the students; they bring into play contrasting features; they represent different Muslim communities in Britain (although many of the families originate from the same area in Pakistan, and this is important); and in each case they have generated a special set of local interests. In one locality parts of the Muslim community have felt it necessary to establish a private school for Muslim girls while in the other locality at the time of the research there was no Muslim girls' school.[1]

The aim of this chapter is to introduce the schools. The first section focuses on the research method, direction and design. It is concerned to make both the process and the progress of the research more explicit. The following two sections describe each school, their establishment, management/governance, and background of staff and the curriculum. In each school a wealth of data was generated, so that the focus is on the dominant issues; that is, the emergent questions which determined the direction and development of the analysis of the research.

The research design

The research started with both practical and theoretical concerns and certain questions. These questions determined the direction and the design of the research, which was placed within a framework of background data supplied by information obtained through a postal questionnaire distributed to the 21 Muslim schools listed in England at the time and a girls' school in Rawalpindi, Pakistan. Within the research design there were four phases: first, to gather any documentary evidence such as governors' reports, school brochures, timetables, curriculum details, breakdown of exam results, destinations of Year 11 students and inspection reports, as well as conduct a postal questionnaire of all listed Muslim schools in this country and one in Pakistan.

The second phase was to interview the head teacher and staff (a representative sample in the case of the state school, as the number of staff is greater).[2] The third phase was to give three related pieces of 'work' to years 8, 9, 10 and 11, and the fourth was to meet informally with some parents and ex-students who were willing to do so. These meetings sometimes took place at school functions such as parents' evenings or fundraising events.[3]

The interviews with the head teachers were aimed at obtaining in-depth information about the approaches of each school to policy and practice in the educational provision for Muslim girls both academically and socially. The interview with the teachers was concerned with their teaching experience and educational background; their views on their present school; the needs of their Muslim students; curricular issues; and issues of equal opportunities. This interview aimed at obtaining a different level of information in terms of attitudes to single-sex schooling, awareness, acceptance and working definitions of equal opportunity issues.

I began each interview with a set of photographs depicting different, everyday classroom activities, group work, an information technology lesson, individual work, and the start of a lesson. I chose four photographs out of four rolls of film that were taken. This phase of the design was based on the Adult Learning Project set up in Scotland in 1979, which was a systematic attempt to implement Freire's approach in Scotland.[4] The pictures acted as visual representations of significant situations in the lives of the participants. I asked people to talk about what they thought was happening in each photograph and what the people in the pictures were doing. Participants commented on type of school, type of lesson in progress, uniform, gender and other equal opportunity issues without the prompt of a specific question, and in this sense provided the 'way in' to the issues that the research was concerned to address.[5]

The 'work' with the students included several stages: first was the same set of photographs that were presented to the staff. The photographs were used in group situations because they gave the students the opportunity to talk in an informal way about different situations in school, different types of school, teaching and teachers. Some of these discussions were taped, although the quality of the recordings was variable, especially when the discussions became heated. The value of this was in allowing me to become a familiar figure doing something with them that was not perceived as 'ordinary' school work and enabling me to explain my work to them. I followed this with different pieces of writing.

Second, an imaginative story was used to gain an insight into the attitudes of students towards high academic achievement in girls. This is based on the standard Thematic Apperception Test (as McClelland 1953). Originally this test consisted of a set of deliberately ambiguous drawings into which the person taking the test had to read their own story. The test has since been adapted (Horner 1972 and Faulkner 1989). I adapted this work by asking the students to write an imaginative story around the clue: 'Nazrah was in a big class in an inner city comprehensive school. After the exams at the end of the year the form teacher announced that Nazrah had come top of the class in all her subjects.' I was also interested in what the students thought about Nazrah as a person and what they thought she would be doing when she was 25, because I was interested in their perceptions of the type of occupation that an academically successful girl can take up on leaving school.

Third, there was a more open-ended questionnaire which was designed to give an overview of students' feelings about their school, their attitudes and aspirations.

The students were invited to participate in the research and to complete the pieces in order. They were told that it was voluntary. They were asked to give their name, age and form but assured of anonymity. They were told that they could ask for any help that they felt they needed and this included language translation. The 'work' was done over a period of a few weeks in the weekly lesson set aside for form business.

For reasons of anonymity I have given each school an alternative name. In the state school, City State, 26 teachers plus the head teacher were interviewed out of a total of 45 members of staff in various full-time or part-time capacities, so 60 per cent of the staff were interviewed. In the Muslim girls' school, Old Town High, seven teachers plus the head teacher were interviewed out of a total of ten members of staff. This meant that 80 per cent of the staff were interviewed.

In City State 125 students from years 8 to 11 completed the three pieces of 'work' they were asked to do. Not all of these were Muslim girls, so their responses were categorized as to whether they were Muslim or non-Muslim. Sixty of the replies were from Muslim students and 65 from non-Muslim students. Those replies from non-Muslim students provide a valuable means of comparison as to whether any of the views about single-sex schooling were attributable to the Muslim students only.

In this school there were several constraints on the research. I was the only researcher and therefore with the resources available I was only able to work with two representative forms from each year group and one in the case of Year 11. These forms were chosen in consultation with the home–school liaison officer, head of year and form tutor. The forms that were chosen had a high proportion of Muslim students from a variety of home backgrounds. They were also those forms whose form tutors were interested in the research and willing to let me take their weekly form lesson. In Old Town High 137 students participated in the study.

It is not my intention to give geographical details about the location of each school because I have promised both schools anonymity. Most Muslim schools are clustered in certain areas, making it quite simple to identify the school from such geographical clues. There are some who have argued (see for example Connolly 1994) that little attention is given to 'looking beyond the school gates' and exploring how a particular locale has provided a site through which broader, national political discourses on 'race' have been appropriated and reworked and how, consequently, this has impacted upon the nature of social relations in the school. I agree. Connolly also argues that in the absence of such analysis the work has unwittingly reproduced an ahistorical and static notion of racism. However, if the research is concerned with sensitive issues, and this is, such considerations become problematic. I would argue that there are ways of 'looking beyond the school gates' so that people's lived experiences are considered without divulging geographical clues. For me this is through the use of a feminist and post-structural analysis which predicates discourse as an analytical tool so that the ways people are positioned in discourses both in and out of school are given due consideration.

The theoretical positions which have already been made explicit guided the analysis for this research, so that post-structuralism seen through the lens of feminism provided the analytical tools which were sophisticated enough to locate the gaps, the commonalities and the tensions in the data. There were of course many stories that the data could tell. The difficult questions for me were, which story was it to be and why that particular one.

Theoretically I was interested in how discourses operate and consequent relationships of power, and the research itself began with two areas that aroused my curiosity: first, the issue of single-sex education and whether or not there were any areas of agreement between Muslims and feminists over this issue; and second, the issue of educational achievement in Muslim girls' schools. For these reasons I began the analysis by looking at attitudes to single-sex schooling. This is also where I felt most at home. I had been to a girls' high school myself, and the issues were easy to locate.

At an early stage the similarities and differences which began to emerge between the two schools led to the next phase of the analysis. It became obvious that there were many areas of agreement between the staff and the students in both schools over the issue of single-sex schooling, but at this point new questions began to emerge.

One question focused on whether the differences between City State and Old Town High concerning emphasis on academic performance were detectable in the responses of the students. Secondly, there emerged a strong commitment by the staff in both City State and Old Town High to gender issues. The commitment of the staff in City State to gender issues in terms of equal opportunities also identified certain tensions as they tried to reconcile their desire to encourage the students to challenge and question the stereotypes of women, their rights and their roles in contemporary society on the one hand, whilst giving due consideration to what they understand to be the religious/cultural beliefs of the Muslim students on the other hand. These tensions were not detectable in the responses of the staff or the students in Old Town High. This began the final stage in the analysis.

The tension and conflict identified in the responses of the staff and students in City State became the focus of interest which was systematically related to other issues, so that relationships between these issues generated three further questions which were addressed in the final stage of the analytical procedure. They were: first, do the Muslim students in the private Muslim school feel more 'comfortable' in an environment where being a woman is not an issue, being a Muslim is not an issue, but being a Muslim woman is an issue because this is the raison d'être of these schools? Second, are the Muslim students in the Muslim school more empowered to 'read', take up or reject the discursive positions offered to them in school in terms of 'race' ethnicity, religion, class and gender? And third, is this different for the Muslim students in the state school, how, and why?

The descriptions of City State and Old Town High which follow represent each school in the years over which the research was carried out, that is, between 1992 and 1995. There have of course been changes in each school and both now have new head teachers, due to retirement and career advancement. Any significant changes apart from this last one are pointed out, but largely these studies are bounded by the physical, spatial and historical contexts in which they were carried out. They are therefore written up in the present tense.

City State

City State is a county comprehensive school for girls aged 11 to 16. It is situated about three miles north of the city centre and is the only maintained single-sex secondary school in the city and one of only a very few in the whole county. City State shares a large open site with several other schools, with access to a neighbouring special school facilitated by linking corridors. The buildings are quite pleasant although in need of some decorative refurbishment, the original main building dating back to the 1950s.

Establishment

City State was established in the early 1930s as a girls' grammar school and catered for a selected intake of 11–18-year-olds. In the 1970s, as a result of reorganization of county secondary schools, to become comprehensive schools it became an 11–16 comprehensive school. It retained its single-sex status but became a neighbourhood school serving the local area for the most part. A nearby comprehensive was also single-sex for boys.

In the early 1980s the boys' school was closed and the plan was to close City State and establish a co-educational school in the locality. This new school was to be formed and housed in City State's original building, situated in an area of high South Asian, mainly Pakistani Muslim population. Parents, governors and staff successfully fought against the decision to close City State, which meant that the school was relocated to its present site away from the densely populated South Asian areas of the inner city.[6] This prevented a protest from South Asian families who maintained that the school met their religious and cultural needs. The continuing presence of a girls' school was also used by local politicians as a reason for refusing a request from local Muslim organizations for a Muslim girls' secondary school. City State is now situated in a pleasant suburban area west of the city but also adjacent to a large council estate. Its original location was in an accessible inner city area, on a road which intersected with two main bus routes into the city.

The school now has no local catchment area. It serves all girls whose parents live in the city and can then offer places to county girls if there are spaces available. All girls therefore come as a result of parental choice. Generally Muslim parents choose City State because it is single-sex and they therefore allow their daughters to travel outside the family situation to attend the school. In fact, significant moves have been made by City State and the local authority to provide buses with a direct route to school, enabling Muslim girls to travel across the city unaccompanied. At the time of the research a contribution was made by the local authority to the cost of the journey.

The admissions policy states that priority will be given to girls living within a five mile radius of City State. In the past it has been unnecessary to apply this criterion as the school has been under-subscribed. However, a good inspection report coupled with an awareness that single-sex education could be beneficial for girls has meant that the numbers on roll are increasing. This makes for a potentially interesting situation. In the past, Muslim families who wished to send their daughters to a single-sex school have automatically sent them to the school, even if they reside outside the five mile area, and they apparently still assume that there will be no problems in this respect. However, increasing numbers could mean that the criterion in the admissions policy will have to be more strictly applied. The girls attending the school are still mainly from inner city areas. Usually about a third come from the original catchment area, especially the Muslim students. In the last 12 months there has been growing interest in the school within the local neighbourhood, which was certainly noticeable for the 1993 intake. These are mostly white girls from the nearby council estate.

The property in the immediate vicinity of the school is owner-occupied bungalows and houses – it is a desirable residential area with many families who would be termed 'middle class' and seem affluent.[7] A proportion of the residents are in the retired age group, especially in the houses facing the school. The council estate adjoining the other side of the school was built in the 1930s. There are some notorious trouble spots.

According to the head teacher the South Asian presence in the local area is very low. The daughters of the one or two affluent local South Asian families do not attend City State, but are either educated privately or sent to a Church of England school which has a prestigious and academic reputation.

Management/governance

School starts at 8.55 am and finishes at 3.35 pm with a lunch break at 12.20 to 1.30 pm. The governing body is made up of eight women and five men. One of the men and one of the women are Muslim. There is a Sikh man who is the Labour Party nominee and the rest are white. At the time of the research there were vacancies for two more governors. A full governors' meeting is held once a term and there are also three sub-committees with oversight of Finance, Personnel and Curriculum. The Chair of the Governors and Head sit on each of the latter together with 'volunteer' governors.

City State has a clearly defined management structure. There are 37 staff in full-time employment plus six Section 11 staff, four of whom are in full-time employment.[8] There are a head teacher and two deputy head teachers, one with responsibility for curriculum and staff development and the other with responsibility for pastoral issues, student welfare and development. These are all 'white' females. The curriculum is delivered via the heads of department and their teams, which may number four or five but occasionally be as low as two or one plus. The pastoral work is delivered via heads of year and form tutors. The heads of department are all white females except for the head of science, the head of technology and the head of music and buildings maintenance administration who are white males. The heads of year are all white females.

Other posts of special responsibility include a finance manager who is a white male, on allowance C and a curriculum coordinator, also a white male on allowance D. The Section 11 team is headed by a white female and a home–school liaison officer who is a South Asian, non-Muslim female. There are two other full-time members of the Section 11 team, one a white male and the other a South Asian female, together with two part-time members, both white, who make up a full timetable by teaching in mainstream departments. Therefore there are only two South Asian members of the Section 11 team, neither of whom is a Muslim.

There are also peripatetic teachers who come in from the central language team to teach Urdu and Punjabi, two of whom are Muslim men. From September 1993 this team was disbanded and the school now employs a full-time member of staff to teach Urdu. One of the Muslim men was appointed to this post. Therefore, at the moment, the full complement of South Asian staff is two Indian women who are non-Muslim and one man who is a Muslim. There are seven men on the staff, none of whom is on less than a B allowance. Three of these are on B allowances, three on C allowances and one on a D allowance.

No one from the ethnic minorities is represented amongst the ancillary staff of secretaries, librarians, kitchen assistants, caretaker/cleaners, midday supervisors or resources technicians. City State is situated in a predominantly white area so the 'locals' who apply for part-time jobs of this status are almost bound to be white.

Very few applications are received for teaching positions from other ethnic groups. There was none for the recently vacant headship and there were two rounds of applications and interviews. In the past five years there have only been two applicants from minority groups for advertised posts, one a South Asian male, and the other an African-Caribbean male. Both were unsuccessful.

City State is helped by contact with education liaison officers. The authority appoints one of these for each ethnic minority community, and the Muslim education liaison officer links with the school as necessary.

Numbers and backgrounds of staff and students

In April 1993 there were 570 students on roll, whose ethnic background was broken down as follows:[9]

White-indigenous English	43%
South Asian	42%
African-Caribbean/mixed race	14%
Chinese/Vietnamese	1%

The 42 per cent South Asian group consists of girls whose families originate from Pakistan, India, Bangladesh, and one or two from Afghanistan and/or Kenya. Most have their roots in a specific region of Pakistan. Many of the parents/grandparents come from rural communities where little formal education was available. There are therefore still parents who cannot read and write in either their own language or English. The head teacher states:

> Some mothers are known to find their lack of skills, especially communicating in English, very frustrating and this is exacerbated by the fact that their daughters are fluent in mother tongue and literate in English. This can mean that with the children communicating in English and the father quite fluent, the mother becomes isolated.

The school numbers are growing, from 422 in 1989 to 573 in 1993, and to over 600 in 1994/5, which has meant that this South Asian group is becoming proportionately less in percentage terms. This group is numerically stable, but increasing numbers of whites and to a lesser extent African-Caribbean and bicultural students are now opting for the school. In the past there has been a year group that was 60 per cent South Asian (52 per cent Pakistan/Bangladesh origin), but the current Year 7 and next year's intake suggest that the proportion of Muslim girls will drop to around 30 per cent.

According to the head teacher, whose subject specialism is religious studies, the religious background of the students is varied. Most of the white girls seem to have no declared faith, although there are a few practising Christians and some of the African-Caribbean students attend gospel churches. The students who originate from India are mostly Sikhs. The students who originate from Pakistan/Bangladesh are Muslim and form the largest 'faith' group in the school (about 34 per cent), the majority of whom according to the head appear to have a natural commitment to the ritual requirements in that they fast during *Ramazan*, they eschew alcohol, and they wear school uniform which ensures they are covered, such as trousers or *shalwar kameez*. A fair proportion attend the local mosque after school or visit a relative for Islamic and Qur'anic studies.

Over 200 students receive free school meals, and of those that do not, a fair proportion are from low income families. The students are mostly drawn from inner city areas. The majority of the Muslim students are from less affluent families, with a significant proportion being poor due to unemployment. These are in receipt of free school meals.

Curriculum

The school offers English, maths, science, modern languages, religious education, humanities, craft design and technology, physical education, art, and personal and social education in Years 7 to 9, supplemented by other subject choices in Years 10 to 11. Careers education operates in the school from Year 9 as part of a fuller social and personal development programme. At the end of Year 10 there is one week's work experience and a further one week's work experience in the Autumn term of Year 11, followed by a careers convention in school together with visits to local colleges. Each student has an interview in Year 11 with a careers officer who is white and linked to the school. Careers officers from the ethnic minorities are linked to the wider team and are available on request. The head teacher states that Muslim families rarely ask for this help.

A wide range of extra-curricular activities is available within school, most taking place during the lunch break such as choir and drama activities (especially when working towards a production) and various sports activities such as football, athletics, netball and trampolining. According to the head teacher, Muslim students very rarely participate in these activities.[10] There is a lunchtime club organized by black youth workers, attended by African-Caribbean girls only, although it is officially open to 'anyone who considers themselves to be black'. Another lunchtime club is led by the Section 11 team. This offers a range of activities and is well supported by younger Muslim girls as by others.

Every Friday there is another lunchtime club run by representatives of a local Asian youth project. Over the years this has been well supported by South Asian girls of all ages, including a period when older girls had an after-school session. The project workers then took each girl home in their minibus. Additionally some Muslim girls take advantage of belonging to the 'Stimulus and Development Programme' groups in Year 8 or Year 9. This is open mainly to the academically more able to help them extend their skills. Attendance is voluntary and extra homework is involved.

Muslim girls join in visits to events of particular educational or vocational significance for South Asian young people as they occur, such as the Careers Convention Day Conference for Muslim and other Asian girls: 'Different Culture; Different Future'.

Old Town High

Old Town High was originally situated off a main ring road about a mile from the city centre. The building opens directly onto the street and is found right at the point where the road comes to a dead end. Adjacent to the school is a maintained primary school. Initially the building had other uses which were not educational. From September 1994 the school became a split site school, the lower school being taught in the original building and the upper school situated some miles away in a building which was formerly a primary school.

Establishment

Old Town High was formally established as a result of parental interest. The building was bought by the Muslim Association. The school is responsible for the maintenance of the building but does not pay rent, and the head teacher directly attributes the survival of the school to this.

Old Town High is recognized by the Department for Education and Employment and has charity status through linkage to a Muslim association. It serves a heavily populated South Asian area of the city, a large proportion of whom also originate from the same region of Pakistan. Most of the students live locally or just outside the boundary; a few travel some distance to attend the school, which is currently applying for voluntary-aided status.

Management/governance

The school day begins at 9.10 am with a 15-minute religious assembly taken by the head teacher or the students themselves. The day is divided into four lessons each lasting one hour and ten minutes. There are two ten-minute breaks, one in the morning and one in the afternoon. The afternoon break is there so that the girls can offer the late afternoon prayer during winter. This is not a consideration during the summer months, but the break remains.

Old Town High is governed by a governing body of ten people including the head teacher. These are all Muslim. There are four parents, and the other five come from a range of backgrounds across the Muslim community. They offer an interest in the school and expertise in financial or education matters or business contacts. The chair of the governing body is a prominent male Muslim educationalist and spokesperson. There are two females on the governing body, the head teacher and one of the parent governors. The head teacher has expressed a wish that eventually the school will be run by a female governing body, but at the moment she is concerned with building up the confidence of the Muslim women in the community and does not want them to feel pressurized into participating in such a role prematurely.

The management structure of Old Town High is such that the head teacher is entirely responsible for the running of the school and all decisions, having recourse to the governors only in situations in which she feels unsure.

The role of the governors is to ensure that what is implemented by the head teacher is appropriate. Other than the overseeing of financial matters there is not much 'interference' from the governors in the day-to-day running of the school and educational decision making. There is continuous feedback to the head teacher and the governors from the community, often from informal discussions in the mosque. The views of the parents and the community are given great weight. It is the community and the parents who will influence the success of Old Town High, and the head teacher feels strongly that it will not serve any purpose if the school tries to move faster than the community in terms of change. Old Town High therefore reflects the community and the community reflects the school, and feedback whether on a formal or informal basis is essential to this process and the success of the school.

The structure of Old Town High is that there is a head teacher and subject teachers with responsibility in consultation with the head teacher, for their own subject area. This less hierarchical structure in comparison with City State is due to two factors: size of the school and lack of finances.[11]

Numbers and backgrounds of staff and students

At this time there are 184 girls on roll aged 11 to 18. There is a substantial waiting list. The increase in student numbers is directly attributable to a steadily improving academic record over the last three or four years which has meant that Old Town High has gained a good reputation amongst the local Muslim community, and there have been transfers of students from local maintained schools who were struggling academically in these schools. Increased student numbers has meant that space is now at a premium even though building work has been undertaken and the existing classrooms have been extended.

At the start of this research there were six classrooms and seven classes, although this class number includes the upper and lower sixth which are taught as one group. For the academic year 1993 three temporary classrooms were sited at the rear of the building, effectively taking up all the space which was previously available as an outside recreation facility. With the move to the other site these are no longer required and are being removed.

There are four full-time staff: one is the head teacher and the others teach science, maths and English. There are seven part-time staff and one cleaner. The staff are paid an hourly rate of £7.21 for qualified teachers and £4.12 for unqualified teachers. They therefore do not get paid over the holidays nor do they receive any additional benefits such as superannuation. Of these staff, five are Muslim and the remainder are white non-Muslims and one African-Caribbean non-Muslim. All the staff are female.

The predominance of part-time staff means that there are no formal staff meetings of the whole staff. Decisions are made on an informal basis by the head teacher, or the head teacher in consultation with the relevant member of staff as far as curricular issues are concerned. This also means that there are no formal discussions concerning the day-to-day running of the school, its ethos or its philosophy.

There are no food facilities in the building, so there are no ancillary staff associated with this. There is help in routine administrative duties from ex-students, but this is done on an *ad hoc* basis.

The students in the school come from family backgrounds where there is financial hardship, with the majority of the parents being unemployed. Often the parents are not formally educated, having migrated to this country in the 1950s and 1960s, mainly from Pakistan and Bangladesh, although there are some students whose parents originate from Iran, Iraq, Libya and India. When Old Town High was first established, the majority of the students had parents who migrated from one particular region of Pakistan, but now they come from all areas of Pakistan from Peshawar to Punjab and the Sindi areas.

There are Muslims from different backgrounds and sects within the school. The students attend a range of mosques, but the majority of the students are from the Deobandi branch of the Sunni Muslims. There are several mother tongue languages spoken in the school; these include Bengali, Urdu, Punjabi and Arabic, but now some students are from mixed parentage so English is their main language. Ninety-eight per cent of the students are first generation British, the remaining percentage coming from abroad. School fees are £500 per year requested in one or two lump sums. In reality the parents pay in small instalments. The head teacher suspects that quite often child benefit is used.

Curriculum

Old Town High complies with National Curriculum guidelines. There are nine subjects on the timetable: science, English, maths, religious education, Urdu, French, art, humanities, and child development. Physical education is done for the required five per cent of the time. There are no option choices at the end of Year 9. Years 10 and 11 take as exam courses the subjects offered on this timetable. Four mandatory subjects are offered at A level – sociology, religious education, Urdu and English. However, when Old Town High school moved to its new premises part of the building work included conversion of existing classrooms to science laboratories. This means that the school now offers Science A levels. Old Town High does not offer careers education or work experience, although the sixth form is being offered ten sessions on Tuesday afternoons with a white female Careers Advisory Service officer, because the head feels that the students should be aware of what is available.[12]

There are no extra-curricular activities available to the students that could be compared with those offered in City State. There have been some local educational visits as part of course work, and the school is in contact with a local voluntary organization which organizes weekend trips to theme parks and offers 'women only' outings. Old Town High is not involved directly in the organization of such trips. In the past, girls from the school have participated in public speaking and literary competitions, but staffing and financial constraints mean that this is not a regular feature. These constraints are also largely responsible for the lack of extra-curricular options.

Conclusion

The aim of this chapter has been twofold. First, it has been concerned to discuss the research design, the methods of data collection, the progress and process of the research, and to relate these to the theoretical framework argued for in the Introduction and Chapter 1 showing that the analysis too is derived from my discursive positioning in interplay with the historical context and focus of the research. The aim of the research was to facilitate a process in which Muslim girls and women are encouraged to voice their own opinions so that positive views are highlighted and disseminated and concerns become goals for change. The selection of participants was neither haphazard nor random; neither should they be viewed as a statistically representative sample. Nevertheless, their opinions are valid because the purpose of the research is to collect subjective information from Muslim girls and women in two Muslim communities. The value of this lies in the depth and richness of the information obtained through people speaking for themselves and through opening up a forum for them in places where they would not normally be heard.

The descriptions of each school taken from field notes and as seen through the eyes of each head teacher provide the context for the analysis of the data collected from interviews with the staff and for the pieces of 'work' and group interviews with the students. The emerging issues and patterns reflected the complexity of the research context. The discursive interrelationships among and across contexts, which both construct subjects and which are constructed by these subjects in the process, highlighted a web of commonalities and differences. This forms the basis of the subsequent chapters in this Part.

Notes

1 A Muslim girls' school has recently been established in this area.
2 The selection criterion used is described later in this section, together with some of the issues generated by the use of interviews in the research process.
3 For these reasons the information gathered was mostly not taped and is not

therefore directly quoted. The insights from these meetings are mainly to be found in Chapter 8, which is concerned to weave the fractured data back together again.

4 A more detailed discussion of the project is to be found in Kirkwood and Kirkwood (1989).

5 For further discussions concerning the use of photographs in a piece of research see Walker and Weidel 1985 and Prosser 1992.

6 This and the following information provided by the head teacher is substantiated by her personal log in which she details incidents and events concerning the school. I was given access to this log book.

7 This interpretation of class is that of the head teacher and as such can be described as a common sense understanding of class. For a theoretical discussion of this concept see Hamilton and Hirszowicz (1987) and Bradley (1996).

8 Section 11 staff are those staff in British schools specifically appointed using funding from the Home Office mainly to help immigrant children learn English and adapt to life in Britain.

9 These are the ethnic descriptors used by the head teacher of City State.

10 This is also corroborated by interviews with the staff. The drama teacher, for example, talked of the difficulties of any after school activity because of lack of transport. She also referred to problems with school productions, even when they were women-only events, because of travel arrangements for Muslim students and their mothers.

11 The head teacher for example is paid at exactly the same hourly rate as the other qualified teachers in the school.

12 Some of the girls expressed some concern that in the initial session the advisor asked them why they were asking for information about certain careers that they would 'never be able to do'. The head teacher sat in on subsequent sessions.

6 Equality in difference?

Kaye Haw

Introduction

This chapter has three sections which introduce the 'voices' of the staff and students in that they surface through my analysis as direct quotes. To preserve anonymity pseudonyms have been used. Each quote is prefixed by the initials of CS for City State and OTH for Old Town High. The staff of both schools are identifiable through the use of a first name only, whereas the students are given a name and their actual year at the time of the research.

The first section describes the ethos and philosophy of each school as seen through the eyes of the head teachers, staff and students, and it is here that the process of highlighting the commonalities and differences, both within each school and between the schools, begins. I have already said that in the spaces, the silences, the gaps there is a theoretical possibility to explore commonalities 'without making assumptions' while also exploring the tensions holding Gilroy's 'changing same' together. The second section of this chapter, 'Dealing with difference', picks up on the tensions that become apparent as the staff of City State reflected on their relationships with their Muslim students in the context of their commitment to encourage the students to question gender stereotyping. The third section discusses the different strategies that City State have put in place to accommodate the needs of their Muslim students. These are the initiatives which the school believes will go some way to providing 'equality in difference'. This section extends the discussion of Chapter 3, which outlines moves that have been made by schools throughout Britain to meet the needs of their Muslim students concerning the formal curriculum, the informal curriculum, and community and parental links by focusing on the experiences of the staff and students in one particular state school, City State.

The ethos and philosophy of the schools

Keeping to the focus of the two main areas of the research, the process of analysis began with the perception of the staff and students in each school of their experiences of single-sex schooling. In this respect some common ground emerged between the two schools which is perhaps best summed up as follows: 'I think the good thing about being with girls is that you can get on with your work without the boys bugging you, and the bad thing is that you don't have any boys to bug you' (OTH, Sofia, Yr 8).

Single-sex schooling was seen by the staff and the students in each school to provide an atmosphere free from male dominance and harassment, with equal access to the curriculum both during lessons and in terms of subject choice and encouragement in terms of positive role models. Both schools emphasized feelings of 'sisterhood' between staff, staff and students, and students. It was felt that this in turn led to a warm, friendly, supportive and non-violent atmosphere. From this base the students **believed** they had the freedom to explore ideas about being a woman, or specifically a Muslim woman in the case of Old Town High. This led to feelings of confidence and assertiveness for the non-Muslim students in City State and the Muslim students of Old Town High, but not necessarily for the Muslim students of City State. '**They [the Muslim students] also tend to be the ones who've got less confidence.** I think they don't aim high. **I feel they're quieter and they need confidence in class to speak up because other students can be louder than they are.**' (CS, Robert, emphasis added). This is not to say that in less structured situations the Muslim girls in City State conformed to the stereotype of the shy, retiring, unassertive Muslim girl.

In contrast the encouragement that the students were given to be confident, assertive, express their own opinions and be women was seen as a definite advantage in Old Town High. The importance of academic achievement within a spiritual and moral framework was identified as permeating the school. The girls felt secure enough in their own identity to question, to challenge and assert their rights as women and Muslims to pursue further and higher education. For example, one student of Old Town High remarked:

> I like the environment of my school and the way the teachers push you to do your utmost to make you produce the results you want, although I don't agree with too much pressurizing. **In this school I like the way some teachers think of you as an individual and not a whole class.** They make you work and try to build your confidence, make you realize that what you do, does matter, it is relevant and your future relies on it. **Since I have been to this school I have learned a lot not just about education but about life, how it could change.** I have gained a lot of confidence although I am sometimes a bit too confident which I shouldn't be.
>
> (OTH, Ambreen, Yr 11, emphasis added)

This is of interest for two reasons. First, because Ambreen expresses her gratitude at being treated **as an individual**. This contrasts sharply with the experiences of the Muslim students in City State because they, like other students belonging to ethnic minority groups, appeared to be treated **as a group** rather than individuals: 'Groups of girls are labelled, particularly Afro-Caribbean girls. If Afro-Caribbean girls are presenting a problem it is an Afro-Caribbean problem, if white girls are presenting a problem it's an individual problem' (CS, Barbara). Secondly, Ambreen's confidence is obviously causing her some confusion and possible difficulties.

The primary purpose of City State is held to be the provision of a 'first rate' education, the best for secondary school-age girls in the area. Girls of all abilities, backgrounds and needs are welcomed to the school and are valued for what they can bring to the community. There is a strong philosophy about the 'person' at the school which is regarded as a 'plus' in such a multicultural setting.

Education is also perceived as being about academic achievement so that each girl is encouraged to reach her own potential. The school aims for high academic standards and encourages those who are weak with the help of a strong Section 11–Special Needs support link. The commitment of the staff is to achieve the best for each student; to encourage the students to develop into positive women who are able to take their places alongside other men and women from all backgrounds and at every level of achievement while also educating them as 'the mothers of tomorrow with all that they will bring to their families'.

Opponents of Muslim girls' schools have voiced concern about such a commitment to 'educating the mothers of tomorrow' and indeed the head teacher of Old Town High also believes that it is a priority to remind the students of their duties as future mothers so that they are 'taught to be a good mother and will be taught within the faith they are the first school for the new generation. Therefore education is even more vital for them than boys.' The difference is that the latter is framed within the context of Islam. For now it is interesting to note that this perspective surfaces in the ethos and philosophy of both City State and Old Town High.

The ethos and philosophy described by the head teacher of Old Town High bears much resemblance to that of City State. Thus the school also emphasizes the need to encourage their students to be self-confident, correctly assertive young Muslim women who will make a positive contribution to the community and as mothers of the next generation. Old Town High also believes that it offers an educational opportunity to a wide range of girls with differing abilities and needs. It emphasizes that it offers an opportunity to provide schooling for some of the most vulnerable and least wealthy Muslim families in the area who would otherwise send their daughters 'back home' rather than be forced by law to attend a non-Muslim school. This is an important point. Thus the school sees itself as offering an opportunity for young British Muslim girls to understand the Islamic way of life within a non-Muslim society. It is here that marked differences between the two schools start to become evident.

Both the Muslim and the non-Muslim staff in Old Town High felt that there were clear advantages for the students in being educated not only in a single-sex environment but in a single-sex Islamic environment. The view was expressed that this lack of constraint meant that the students were free to question and explore a whole range of issues concerned with being women, being Muslims and being Muslim women 'without necessarily rebelling against their own system and their culture but to see how to change things within the culture for the better'.

In Old Town High the feeling of a **calm, warm and friendly atmosphere** in the school where girls could test their strengths in a non-threatening environment and express their opinions without ridicule was constantly referred to. In this environment they were nurtured and supported by the staff. The girls also showed the same feelings of support.

However, marked differences also began to emerge between the schools at this point. These were, first, a religious dimension; second, community responsibilities; third, an academic reputation; fourth, a 'pioneering spirit'; and fifth, dealing with the issues of woman/Muslim woman.

The religious dimension

'Feelings of sisterhood' emerged very strongly in both schools, but in Old Town High they had a strong Islamic slant and were referred to as the major underlying factor which contributed to the positive advantage that the students gained from being educated in a single-sex Islamic environment. **In this environment being female was not an issue and being a Muslim was not an issue.** 'I like this school because it is an Islamic school where I am accepted for my religious behaviour and I am provided with facilities to practise my religion **without any care**' (OTH, Khadija, Yr 12, emphasis added).

As would be expected, the religious dimension is much emphasized. It permeates the school from adherence to religious duties throughout the day, to assemblies with a strong religious and moral dimension, and through to the curriculum with all students taking religious and Islamic studies throughout their school career. This is the first marked difference between the two schools.

The individual and the community

This second marked difference between the schools is that the emphasis in City State is on personal autonomy or 'the person' whereas in Old Town High, although the importance of personal achievement is stressed, a greater emphasis is put on responsibility to the community. In Old Town High the students are encouraged through a strong moral framework to realize that 'it's not morals for me, it's not education for myself, it's education for everyone'. The expectation is that once the students have left the school, they 'give something back'. This is linked to the strong religious ethos of Old Town High and is consistent with the theoretical context of the 'community', Islamic knowledge and aims of Islamic education discussed in Chapters 2 and 3. It is this consideration of the meaning of 'knowledge' which defines the dividing line between Islamic and western concepts of education. The difference in perception rests on the fact that whereas western philosophy allows religious knowledge as a distinct form of knowledge in isolation, Islam only acknowledges the validity of the true faith and believes all knowledge, both revealed knowledge and acquired knowledge, is to be found either within the parameters of the Qur'an, or sought using the Qur'an and the *Hadiths* as guides: one system seeks individual autonomy by which the educational process invites young people to think and act for themselves within society, whilst the other attempts to maintain a strong sense of community and family solidarity within a religious framework.

Proving itself academically

Old Town High needs to prove itself not only to society at large but also to the local and wider Muslim communities, and has a commitment to overturn the stereotype of what it means to be a woman and Muslim. The ethos of the school is based on the very strong belief that an academic background is one way of giving the students the **power** to survive in different situations and a means of moving forwards and combating the stereotype of being a woman and Muslim. The expectation is that the students will 'show that Muslim women can get an education, can think for themselves, that we are all decision-makers and the way we look and dress up has nothing to do with mental ability'. This is the third difference between the two schools.

Stereotypes about the educational standards in Muslim schools are not just the province of the indigenous white society. In this sense the head teacher sees her role as one of informing the public, and this includes the Muslim community, about the school in general and its educational philosophy in particular. When stereotypical judgements about the school are made by the local Muslim community this is felt very keenly by the head teacher of the school.

The intention is to encourage each student to maximize their talents and abilities through emphasizing the positive. This is tempered by a recognition that those students who wish to go on to some form of higher education may face cultural constraints, family pressures and institutional barriers when they leave school. It was felt that there were four main issues here: first, the assumption that in Muslim schools academic performance is seen to be of secondary importance to an Islamic way of life. Old Town High therefore has a strong commitment to not only overcome the **stereotype of what it is to be a woman and Muslim but also the stereotype of being a Muslim girl who attended a Muslim school.** Second, the students are automatically considered not to have the language skills to cope with a degree course. Third, there are those factors which revolve around institutional racism. In this regard the head teacher of Old Town High believes that even though her students sit the same exams, their high grades are perceived as good fortune rather than as evidence of academic ability. Fourth, there are the cultural constraints of the community and therefore their parents. This is a debate which has to be placed within the context of the discussion and arguments offered by Saeeda Shah in Chapter 2.

The strong commitment to challenging mainly white stereotypical views of Muslim women, and the necessity of proving itself as an academic establishment to both the 'host' and the parent communities, contributes to this difference between the two schools. Although City State does emphasize the academic achievement of the students, it is embedded within an ethos which centres around 'a very strong philosophy about the person' which springs from the 'comprehensive ideal' of the school. The 'pioneering spirit' which influences the ethos and philosophy of Old Town High means that academic achievement is stressed very strongly as being concrete and incontrovertible proof to a sceptical indigenous society and to the Muslim community in the locality that it is an educational establishment because 'that's how the judgement is made'. In Old Town High the students and the staff work hard for GCSEs because 'without that we would not have the power to say we are intellectuals, we can think for ourselves, we can make our decisions'. This is achieved within a 'spiritual dimension. You can't measure it, but it is there.'

The 'pioneering spirit'

In Old Town High the attitude fostered by the ethos of the school which places much emphasis on the development of the individual academically, morally and socially was equated with the eagerness of the students to learn and to work hard. A consequence of this cooperative student attitude for the staff was job satisfaction, which outweighed the disadvantages of poor pay and meant that staff 'go home feeling at the end of the day that I've actually done something worthwhile'. This links to this fourth marked difference between the two schools.

In this context there emerged a pioneering spirit amongst the staff: 'I feel it is something of a "cause" ', 'it seems unjust that they do not have voluntary-aided status', 'I wanted to know more about the Muslim community'. This was also felt to be reflected in the attitude of the students towards the school who were 'maybe at the present time almost sacrificing themselves in order for the next generations to have more opportunity; they see themselves as pioneers in many ways'.

The head teacher sees her role as one of discussing religious/cultural issues with the parents, challenging their assumptions but **not** going against their wishes. The student who features in the following extract went to university after much discussion with her parents and once she had got married. The head teacher believes that the way is then eased for the students following them and in this sense the 'pioneering' spirit is further evident.

I have got a candidate in university who wasn't applying initially because she wears a full *hijab* and because of her family. I said to her, 'Look, do you want to get a good education? If yes, then apply and see what they offer you. Then try to get those grades and then go in and see how the relationship is. If you can't cope with it obviously you'll have to make a decision but you can't just give up. This is you and you're going to wear a *hijab* because you believe in it and therefore you've got to fight for it. Maybe by your presence the next candidate will have an easier task.'

(OTH, head teacher)

Woman/Muslim woman

The importance of academic achievement within a spiritual and moral framework was identified as being the ethos which permeated Old Town High in an environment where the girls felt secure enough in their own identity to question, to challenge and assert their rights as women and Muslims to pursue further and higher education.

Well it's to bring out the best in every girl and try to develop that to its fullest potential in very difficult circumstances. It's also to help them adapt to western life within their own faith which quite often might be at conflict. I think they enjoy the work they do and the main ethos is always based on hard work. To try and achieve the best that they possibly can. For a lot of the girls they do achieve that and they are quite positive about it. The main advantages are that they can work within the Muslim set and so I think that they probably have less bullying, less taunting, particularly mainly from western boys and so they have a much better understanding themselves and they don't get the negative view from our society. That's a big advantage.

(OTH, Mary)

This leads to this fifth and crucial difference between the two schools. City State is concerned with the category 'woman'. In this school there was a desire to encourage the students to challenge the traditional expectations and stereotypes of women and their roles through equal access to the curriculum and widening their aspirations on leaving school. The staff of City State therefore placed great value on their ability to encourage the students to be self-confident, assertive and independent through nurturing the self-esteem of each student, and here tensions begin to emerge very obviously because of the multicultural nature of the school. There was some concern that although they as a staff were committed to ensuring that their students challenged and questioned and analysed gender issues, at the same time they were 'treading on the cultural toes' of their Muslim students and perhaps more importantly their parents.

The problem is how to deal on an everyday level with a commitment to a universal category 'woman' when in the case of the Pakistani Muslim students the fragmentations and differences are plainly visible. They are always there, in terms of class, ability and sexual orientation for example, but these fracturings are not as immediately obvious and therefore there is not the pressure to deal with them. This is a theme which runs throughout this book and which is also the focus of the following section.

Dealing with difference

The staff at City State voiced concerns about their Muslim students in terms of conflict and dilemma. At this point I felt that there were several questions that needed answering. These were questions which were generated by strong 'presences' in the interviews of the staff of City State of phrases like 'fall into the pit' or 'you've got to be on your toes' or 'wary of being pushy'. At the same time I was also struck by the equivalent 'silences' in the interviews with the staff of Old Town High, even if they were also white, non-Muslim teachers.

> I think because they are in a safe environment they're more able to ask questions that they might not ask in a more supposedly open environment. So I think they're able to criticize and question and get their doubts sorted out while they're still within a safe community . . . I feel comfortable about discussing these issues because I don't see that it is against any of the ethos of the school to develop. I think this is why I like working here because I do feel girls are taught here to fulfil themselves without necessarily rebelling against their own system and their culture but to see how to change things within the culture for the better.
> (OTH, Mary)

Where did such tension and conflict arise in City State and why did it arise? The commitment of the staff to equal opportunities emerged very strongly in City State despite initial impressions that it appeared to be a school with all girls attending it rather than a girls' school. The school was seen to be a place where the students needed to be encouraged to question gender stereotypes and the division of labour, often in the face of increasing pressure from outside influences such as the media.

This strong commitment to equal opportunities in terms of gender is also the point where in City State the discourses of 'race' and gender articulate on a daily basis. It is here the staff voiced their anxieties about giving due consideration to the needs of the girls as a whole and the needs of their Muslim students. They did not feel 'comfortable' in this area. They used terms like 'worry about saying the wrong thing' and they clearly felt less comfortable with the 'race' aspect of the situation.

> I don't want to stereotype to be quite honest, as I said before I believe this school and the home conflict. I feel, **I didn't fall into the pit** but I was aware of going to ask the questions of what are you doing when you leave here, what would you like to do, and I learned to maybe put these questions in a different light or not assume that they were going to do anything. I find that when you are in a smaller group, when I do course work with them [the Muslim students] they ask about me, you give a little bit but **I feel that I would not say things to them that I would say to a white girl or a black girl because I couldn't say that my husband does the dishes or, or I feel I don't want to because that could create problems.**
>
> (CS, Liz, emphasis added)

The staff articulated what they felt to be a clash between the expectations of the Muslim parents of what the school should provide, and the expectation of the school for its students. It was either felt that the school was seen by the Muslim parents to be a 'dumping ground' for their daughters until they reached marriageable age; or that the Muslim parents had unrealistically high expectations for their daughter in terms of future educational pathways and career patterns. Either way the staff appeared to feel that this clashed with the expectations of the school. Such comments often prefaced perceptions that inevitably such clashes of expectation led to tensions, conflict and dilemma. Here the staff felt that they were in a 'dichotomous situation where the school is leading the girls along one path and it can be at a tangent to what is actually required of them at home'. The 'trick' in negotiating this difficulty was through 'presenting what is available without offending parental opinions'. The difficulty lay in 'reaching a balance'. In this context the staff were also anxious to point out that parental background and the time of their arrival in this country was a major contributory factor affecting their expectations of school.

Some staff felt that on leaving school the girls retreated back into the family and 'we have done them little service really'. This circle of confusion and tension also appeared to lead to a lack of communication between the staff and their Muslim students, with two effects: first, some staff commented that the Muslim students tended to group themselves together, especially during lesson time, so that they could operate from a position in which they felt 'comfortable'. Interestingly this is also seen by the students of Old Town High as being a major advantage of their school. Second, the staff remarked on the resultant difficulties of encouraging the Muslim students to participate in lessons.

> The Asian girls will work in one group and there's usually an ethnic mix amongst the others. The Asian group of girls usually, given a choice, will tend to work together and resent being ungrouped. **Sometimes I will mix the entire class up. I often find then that if you get one or two Asian girls in a group with other girls the couple of Asian girls will tend to go extremely quiet, more quiet than they are normally and not join in, not contribute even to discussion. Just do as they're told as it were.**
>
> (CS, Marie, emphasis added)

In City State the failure of the Muslim students to participate in lessons was attributed to two reasons: first, peer group pressure; second, failure of the curriculum to adequately provide for their needs.

Peer group pressure in a multicultural sense does not apply to Old Town High in the same way. The staff at City State referred to the difficulties that they believed the Muslim students encountered at being confronted on a daily basis with western cultural norms. By this the staff meant not only that the girls questioned and felt resentment at their own cultural restrictions, but also that they did not feel able to discuss this amongst themselves because of community pressure. Nor did they feel able to talk about this to other students or staff from outside the community. The staff also felt that their Muslim students saw and resented the 'freedom' that other girls have outside of school without realizing the depths of the responsibility that goes with the freedom. To deal with this perceived difficulty, counselling sessions with a trained counsellor were seen to be a possible way forward – 'someone to be able to talk to about the things that frustrate them or the things that they don't agree with. They really need to be able to, if they can't talk with the family at home. It is a very close knit cultural group, and they are aware that they have to be careful what they're saying in case someone passed it on or someone heard.' This was perceived as a major contributory reason for the Muslim students at City State forming themselves into tight groupings.

A 'felt lack' of cultural knowledge was constantly alluded to by the staff of City State. It was an area in which they clearly felt ill at ease, worrying that they would say the 'wrong thing' or be 'too pushy'.

> I'm not totally au fait with everything to do with Muslim students but because I've seen Muslim girls go away from school and get married and things like that I think perhaps in some of the more fundamental of the Muslim community they are still more encouraged to go towards marriage rather than going into further education and allowed to do a career. **So I think it's hard to sort of push education to the limits with**

**them. I still think they need to be encouraged but I'm very wary of
trying to be too sort of pushy about it because I know they've got other
pressures from home and that, that will make them slightly different.**

(CS, Jane, emphasis added)

Such tensions clearly affected their Muslim students, who also used words
like pressure, stress, confusion and 'not knowing who to listen to'. Interviews with the ex-students of City State revealed that they felt that they were
not sufficiently encouraged by their teachers. One ex-Muslim student now
studying for exams at college, having persuaded her parents to allow her to
do so, felt that she had been allowed 'to drift away' at school. She attributed
this to her non-confrontational behaviour and lack of confidence in school,
which meant that she was allowed to coast along in lessons. The less she felt
the teachers encouraged her, the more she drifted away. The comments from
the staff in the school show how this becomes a vicious circle because of
their wariness to push their Muslim students into areas assumed to be closed
to them for cultural reasons. As her performance at school dropped off she
shielded her parents from that knowledge by failing to pass on letters noti-
fying them of parents' evenings where they would have had the opportunity
to discuss her progress, or lack of it. It became advantageous for her to keep
the school and her parents separated. Her parents, seemingly content with
this, were equally happy about leaving the education of their daughter to the
professionals.

Conversely those areas of concern which are voiced by the participants in
City State and which, it would seem, lead to feelings of tension and doubt,
are those areas in Old Town High where the staff and students felt secure
and comfortable. They identified several reasons for this. First, they felt that
being all Muslim girls meant that they felt comfortable to practise their
religion and discuss cultural norms and constraints from a feeling of security
without having to worry what others might think. Second, a mixture of both
Muslim and non-Muslim members of staff meant that any felt lack of knowledge of culture could be discussed with them. This was facilitated by an
Islamic ethos which permeates through the school and the curriculum.
Third, and importantly, there were strong and informal links between the
parents and the school founded on a relationship of trust.

The staff of City State were unsure in their relationships with their
Muslim students and their parents. There are students from other ethnic
groupings as well as from the indigenous white population in the school.
These girls are often from a different class background from the staff, and
some of them also see their future in terms of marriage, children and possibly some form of low status employment. Here, as confirmed by Davies
(1984), the staff appeared to have fewer problems in subsuming the discourses of class and 'race' beneath the discourse of gender in the interests of
their aim of encouraging students to be self-determining individuals and feel

comfortable doing so. However, because of their cultural assumptions about their Muslim students and their parents, particularly those who are first generation and who also come from low socio-economic backgrounds, the discourses are assumed to be in open conflict. In a busy and increasingly overloaded school day the staff often have to make practical decisions over which students receive their help, attention and encouragement. This is necessarily often those students who make some attempt to help themselves or bring themselves to the attention of the teachers for many and varied reasons.

Those students who are not perceived to be committed to academic achievement, further education and a career, or who do not bring themselves to the attention of the staff, or who appear to have switched themselves off from school for many and varied reasons, are the ones who fall by the way-side. In the case of the Muslim students who fall into these categories and who need a great deal of encouragement to participate in lessons, stereotypical cultural assumptions are an additional factor. This results in a vicious circle which is amply illustrated by the following comment:

> . . . so they just stand back and the sad thing is that sometimes even the teachers themselves **having this viewpoint don't encourage our Muslim girls to achieve their potential**. They have low expectations as well I feel. True, this is it, this is the danger and the thing is now it's come to the point now where the child has stopped believing in herself.
>
> (CS, Rita, emphasis added)

To this point this chapter has highlighted the tensions of the staff in City State in their relationships with their Muslim students. This is made more evident by the comparison of the experiences of their counterparts in Old Town High. It has also made clear that the staff of City State are aware of the needs of its Muslim students and the necessity of providing different strategies to deal with their perceived difference. To this end it has put in place several structural initiatives which the school believes will go some way to providing 'equality in difference'. This is the focus of the next and concluding section of this chapter.

Initiatives to deal with difference

Chapter 3 outlined those initiatives that small scale studies indicate have been implemented by schools throughout Britain to meet the needs of their Muslim students concerning the formal curriculum, the informal curriculum, and community and parental links with the school. This section aims to put these studies in the context of the experiences of the staff and students in one particular state school, City State. At the time of the research City State had implemented some of these approaches and not others. The responses of the staff in City State to these issues indicate that in this school some of these needs are more readily addressed and accommodated than others, and the reasons for this become especially clear as these experiences are compared with those of the staff and students of Old Town High.

Formal curriculum

With regard to the curricular needs of the students in City State, the staff emphasized the multicultural commitment of the school. In this area they talked about appropriate subject matter across the curriculum and in relation to their particular subject area, language needs, religious education and withdrawal from certain lessons such as religious education and personal and social education.

Questions concerning the use of appropriate and culturally specific subject material met with variable responses commensurate with the requirements of the National Curriculum in different subject areas. Although teachers of some subject areas, such as humanities, felt that there was room for an Islamic orientation in the curriculum, it often took the form of a specific module, or it was introduced as part of a multicultural approach where a variety of subject material was made available. The latter approach figured fairly consistently over the range of disciplines, in keeping with the equal opportunities and multicultural commitment of the school. Alternatively some teachers of subject areas, such as science, indicated that they had very little room for manoeuvre at all.

The staff at Old Town High were also committed to this multicultural approach and equally constrained by the National Curriculum, but the difference is that the Islamic dimension could always be addressed in Islamic Studies or in discussion with the Muslim staff should the need arise, an opportunity not available to the Muslim students in City State. In contrast, the staff in City State voiced their concerns of finding subject matter appropriate to their Muslim students which would encourage them to participate in the lessons.

They find it quite difficult when we do things like looking at women in society. To begin with they often don't contribute. **You've got to try to find ways to get the Muslim girls in particular to make a connection between them and the subject matter because quite often they turn off.** I don't know whether it's because the system is white predominantly that the Muslim girls very rarely will bring into the lesson anything from their own backgrounds unless specifically invited to do so. Even if it's just something generally about home they don't go into anything that might be specifically common to Muslim families. They will go along with all the other things such as going home late, they'll go along with what they think I want from them or what they think the other girls will want from them as well. I think they're very careful not to bring their own cultural issues into the lesson because I don't think they want to be mocked and sometimes I don't know how much to encourage them because you know that they do get mocked when they do it.

(CS, Marie, emphasis added)

Both schools are constrained by the National Curriculum, but the students in Old Town High have the advantage of having Muslim teachers who are able to provide an Islamic dimension as and when the need arises. They also have the benefit of being able to discuss a variety of concerns in Islamic studies. The Islamic dimension permeates the curriculum, it is not 'bolted on'. The staff at City State believe that there is still a lot of work to be done 'in the curriculum subject areas in essence, not bits added on but really the whole thing be embedded so it becomes so natural'.

The staff at both City State and Old Town High voiced concerns about the language needs of their students. In both schools the cultural context of the majority of the Muslim girls is that they are double and sometimes multiple language users. This has implications for academic attainment in terms of assessment and testing. Encouragement to develop their communication skills in both an oral and a written sense is therefore given high priority in both schools. In Old Town High there was an additional concern that the students would face problems when applying for higher education because of the assumption that their language skills would be insufficient to cope with the demands of a degree course.

In City State language barriers were referred to in two senses: first, as being to an extent responsible for encouraging the Muslim students to group together whilst in school:

One of the reasons that the girls like to stick together is that I have noticed that although they speak very good English there's still this language barrier. **They'll say, 'Miss, I can't explain to you, I don't know the words to be able to tell you' or 'Miss, if I told you, you wouldn't understand'. There's this thing amongst them that they understand each other obviously but that we are not going to understand their little ways and we are not interested in their ways.** I mean I'm fascinated and love to hear but it takes a heck of a lot of encouragement to get them to tell you something about their background. I suppose therefore they stay together to protect that.

(CS, Marie, emphasis added)

Secondly, language barriers were mentioned in the context of difficulties in communicating with parents. This is not a problem at Old Town High. Parents' evenings at City State, however, were described as being poorly attended by the parents of the Muslim students, although there has been some improvement since the school adopted the policy of directly contacting the parents by phone through the home liaison teacher, who speaks several community languages. Where Muslim parents attended the evenings, teachers often noted that it would be the father, brother or uncle who spoke directly to the teacher with the mother in the background.

City State was felt by the staff to offer the best language resources possible to its Muslim students within the confines of the funding available. In this respect the Section 11 staff were concerned to point to the reduction in their funding. Although they believed that language needs would take priority they felt that the prerequisite of good home–school links with Muslim parents was good communication between the parents and the school. This also needs adequate resourcing but it is here that the Section 11 staff believed that cuts were inevitable.

The question of withdrawal from certain lessons such as religious education and Physical Education has not proved to be a problem in City State after a sensitive consultation procedure; however, the religious needs of the students are not addressed by City State because there is no member of staff in City State who is a practising Muslim apart from the male Urdu teacher. This is a difference between City State and Old Town High. It was an expected difference, but not one that the Muslim students in City State appeared to feel the lack of. It is, however, the moral dimension of their religious faith which spills over into cultural needs where problems are seen to arise and about which the staff of City State voiced concerns:

> In terms of an ongoing developmental thing I think a lot has happened. We started off with the very basics and parental requests in terms of dress, even a place to pray. Food as far as possible has been met. The girls are quite confident and forthright in asking for their needs. Where there is a slight concern is on the values. Sometimes parents feel, and rightly so as well, that the values which they stand for are not reinforced in schools. In Islam the religion is the essence of life and they would like especially in curriculum areas like RE, more first-hand input from people themselves to come and teach the subject.
>
> (CS, Rita)

Informal curriculum

In this area of the informal curriculum the staff of City State claim that there have been some advancements in terms of provision of vegetarian meals, respect shown other languages by use of dual signs and letters if necessary, celebration of *Eids*, sensitivity during *Ramazan*, provision of prayer facilities if requested, and permission given for visits back to Pakistan. The physical education department was also sensitive to the needs of the Muslim students in terms of dress, facilities and showering arrangements. School uniform is presented and offered for sale at the parents' evenings for new students in different forms, including *shalwar kameez*.

There have been some difficulties with scarves in science and which 'dangle in the paint' in art but generally such issues have been tackled with little fuss. There is also provision of extra-curricular activities and although there is no Islamic Society, there is a lunchtime club specifically aimed at the Asian students. The school has instigated women-only evenings to encourage the Muslim mothers into the school. Muslim students have also participated in drama and dance performances at these evenings and they have been extremely successful although transport has been a difficulty. Work experience for Muslim students is also approached in a sensitive manner, with due consideration given to the wishes of the parents and the student and counselling offered where these wishes do not coincide.

Community and parental links

This is an area that the staff of City State have targeted as being one which is in need of some improvement and one which comparison with Old Town High reveals as being crucial to the educational well-being of the Muslim students. The parents need to have the confidence to be able to work with the school on both a formal and an informal basis and in an attempt to facilitate this, City State has two Muslim governors on the governing body, although there was no evidence of regular consultations with local mosques or other Muslim community groups.

The staff at City State indicated that their inability to communicate with the Muslim parents was a major problem. This is not a problem at Old Town High, where strong and often informal links between the school and the local Muslim community meant that parents were able to voice their concerns in a way that was non-threatening to all parties.

> I also hear from my parents asking about certain textbooks which we have covered, 'Do you think it will be appropriate, I mean is it appropriate for a Muslim school to be studying so and so book?' 'Exactly,' I say, 'we are in a safe environment, we can do it, in another school I would question it myself but in this school I can do it because there's always the other dimension coming into it.' So I mean I've had queries like that from my parents which is good.
>
> (OTH, head teacher)

Communication between the home and the school is an important factor here. Again it is an area where the staff in City State felt both tension and concern. The perceived clash of expectation between home and school, complicity on behalf of the Muslim students in shielding their parents from their own performances and misdemeanours, and also the different codes of behaviour of their peers, of which they know their parents will not approve, inevitably become factors which contribute to weak home–school links. In City State this is complicated by the fact that it draws its students from a geographically diverse area, and limited by the fact that there are insufficient numbers of staff with either the language or the cultural expertise.[1] Neither does the school have a ready-made network from which to build and strengthen these links.

In contrast, Old Town High has links with parents and the community which are both strong and informal, partly because the school is centred in the community from where it draws its students. Here, concerns voiced in the mosque or on the street corner are passed back to the head teacher. The parents are quite confident to communicate over the phone or to 'drop into' school.

> **I think mainly the reason that I have succeeded is that I am one of them.** I think that plays a part, it's like you can understand me because you know the background. The second is that in other schools students are embarrassed to bring their parents because their mothers are simply dressed and the image they have. In my school the students are not embarrassed by their mothers. They're quite happy to introduce their mother to their sisters. I came from Pakistan at the age of 13 and I was embarrassed to take my mum around and say this is my mother. These students are quite happy to take their mothers around.
>
> (OTH, head teacher, emphasis added)

These needs have been identified by the staff in City State as areas which require attention and improvement. These are also needs which multicultural initiatives and equal opportunity policies have failed to meet. They constitute the 'real' needs of Muslim students which move beyond practical, more readily achievable and pragmatic changes in the school.

Although they were given opportunities to address these issues on a series of staff INSET days, some staff, particularly the more experienced ones, felt that all these did was repeat 'common sense' knowledge which failed to furnish them with a working and in-depth knowledge of the needs of the Muslim students and their parents.

> I don't know whether the Muslim community is leaning more towards women working. I assume not. It could equally be I was wrong about that but you never have the time to find out. I often think that when we have INSET days and we do racism awareness I think for me to find out about the different ethnic groups, particularly the Muslim girls, here because there are so many of them and things about their culture, that would be helpful. Far more helpful than trying to go over the same ground of racial awareness because we're still getting racism from the staff. There is no two ways about that. We don't have that knowledge of their backgrounds. **It's very easy to moan about their parents again, and a lot of that does go on, even though we are supposed to be racially aware here,** and are so compared to a lot of other schools. But still we

don't bend the system to meet their needs at all. We're still plodding along in this very English old-fashioned system.

(CS, Marie, emphasis added)

At this point it must be emphasized that City State enjoys an excellent reputation with the local education authority and Ofsted (the school inspection service) concerning its multicultural approach and initiatives. Further, the staff are generally committed to both the policy and its implementation through a high level of pastoral support within the school.

Conclusion: can state schools provide equality in difference?

The concern of this chapter has been to emphasize the similarities between City State and Old Town High which are in keeping with the aims of particularly liberal and radical feminisms in terms of equal access to the curriculum, the questioning of gender stereotypes, enjoyment of working in a predominantly female environment, the employment of female staff as role models and the adoption of an approach which seeks to make the actual experiences of women more central to the education of the students. However, it has also highlighted that the equal opportunities policies and practices on 'race' and gender adopted by City State have served to promote anxiety in the staff concerning their dealings with their Muslim students and their parents. This in turn is reflected in the confusion and tension expressed by their Muslim pupils, and affects their attitudes to academic achievement and success and their expectations on leaving school. The question is, can state schools provide equality in difference?

In comparison it would seem that the staff and students in Old Town High feel 'comfortable' and confident enough to shift their discursive positionings with respect to the discourses of 'race' and gender as and when the particular moment requires it. This is in contrast to the staff of City State, who appear to be immobilized by many different concerns in their dealings with the Muslim students. The Muslim students in each school are not homogenous in terms of religious adherence, class, physical and mental ability and linguistic ability, but they do share the experience of being Muslim women who at present belong to a disempowered group in Britain. The analysis suggests that it is the Muslim students in Old Town High who are potentially better placed to challenge this positioning than their counterparts in City State. Here the idea of equality in difference is central, for it is in Old Town High, where the Muslim students are comfortable in their difference, that there is the potential for the process of exploration and questioning and challenging from within an Islamic framework to begin.

In City State the discourses of 'race' and gender, particularly, are in open conflict. Not only this, but because the Muslim students in City State do not benefit from a shared and secure environment, a shared conversation, a feeling of belonging, they do not have the advantages of the Muslim students in Old Town High. This means that in City State there is not and cannot be equality in difference, which has repercussions for the academic achievement of the Muslim students in terms of expectations and self-confidence. In Old Town High the lack of equipment, resources, subject options and extra-curricular activities is more than made up for by the value and experiences of sharing a common identity. From this point of reference the Muslim students in Old Town High are then empowered to concentrate on educational achievement and academic success, although this could be further capitalized on if the school had the educational equipment and resources to extend their range of options and other educational opportunities. Here, there is the **possibility** for academic achievement leading to further and higher education.

There is a concern that Muslim girls' schools reduce educational opportunities because they reflect a cultural tradition which relegates their students to an inferior position by 'educating them for marriage and motherhood in a particular Islamic sense'; encouraging an ethos within them which is conducive to the perpetuation of the traditional sex stereotypes of girls and women. This was highlighted in Chapter 3. It was considered by the Swann Committee thus:

> We believe that it is important to recognise that the concept of a single-sex school in the Muslim context differs in certain fundamental respects from the philosophy underlying existing single-sex schools in the education system. Girls' schools in this country – apart from their pupil populations and to a lesser extent their teacher populations – have in practice differed little from coeducational schools in that the core curriculum has been the same and the same educational standards in terms of public examinations have been sought. Traditional 'girls' subjects' such as home economics have of course tended to be included in the curriculum at the expense of 'technical' boys' subjects, but in recent years even this difference of emphasis has become less clearly defined with the greater acceptance in society as a whole of a broader role for women. From the statements which have been made by **spokesmen** of the Muslim community, however, it is clear that the form of single-sex education, which at least some are advocating for girls would entail a far more central focus in the curriculum on education for marriage and motherhood in a particular Islamic sense, with other subjects receiving less attention and with the notion of careers education being seen as irrelevant to the pattern of adult life which the girls are likely to pursue.
> (Swann 1985: 505, emphasis added)

The analysis of the data in this chapter challenges these views.

Finally, it is now clear why some of the needs of Muslim students are more readily addressed and accommodated than others in City State. The comparison with Old Town High highlights how the multicultural aspect of City State and its commitment to equal opportunities in terms of gender and 'race' presents problems for the staff when dealing with the Muslim students, which are in turn reflected in their approach to school life. It is here that clear differences emerge between the students in these schools concerning questions of identity and self-knowledge of their Muslim students. It is evident from this analysis that although City State has implemented a number of such pragmatic structural initiatives such as a dress code, language provision, food requirements, prayer room and sensitivity to requests for withdrawal from certain lessons, this can mean a reification of culturally held stereotypes formulated within historical, spatial and political contexts which do not allow for diversity of opinion, complexity and change. **Such initiatives also mask the deeper issue of what it actually means to be a British Muslim in a state school and in a plural society which is fluid, fractured and shifting.** It is these issues which the next chapter is concerned to explore further by looking at students' attitudes to Nazrah, a fictitious Muslim girl who is academically able.

Note

1 There is a female Asian teacher who has responsibility for home–school liaison who is employed as a Section 11 teacher.

7   The Nazrah story

Kaye Haw and an analysis by Saeeda Shah

Introduction

The aim of Chapter 7 is to introduce the 'voice' of the students through the Nazrah story. These are the stories written by the students concerning the high academic performance of a fictitious Muslim girl. The stories that have been chosen are included in their entirety. There are four reasons for using these stories in this way. First, because they represent the 'voices' of the Muslim students without the constraints of the interview procedure and for this reason I only impose my analysis upon them as they are introduced. Second, Saeeda Shah is given the opportunity to interpret them from her perspective and this adds another dimension to the book. Third, and more specifically, they raise and reiterate several important issues; and fourth, the stories show the students that wrote them as complex human beings and active readers of their cultures and contexts both in and out of school.

These stories highlight the more general issue of how girls place themselves within a discourse of femininity which views competence, independence, competition and intellectual achievement as inconsistent with femininity and 'positively related to masculinity' (Horner 1972). More specifically the stories also bring out issues of racism, arranged marriage, status as a sister in the family, honour (*izzat*) within the kinship group, *bradari* gaze, and progression to further and higher education, while highlighting the issues of difference and fragmentation within these two groups of Muslim students themselves.

The Nazrah story

The Nazrah story was the first piece of writing that the students participating in the research were asked to do. It was designed to reveal their attitudes to academic success by asking them to write an imaginative story about Nazrah, a girl in an inner city comprehensive school, who had come top in all her exams at the end of the year. They were also asked to write about what they thought Nazrah was like as a person and what she would be doing when she was 25.

As we have seen, the Muslim students in both City State and Old Town High come from similar socio-economic backgrounds and many of their parents migrated from the same areas in Pakistan. If the premise of the Swann Report, that girls in Muslim schools are educated for marriage and motherhood in a particular Islamic sense with careers education being seen as irrelevant to their adult life, is correct it would be expected that the students in Old Town High would show less positive attitudes to the high academic achievement of Nazrah and to Nazrah herself. Faulkner also suggests school type is important: 'The result appears to suggest that the type of school attended was the major influencing factor on the development of the attitudes of these pupils' (Faulkner 1991: 216).

In a statistical analysis of the stories, I concluded:[1]

> The students in the private Muslim school were significantly more positive to the high academic achievement of Nazrah and to Nazrah herself. However, both groups produced a favourable response. The Muslim girls and non-Muslim girls in the state school were separated out as well as the Muslim girls in the private school. Again there was a highly significant difference between the three groups with the Muslim girls in Old Town High scoring most positively in their attitude towards the high academic achievement of Nazrah, followed by the Muslim girls in City State and then the non-Muslim girls in City State.
>
> (Haw 1995a: 323–6)

Signs that the students were concerned about conforming to traditional stereotypes of femininity can be clearly traced in their stories about Nazrah's high academic achievement. In many of the stories Nazrah appeared to experience inner doubts and conflict. This was often expressed in terms of disbelief and not feeling able to show their joy. Fear of negative consequences such as loss of friends or being considered 'different' and suffering as a direct result of that success was also in evidence. Sometimes this was also expressed in racial terms or with a specific cultural slant such as the issue of arranged marriage, status as a sister in the family, honour within the kinship group, the issue of going on to further and higher education, and parental attitudes to educating girls. The stories also illustrate differences and fragmentations in explicit ways; some stories, for example, portrayed parents viewing the education of their daughters as not having relevance or importance for them, while other stories revealed parents as both educationally ambitious for their daughters and supportive of them, and their aspirations.

Further, the stories show that as these young Muslim girls and women negotiate their own personal and social contexts they make intentional decisions while at the same time being objects of the discourses which make up their lives. These are the discourses in school which are associated with the schools' cultures and subcultures and those out of school, which include: the discourses of the family and generations within the family influenced by their contemporary and historical socio-economic/political positionings; the *bradari*/kinship network; the local community; local and national politics; and those associated with the student's ethnic/racial/class/cultural/religious positionings. More generically these discourses can be described as discourses of 'Muslimness'.

I do not want to impose a more in-depth analysis than this on these stories. I believe that they should speak for themselves in their entirety. I have also generally left the spelling and grammar intact. The selection of the stories has been made on the basis that they are particularly evocative examples of the issues I have just raised rather than length, style, neatness or overall merit. The selected stories appear as two collections which begin and end with a brief introduction and summary.

Collection one

The first collection of six stories highlights the issues of racism, bullying and isolation, with the recognition that these are issues which equally affect girls from a variety of groups and backgrounds.

Shameem's story

Nazrah was very happy she had come top of the class. But a few of her friends got jealous of her because they wanted to come top of the class. They wanted to be better than an Eastern girl. The teacher was proud of Nazrah because she had come top. A few of the other teachers were very unhappy that no western girls had come top. Nazrah's family were very happy to know that their sister or daughter came top of the class. They invited Nazrah's friends and also all her family and her cousins to a celebration party but only a few of the cousins and a few of her friends came. Next day in school, her friends made life difficult for her. Soon she started regretting coming top.

Nazrah was a clever, hard working person who didn't like to upset other people and tried her best to please everyone. Nazrah will be a teacher at the school where she was taught.

Nazia's story

When she heard that she had passed she was so happy and got excited about what her parents would say. When her friends found out, they were jealous and would not talk to her but it didn't matter because she was top of the class and when her parents found out they were so happy that they said 'what would you like to do or where would you like to go' and her brothers and sisters were happy with her because she had done good and given her parents a good name.

Nazrah was a nice and pleasant person. All the staff were happy with her and she wasn't interested in friends because she was happy in work. When she was 25 she would like to carry on and get a job and earn money. She would like to work all over the world.

Sameera's story

She was overjoyed and very happy but felt sorry for the other people who had failed. Some people got jealous about Nazrah and broke friends with her so she was lonely. But her close friends stood by her whatever happened. The people would start trouble on her and she would get bullied and then she would get stressed. People would say she is a snob, a show off, or that she cheated but then people would start hitting her and then start calling her racist names. She would not be able to take this. People would call her disgusting names and use racist language. Her parents were proud of her, but her school mates were jealous of her because she got top marks. If I was her, I would be proud of myself and ignore these horrid people. Her family were proud of her and told her to ignore people because they were jealous.

Nazrah was a caring person who had a good personality, she only cared for her work and was sensible. She cared for other people as well. Her family cared for her and told her not to worry and that she would get a better job than anyone who bullied her badly. She will be settling down with her high paid lawyer job, with a caring husband who understands her feelings and two children who she really cares for. She has become famous and very rich. She is proud of what she has done and she is writing a book on school bullying and has opened a bullying free line so that she can help other people who have suffered the pain that she suffered.

Rizwana's story

Some people who are racist towards her. A few will be happy for her. Some will turn their back and bully her. Her parents will be proud of her, but they could think she could have done better and could have got higher marks.

She was a down-to-earth person. She probably had high hopes and thought she could do whatever she could do. When she is 25, she probably will be married and have started a family because she is Asian.

Zarka's story

I would imagine that unless she had a friend who was on the same 'level' as her, she would be left on her own. The other girls may feel inferior to her and so keep away. She may be emotionally bullied and called names by some yet a few may genuinely be pleased and congratulate her. Although the class may have mixed reactions, her family, I would imagine would be extremely pleased. They may reward her in some way. The girl could have also achieved these grades by continuous studying and staying in each night instead of going out with her friends, which no doubt, she would rather do.

I would imagine Nazrah to be 'over the moon' at achieving these grades. She would have so many possibilities to consider. She could do almost anything she wanted. The reaction of the class, though, well, some of them could purely be just jealousy. They probably wish it was them who had these wonderful grades in place of her. They don't realize all the hard work she did to get where she is now. If they had studied as Nazrah did then, maybe they would have done well too. I think that they feel that if they can hurt her in some way, then it will make up for them not doing as well as they hoped.

I imagine Nazrah to be quite a reserved sort of person. One that cares about her future and wants to do well. She sounds like extremely hard working and prepared to give up her spare time to study. She seems level-headed and knows what she wants. She also seems to be the sort of person who would not care what other people said about her. I would imagine Nazrah to have gone through college and got her A-levels, gone through, or still at University getting a degree, and probably in a highly paid job. She may have a 'flash' car, a beautiful home, but without any children yet! She may be married or have a boy-friend. Judging by her character, I would imagine that she wouldn't have a boyfriend at present.

Shabana's story

When the teacher announced that Nazrah had come top of the class all her friends started being horrible they said to her brain box, she thinks she knows everything Miss Know It All. Nazrah hated her teacher for saying she came top. Her teacher told Nazrah that in front of the whole school she was going to get a prize but she told her teacher she didn't want the prize. Her teacher felt disappointed at what she said because Nazrah had always agreed with the teachers and what they had said all her teachers had said to her, that they were proud of her but Nazrah wasn't proud of herself when she got home, her mother told her 'why didn't you walk home with your friends?' Nazrah shrugged her shoulders and went upstairs then there was a phone call and Nazrah's Dad answered the phone and it was the Head Teacher, he wanted to congratulate Nazrah's parents on her results when her father had finished talking, he called Nazrah and said 'why didn't you tell us about your results?' 'Oh, because I forgot'. 'You forgot?' replied the mother. 'It is a wonderful news' said her father. 'Let's celebrate' they said. Her mother cooked a special dish for Nazrah then her mother said 'you don't have to do the washing up, your brother can do it'. 'Oh, Mum' he said. Then, Nazrah went up to bed.

Nazrah is the type of person who doesn't like to hurt others feelings. She likes people to treat her like a normal person especially her parents. She is a neat and tidy person and likes to help people in any way that she can. I think Nazrah will be in college and getting a degree in Law with her parents support and help from the teachers.

Summary

Although the issues of racism and bullying come to the forefront in this first collection of stories the complex reactions of Shameem, Nazia, Sameera, Rizwana, Zarka and Shabana to academic achievement as they shift their positioning to cope with their success and the reactions of their friends, family and extended family, are also highlighted. The issue of *izzat* is raised by Nazia in her story so that 'her brothers and sisters were happy with her because she had done good and given her parents a good name', while *bradari* 'gaze' and their reaction to a successful Nazrah is evident in Shameem's story.

Bullying, peer group pressure and isolation were also evident in many of the Nazrah stories irrespective of whether they were written by Muslim or non-Muslim white, African-Caribbean or bicultural students. These last issues also feature again in the second collection of five stories from Maryam, Irfana, Riffat, Fozia and Saffia.

Collection two

The focus here is on the interwoven issues of further education, arranged marriage and the status of the sister and the woman in the Islamic family. In Chapter 2 Saeeda Shah describes the differing patterns and standards of behaviour/character applied to men and women in Islamic societies. Historically this dichotomy has 'relegated women to spaces of "otherness", making them invisible, behind "veils and walls" (*chadar* and *chardewari*)' (see p. 60). In Islamic societies these symbolic 'veils and walls' (*chadar* and *chardewari*) came to operate beyond physical spaces so that education for women was interpreted to be violating the assumed sanctity of veils and walls. These boundaries are reinforced by the threat of social stigma so that the discomfort and uncertainty which result are evidenced in the following stories.

Maryam's story

Nazrah, obviously a hardworking student, would have been pleased, all her time and effort had been worth it, yet be disappointed that they have been wasted maybe because of her parents' 'backward' ideals that education is not so important and that girls like her should be married as soon as they reach the age of 16. Nazrah would feel confused and unsure what she would do with the results but not letting her teacher down who had high hopes for her made her feel good. Higher education was what she wanted and what she worked for but making her parents realize this would take a bit of time.

She probably would have expected these results as she knew she had worked hard and usually came first in class tests but it would be a shame to let her efforts produce no good future for her in later life. She would want to build up a career and become something good but scared her dreams may be shattered. The results might give her more confidence and determination to reach the top despite what her parents may think.

Nazrah was a hard working individual, hoping to reach the top. She may have not been so popular but instead regarded as a 'swot' because of her continuous visits to the school library and more interest in what the teacher had to say. Nazrah would become a doctor, lawyer or something that is if her parents agree for her to go for higher education, but if not she would be married, looking after her children and doing the housework. In both cases, she would be married by this age.

Irfana's story

At first she couldn't believe it. She thought she had misheard what the teacher had just told her, so just to make sure, she asked if she really had come top of her class. When the teacher answered in the positive, Nazrah's face lit up with pride. She really had tried her best and worked continuously these past few months before the exams. She couldn't wait to tell her parents. Maybe this will persuade them to let her study further. After saying goodbye to the teacher, she gently replaced the receiver and headed back to the dining room, where her parents and elder brother were having breakfast. She tried not to look too excited because she didn't want to give the wrong impression. Her brother asked her what she got and when she told them that she came top in her class, the dining room was filled with the sound of congratulations. Nazrah looked cross to her brother, who understood what

Nazrah expected him to say. He took a deep breath while Nazrah held hers just in case it was bad news. 'Dad', begun her brother, 'do you think you'll be sending her to university now? She proved that she will come top in her class, and I really think she will make a brilliant lawyer. There was a sudden silence, that engulfed the room. Nazrah could hear her heart beating. She just couldn't meet her father's eyes, in case they held the wrong answer. She heard someone replace their tea cup on the table. The few seconds that it took her father to absorb what Nazrah's brother had just said seemed to take an eternity. 'Well'. The silence was at last broken; and it was her father who had spoken. She was dreading what the answer was going to be. 'Well, it is worth thinking about. She has really proved that she can work hard, but is she going to keep it up? I will however think the matter through and let you know as soon as I reach some sort of a conclusion' and with that he left the room.

Nazrah seems like a very hard working girl who wants to prove to her parents that she is capable of getting good grades and achieving the top position in the class. She was also determined to convince her parents to let her attend university after leaving the comprehensive school. She however relies rather on her elder brother to do most of the talking on her behalf. But she would not let others walk over her. At the age of 25 Nazrah could be doing any of the following. Either married or studying at university. If she is really a very strong willed person by the time she is 25 she would have probably convinced her parents and got in to university to study whatever she wants or she could be married at the time looking after a child or two.

Riffat's story

When Nazrah was told that she had passed her exams, she felt very good and pleased with her achievements. She did not want to boast to her friends but she could not help smiling as she was very happy. When she got home and told her parents they were not surprised and did not react. All they said was 'don't get too happy, your sister got the same sort of grades as you but they became useless in the sort of life she was going to have'. Nazrah was shocked at her parents words and then realized that she could not take her education any further, as at the age of 17 her sister had an arranged marriage, and became a housewife. Nazrah was disappointed, all her hard work had gone to waste. She could not believe that all that work had resulted to nothing. Her parents had arranged for her to get married and she did. When she had married her husband and her got on well together and he agreed for her to go to college and get higher education and even go to university to get a degree. Nazrah was astonished at her husband's decision, but she was very pleased it was like passing all her exams over again. At this point Nazrah thought that if she had not worked hard and got her GCSEs she may not have been able to continue her education at college studying A levels. So it was good that she had worked as hard as she did.

Nazrah was an outgoing and hardworking pupil. She was very ambitious but would not upset her parents by disagreeing with their decisions. At the age of 25 Nazrah would be married and probably have a good job that was well paid. She would hopefully be well-off. But most of all she would be happy.

Fozia's story

Nazrah was very surprised and was stunned when she heard about the results. She had never expected it. She had always thought of being one of the less intellectual type of pupil but this was great. Anyway, she deserved the results she had achieved, she had worked extremely hard for the exams. The class continued with their lesson but Nazrah was in a dream world, thinking of all the opportunities that were lying ahead. She could become anything she wanted. The bell rang and Nazrah and her friends left the class. All her friends were very happy for her and congratulated her on her success. The only person who envied her was her brother, Ismail, who had become the top pupil of the class. He was expected to achieve a very high result but he had come fourth in the class and he was disheartened. Soon the bell rang for home time and all the pupils left for their homes. Nazrah and her brother waited at the bus stop for their bus. Nazrah looked at her brother, he was very quiet and quite frankly she didn't know how to break the ice. The bus came and they both got on and then got off at the bus stop near their house. They both entered the house and went to their parents. Nazrah's Mum wasn't in but her Dad was. Their Dad asked: 'Ismail, my son, how did you do in your exams, I hope you achieved the results you are capable of achieving'. Ismail stood in front of his father in silence. Nazrah now knew why he had been so quiet, he was ashamed of his result. 'Well' exclaimed their father 'tell me'. Ismail managed to answer and said 'five Bs, one D, one E and one A'. 'What happened to you, I expected a promising result, I expected all As from you'. Ismail walked away mumbling something about him being sorry. Nazrah stood there expecting her father to ask her the same but he didn't ask. She went away upstairs and sat in front of her mirror taking a good look at herself. She thought about why her father hadn't asked about her results. Maybe it was a bad time, with Ismail getting such marks. She would wait till supper time and if no one asked she would tell them her result.

Supper-time came and no one asked so she started the subject and told her result to her father. Her father was pleased and set her as a prime example to Ismail. She talked about all the options open to her and how she could do any job she wanted to. Her Dad listened and didn't say a word. When she had finished she asked her Dad his opinion. He looked at her and said 'you are 16 years old and you know what girls at your age do, the only reason I let you continue on with school was because your Mum wanted you to get a good education. In two years time, we are planning to get you married to your cousin'. She looked at her Dad and couldn't believe what she had heard. She walked away and went to her bedroom. She felt pain and regret, the opposite of what she had felt when she had heard about her exam result all her hopes and her dreams had been shattered.

She had always thought her parents were different from other Asian parents and now this had all happened. Now she could never do anything that she wanted with her life, she was the same as all her friends. Nazrah is a quiet and determined person. It is obvious she had worked hard for her exams. She also does not stand up to people. She accepts everything coming to her. She has no confidence in herself. When she is 25 Nazrah will be looking after her house, husband and children.

Saffia's story

Naturally Nazrah was overwhelmed at the news of her coming at the top of the class in all her subjects. She knew that all the study she had put in had paid off. Nazrah, a popular girl in the class was last year told by the form teacher that unless Nazrah wasn't prepared to study she would be placed in the bottom set of her class. From then, Nazrah knew that with her being in a large class and not getting enough attention, due to interruptions, she would have to do a lot of private study at home. The feelings that ran through Nazrah were undescribable and the news was a shock to her. She had only expected to pull her grades up a little bit, but now she had the top grade. All the members of her class were pleased and happy for her, except for one. Amreen, who was the popular girl of the class and who was always the top of the class before Nazrah had started to make the school envious of her. Amreen hated Nazrah for ruining her position in class. Nazrah became popular and after the results were told, she had proved to be successful as well. Nazrah's teacher was also proud and congratulated Nazrah on her results. When Nazrah got home, she informed her parents and sisters. Her sisters were very pleased for her and so were her parents. Nazrah had many plans for her future, including going to university if she had the right grades. But she knew this would not happen as her parents disapproved of her having any further education. Beyond upper school, Nazrah would try to discuss it with her parents. But her mother would clarify her point that women belonged at home and that men had the role to play in the outside world. On the other hand, her father liked the idea of having an educated daughter, but disapproved of her attending a university with grown men present. Nazrah was pretty sure that these grades that she had attained would help change her parents' mind, but they hadn't as another argument got them all nowhere. That night, thoughts revolved around Nazrah's mind.

What was the point of working so hard if you couldn't go anywhere with it? She spent time thinking about the answer to this question but soon dozed off!

Nazrah is a determined person from the character I have given her. I don't think she likes people putting her down (like the way her teacher had done) and is determined to prove them wrong otherwise; she succeeded in her determination. Not only this but Nazrah also has the skill to socialize and this is shown because she seems to be very popular in her class. Nazrah is fairly confident and knows what she wants in life even though her parents oppose her plans she continues to ask them why. This proves that she is confident. I think Nazrah will be a married woman with maybe two children. The reason for this is that her parents were strongly against her going to university. This would have affected the decision that Nazrah would have to take and judging from the last question answered I think Nazrah decided to live the life of what had her mother said 'I think women belong in the house and men in the outside world'.

Summary

This last sentence is a particularly appropriate one with which to end this section. This collection of stories has not only brought generational differences in attitudes towards further education and marriage into sharp focus, but it has also highlighted the overarching issue of the private and the public spheres in Islamic communities and the consequent shaping of gendered roles which are now explored further through the reintroduction of the 'voice' of Saeeda Shah.

Saeeda Shah's analysis – a muddled maze: reworking the routes

Kaye Haw argues in the Introduction and Chapter 1 of this book that every piece of research is positioned in time and space. Her discussion is intended to explain certain shifts and developments in her work over time. Her argument certainly carries weight, as understanding and interpreting multiple shifting discourses, and the discursive practices involved therein, cannot be a fixed activity. Meanings are layered and multidimensional, invalidating any analysis as absolute. Accordingly, my version is also a situated interpretation with its own limitations. It is an effort to explore the issues from a specific positioning, aimed at enhancing the understanding of the research context, and the issues involved.

Education of immigrant, Pakistani Muslim girls is a complex issue and both Kaye Haw and I believe that it is simplistic to analyse it merely against the backdrop of more pragmatic needs like language provisions, dress code, food requirements, prayer rooms, or a nominal religious education (see page 67 of this book). The educational needs, situational barriers and actual achievements of these girls are all influenced by the multiple forces, discourses and powerplays active in the host and parent contexts. Besides the obvious, heavily symbolic divides of East/West, white/black, and Muslim/non-Muslim, there are diverse 'secondary discourses' within and surrounding each construction. It is **a muddled maze** and, to me, any perspective in this context can be just another effort at **re-working the routes**.

My access to the research data regarding 'the educational experiences of Muslim girls' was limited. Although I had many discussions with Kaye Haw about her completed research, it certainly is very different from having access to 'raw data'. I have tried to explain my positioning in 'Why contribute to this book' in Chapter 1 section 2. Also, I have read only a selection of Nazrah stories and the thesis for which the research was undertaken. In my view, open-ended interviews are a highly subjective construction, and in a way 'processed data'. Accordingly, the analysis which follows focuses on the Nazrah stories as authentic data pointing to 'the **educational** experiences of Muslim girls'. This part looks first at the issue of 'Muslim identity' because this research focused on the 'Education for Muslim girls in contemporary Britain', and in that context it becomes important to understand the participants' perceptions of their identity. Next I consider the role **and** status of women in Islam, and how it relates to their education in this specific research context; and finally I briefly consider the concepts of marriage and sexuality, male/female relationships within Islam, and the multiple discourses surrounding them. The aim is to explore the 'tensions and conflicts in the research context'. These elements reflect the power play which, broadly speaking, determines the priorities concerning the education of Muslim girls, in a situation where decision making and passing judgements have exclusively become male domains, in direct contradiction to Islamic injunctions and Qur'anic teachings.

Islam and Muslim identity

The participating students were selected as a group, specifically for being Muslim. One interesting aspect of these Nazrah stories is that very few of the storytellers referred to Nazrah's faith or religious orientation as one of the determinants of her present achievements or future plans. In the British context where the question of Muslim identity has emerged as a highly political and politicized issue, particularly in the last decade, it would be interesting to explore whether this decision is unconscious or calculated. In both cases this suggests a whole web of interacting elements determining a stance. It is my belief that even a seemingly unconscious utterance reflects a particular subjectivity and positioning and needs to be investigated in that context.

The references that the young Muslim girls make to their ethnic identity have social or regional orientations rather than religious or ideological. Why are they consciously or unconsciously hiding their 'Muslim identity, the only thing that defines them' (Whitehorn 1997)? There can be diverse contextual and personal factors involved, but for the purposes of this brief discussion I will consider two.

First, these respondents may be afraid or hesistant to claim their 'Muslim identity' in this specific context because of a response which they anticipate will be unfavourable or because they fear undesirable consequences. In this sense there is the possibility that they are responding to their construction of the white non-Muslim researcher as someone who, like others of the host community, is hostile to and critical of Islam. At the same time, the girls experience a vulnerability if called upon to defend it. There are multiple references in the Nazrah stories to the negative remarks made by other students and their being 'jeering and jealous', which to some extent are interwoven with her 'Muslim identity'. Nazrah is doubly victimized; first, by the 'jeering' indigenous students who construct her as a stereotype for multiple and complex reasons (and this is so even of the supposedly better-informed and sympathetic teachers who construct Muslim girls as stereotypes and indirectly push them back into their cocoons as in Haw (1995a Chapter 9, 1995b); and secondly, by the 'jealous' community fellows who have their own reasons, social and psychological, for victimizing an out-performing Nazrah. Caught between the two cultures (Ali 1996), and not exactly fitting into either, can be a very discomforting and alienating experience. A situation like this can lead to a chain of reactions against the parent culture as well as the host culture(s). It can be anything from mute passivism to violent aggression, even involving what Whitehorn calls 'a risk of rabid fundamentalism – to fuel white Islamaphobia' (1997: 5). It can further add to problems in the local school context and in an educational context. This silencing through fear of ridicule is in itself problematic because it hampers a healthy growth of young minds and personalities, and can be a serious barrier to educational achievement.

Second, these young Muslim girls may not **choose** to claim their 'Muslim identity' for more personal reasons. They might be attempting to avoid proclaiming a religion whose followers, as their parents obviously claim to be, are anxious to hear about their brother 'Ismail' but do not ask 'Nazrah' how she has done. This is the role-socialization endemic to this Muslim community and in others, where the boy is the breadwinner for the family. Importance is placed on his career destinations and developments in preference to those of the daughter. Here, the complementary nature of male/female roles in Islam is converted into a gender-specific role divide which is oppositional and dichotomous rather than integrated and complementary, as intended in Islam and revealed through the Qur'an. The cultural traditions tend to perpetuate such role socialization, restricting female career developments.

The patriarchal practices and male authority experienced within homes, which is often falsely justified and legitimized in the name of Islam to silence all opposition and reasoning, can cause a reaction among the young school-going girls. It may be further reinforced by the media and the host community's jeering comments and constructions. In the indigenous social context and through the media, Islam is presented as a faith imposing intellectual slavery, female oppression and terrorism (Said 1981; Ahmed 1992). The dominant social attitudes and interpretation within the community partly validate such constructions, discouraging and distancing the younger generation by the rigidity and irrationality of these practices. A religion whose essential injunction is *la ikraha fid-d-din* (no compulsion in (choice of) religion) in practice is exploited to impose cultural interpretations, and regional customs and traditions, in the name of God's commands. The thing which disappoints me as a Muslim is that these young girls appear to be suffering under given interpretations of Islam, rather than living confidently with an ideology.

As Muslim girls, theoretically they have an equal right to education because knowledge is a part of *Imaan* (faith) in Islam, and seeking knowledge is 'incumbent upon every Muslim man and woman'. As particular Pakistani immigrants in Britain, these girls face multiple barriers from within the community and from the host context. The socio-educational structure and system in Britain present certain barriers to the educational achievements of Muslim girls in Britain, but these are also embedded into deeper issues of female role and status within Islam and the current practices within the community, which further influence the schooling of these girls. The next section looks into these and related aspects.

Female role and status within Islam

The schooling of Muslim girls in the British context and their specific needs, asks to be viewed against the backdrop of the present and future role of these girls within their community. According to these respondents, a considerable number of parents appear to believe 'that education is not so important and that girls like her **should be married** as soon as they reach the age of 16', introducing a dichotomy between marriage and career which is never even hinted at in Islam. There is no denying the reality that in Islam, any relationship between man and woman has to be within *Shari'ah*. However, there is not a single reference in the Qur'an or *Hadith* negating women's right to education or work, or even delegating less importance to it. Limiting girls to a housewife's role can have diverse sociocultural determinants but 'the practice of excluding women from public life was not the original intent of the prophet' (Smith 1984). Siddiqi argues that 'according to strict Islamic injunctions, it is not obligatory for a woman to cook the food for her husband or children, or to wash their clothes or even to suckle the infants' (1982: 57). My caveat is that in Islam, roles are complementary, subject to individual potential and positioning, flexible, and equally important.

The earlier quotation from a Nazrah story where a father claims that education is not so important and that girls like the subject of the story **should be married** as soon as they reach the age of 16 needs to be understood in its specific context, which is influenced by the parent regional cultures and social pressures rather than informed by the Qur'an.[2] Marriage is an approved Islamic practice, but to negate the importance of education is a direct contradiction of Qur'anic teachings and Islamic philosophy of knowledge. Issues can be raised around the nature and venue of education, but none against education as such. Instead of discussing and explaining the issues and perspectives, closed statements like these discourage and distance the younger generation, perhaps more than education in a 'secular' context itself can do.

For the majority of the stories, Nazrah is married by the time she is 25, with or without children, working or not working. Only in one story, Zarka's story (see p. 141), is she viewed as 'may be **married** or have a **boyfriend**'. Broadly speaking, a single girl having a boyfriend is not an issue for parents of the host community in Britain, but it can be for Pakistani Muslim parents, as well as their extended family. Dating, moreover, is not just 'alien to their culture' (Ali 1996: 415) but goes against the value system suggested by their religion. The last sentence of Zarka's story is interesting and thought-provoking: 'Judging by her **character**, I would imagine that she wouldn't have a boyfriend **at present**.'

What does **character** signify here? And why is it a deterrent **at present**, leaving a possibility of having a boyfriend when she is 'probably in a highly paid job', after finishing her higher education. Is this what the Muslim community in Britain is afraid of? Is this 'character' an external imposition for these young girls which would change if the controlling authority or disciplinary forces loosen their hold? Do the Muslim girls perceive having a boyfriend as a liberation from male authority which has denied them 'equality'? Conversely, do the parents foresee it as a rebellion against parental authority? Where does Islam enter into it? Why is there tension and conflict in the City State context? Are the Muslim girls' schools 'infiltration free' zones defended from the cultural penetrations of the host community and so consequently spared '**tension and conflict**'? I do not think that there is any single answer to these questions. I would like to quote here two recent cases to explain my point.

The first example is the much publicized case of Saima Waheed (*The News* (international) London Edition, 15 March 1997). This involved a Pakistani girl of 22 who, in claiming the 'right to marry the person of her choice', against her father's wishes,[3] sought help from national laws in a challenge to her parents' opposition. After a year-long struggle she won her case at Lahore High Court (Pakistan) and was judged as having acted within

Islamic law, inviting comments from national and international media (BBC, *New York Times*) and initiating a whole chain of reactions within the country and community. Two questions were posed: one, will the successful litigation lead to female emancipation within an Islamic framework; or two, will it result in further oppression at the hands of a threatened patriarchy?

The second example is from another news item (*The Daily Jang* (Urdu), London, 16 March 1997, p. 6) about Shahzad, a 23-year-old Pakistani Muslim assistant teacher from Peterborough, who fabricated 78 letters showing that she was being followed. Thirty thousand pounds of public money was spent on police investigations into the case. The news item claimed that resultant investigations discovered that Shahzad fabricated the letters in order to maintain contact with a particular policeman because she was 'emotionally involved'.

Each case can be perceived as a reaction to rigid patriarchal structures which close the possibilities of debate and discussion. Saima, born and brought up in Pakistan in a religious family (her father is a well known religious leader), and Shahzad, born and brought up in England, both signal rebellion against rigid oppressive structures which tend to deprive women of their equal status within Islam. However, the examples cited are strictly speaking not rebellions against Islam, because Saima requests validation of her marriage from within Islamic law, and Shahzad seeks satisfaction for her suppressed emotions without violating *Shari'ah*. Rather these are signals pointing to an increasing need to differentiate between Qur'anic teachings and sociocultural patterns and not to equate the latter with the former. Sociocultural traditions and patterns are a changing phenomenon, and fusing them with religious principles leads the critical minds of the younger generation to drift away from religion.

My intention in quoting these examples is to show that an increasing awareness of rights is an emerging feature of the present globalized context and not just a British phenomenon. To convince the younger generation to enjoy their rights in the best interests of *Ummah* needs to be debated as informed by the Qur'an and *Sunnah*, rather than through hampering access to education. We, as Muslims, need to work to bring back the faith and pride of the younger generations in being a Muslim, in a situation of challenge and questioning, rather than through dictating to them what to eat and drink, how to dress, how to socialize and whom to marry. They need an enhanced awareness of religion to develop their socio-religious identity, which requires facilitating their access to the teachings of the Qur'an and *Sunnah*, but not imposing vested interpretations.

I believe that the younger generation of immigrant Pakistani Muslims appreciates Islam and its spirit of justice and equality, and that they are willing to submit to its injunctions, and even to cultural interpretations, for the sake of preserving their 'Muslim identity', as is reflected in another newspaper article 'Blaming the Asians: Whatever happened to the melting pot?' (Whitehorn 1997: 5). Katherine Whitehorn writes about two young Muslim girls, one studying Polymer Science and Systems Analysis, and the other who has just finished a solicitor's training course. Both girls went back to visit their old school in Bradford. She writes:

> Asked by their head teacher Q.R. Thompson, 'What would you do if you fell in love with a white boy?', each said with certainty: 'It would not happen.' Indeed, none of the bright Muslim girls I talked to, up to and including Zahida Mansoor, chairman of the local Health Authority, had any difficulty with the idea of an arranged marriage. A knee jerk British reaction of horror at the very idea of such a thing is greeted with amusement: 'just look at the state of British romance!'

Thus, in accordance with the teachings and spirit of Islam, women and girls need to be treated as equals and as responsible members of the community in Muslim societies. Instead, much-publicized events like the Saima case send negative signals in many directions and to both Muslims and non-Muslims. Parents feel threatened at the possibility of a similar situation arising for their own daughters and the subsequent humiliation and loss of *izzat* within the family, *bradari* and society at large. It could also jeopardize the chances of marriage for other daughters in the family, leading to serious social problems. They generally believe education in mainstream schools to be responsible for such ills, which disrupt the social fabric of their lives and accordingly increase restrictions for their daughters. It is felt that the media uses such cases in sensational exploitation for its own ends, adding to the shame and ridicule for the affected family within the parent and host communities. The 'quiet', 'no-nonsense', 'hard working', 'interested only in work' 'Nazrahs' are driven into islands of isolation as a result of interplay between complex and multiple discourses in the parent and host cultures and subcultures. A suppressed Nazrah may turn into a Shahzad, finding consolation in activity which she may perceive as socially harmless, or may stand up like a Saima to claim validation from Islamic laws. Both situations will be unpleasant, to say the least, for the concerned parents, and would be perceived as bad examples for the community. Blaming such developments on the British school system fails to acknowledge that similar events are taking place in Pakistan as well, even if on a smaller scale. Questions like what to eat and drink, how to dress, how to socialize and whom to marry are not major issues in the Pakistani context, and this indirectly implies that there must be some deeper issues involved in preserving the essential fabric of Muslim identity.

Male/female relationship and sex

There is a need also to understand male/female roles within Islam, which produce and are produced by the nature of their relationship. Each has a primary and intrinsic role which does not negate other options. The creation of man and woman from a 'single soul' (Qur'an: 4: 1; 7: 189) and in 'pairs' (Qur'an: 42: 11) was determined by the 'Creator', 'that you may dwell in tranquillity with them: and has put love and mercy between you' (Qur'an: 30: 21). This male/female relationship within Islam is a focal point which serves as a basis for the development of its wider social structure and the web of relationships. Marriage provides legitimacy to these relationships. Only a bond sanctioned by God between a man and a woman validates other relationships. It has three aspects: religious, social and legal. Marriage needs to be contracted in accordance with the teachings of Islam; it must be a social event with at least two witnesses to it; and it controls all the legal rights to property and other possessions. A child outside this legal union has no claims to parental possessions or property in Islam.

In different Muslim societies, this focus on marriage interacts with regional discourses around the subject, constructed by local relevant laws, customs and traditions, leading to further developments and interpretations within an Islamic framework. On the other hand, in contemporary British society, specifically among the younger generation, marriage does not seem to hold the sanctity ordained by the Qur'an and the prophet Mohammed. It is a threatening situation going against the basic principles of Islam. Marriage is the *Sunnah* of the Prophet (Farah 1984: 48), and 'half faith' and even divorce (although to be conducted in kindness and fairness) is an unpleasant act according to the Qur'an. In Islam the rights and wishes of an individual are interwoven with the welfare of *Ummah* and subordinate to God's favour. In the West, an emphasis on individual liberty has introduced such developments as a breakdown in family structures and male/female relationships in those societies which contradict Islamic values and consequently make Muslims feel threatened through exposure to them.

Islam delegates to women all decisions relating to marriage, with one condition: that 'a Muslim woman should not marry a non-Muslim', unless that non-Muslim willingly turns Muslim. The fourth sura of Qur'an titled *Ai-Nisa* (women) discusses in detail matters relating to marriage, rights and duties within marriage, laws of inheritance, divorce, widowhood, remarriage, and other issues concerning marital life (see also Al-Ghazali 1995; Farah 1984; Haneef 1979). Marriage has existed as a central and sacred institution in an Islamic social structure, but it has been incessantly manipulated as a tool for oppression and suppression by patriarchy in Muslim societies. An exploitation of Islamic practices and a strong influence of related traditions and customs in the parent culture has created a specific discourse of marriage and family for the Pakistani immigrants. The notion of *izzat* demands that a girl should be married according to the *bradari* traditions, to the person most suitable according to the *bradari* criterion, with no preference for her personal choice or opinion in this matter. They hear to whom they are to be married, and submit. This is in fact a contradiction of Qur'anic teachings, which emphasize willingness and the independent consent of those entering into marriage. Education in a British context is seen as further increasing this awareness of free consent, leading to the girls rebelling against arranged marriages which their parents view as being in the best interests of their daughters, securing a happy and protected future for them. It is not the formal academic curriculum and a professional education which is threatening to the Muslim community. This is reflected in the overall attitudes towards the academic achievements of Nazrah and her future plans for work, which are more positive in the case of the students in the Muslim girls' school. The threat is the hidden curriculum, the behavioural norms, social structure and moral values of the host culture, which are perceived as having the potential to disrupt the whole fabric of the immigrant community's social existence.

Further, there are issues around the notion of 'sex', 'sex education' and 'sexuality'. Chastity is a great virtue, highly stressed by Islam with a promise of 'forgiveness and reward' to 'men and women who guard their chastity' (Qur'an: 33: 35). In Islam, sexual activity is highly proscribed and circumscribed, and any sex outside marriage is strictly forbidden with commands of severe punishments like flogging and stoning (see also Al-Ghazali 1995). Even Muslim feminists 'strongly and explicitly disavowed sexual liberation as part of women's lib', not basing feminism 'on the liberation of individual women but part of an effort to liberate society' (Haddad et al., 1984). The reason is that Islamic injunctions regulating sex are very explicit and apply equally to men and women.

Current discourses around sexual practices in British society are mostly contradictory to the teachings of Islam. The value system does not allow for Prince Charles and Lady Diana to justify having sex outside of marriage because they were not satisfied or happy with each other. Islam confines sex within the institution of marriage, for the explicit purposes of a social structure-Muslim *Ummah*. Pakistani communities in Britain fear that their children, and more especially the girls (for sociocultural reasons), will engage with these discourses which have the potential to undermine their socio-religious identity. They are not averse to education or academic achievements, as reflected by the positive responses to the academic achievements of Muslim girls (Basit 1995; Haw 1995a, 1995b), but they are apprehensive about the wider social context within which education is provided, and the popular notions of sex, morality and marriage active in the host society. I know many Pakistani immigrants settled in Britain who have sent their young daughters back to Pakistan to be educated in a single-sex context, incurring the cost of huge air fares and maintenance for many years.

The need for Muslim girls to avoid mixed-sex situations whether social, educational or professional, is attributed to their role socialization as wives and mothers, and as contradictory to career aspirations (the Swann Report as quoted in Haw 1995a). There is no denying role socialization in patriarchal societies, but believing this factor to be solely responsible for girls' behaviour in the present context would be unjustifiable. In view of parents' fears of sending girls to mixed-sex youth clubs (Ali 1996: 377–8) and the apparent promiscuous sex and condom machines in some such clubs, Roger Ali writes: 'Overall, Asian parents are very protective of their daughters because of their perceptions of English society's problems with drugs, alcohol, and undue emphasis on sex. I believe that the parents' fears are quite genuine' (p. 411). It is these 'protective inclinations' in a context of 'genuine fear' which in many cases determine the parents' strict control and the girls' social behaviour.

Muslim girls are measured against a different value system, and accordingly are stereotyped. My argument is that in Islam there is no dichotomy between domestic and professional roles of women as such. An Islamic family context is perceived as supportive to pursuing a career with shared responsibilities and mutual regard. It is my view that if Muslim girls were provided with a context which was non-threatening to their value system they would emerge as even more positively aspiring. I do not deny problems around food, dress, prayer room, language, 'religious studies' and home–school liaison. These can be accommodated, as is happening in certain state schools such as City State; but as Kaye Haw's analysis shows, there is no resolution of the 'deeper issues' which include the multiple hidden curricula in these schools determined by different value systems and diverse social structures. I would therefore argue as Kaye Haw does that these are the more 'surface issues which cloud debate and place barriers to understanding and more effective practice'.

In Islam, gaining knowledge and entering into marriage are both 'favoured acts', and both are incumbent upon Muslims. Education or a career are not seen in opposition to marriage and its responsibilities. The problems in Britain emerge when education is perceived by immigrant Muslim communities as adversely affecting the approach of its youth towards the institution of marriage that forms the religious fabric. The responses of the Muslim girls to the question 'What do you think Nazrah will be doing when she is 25?' predominantly reach the consensus that she would be 'working' and 'married'. These opinions must have evolved from their social experiences where career and marriage are not viewed in opposition. Marriage is the Prophet's *Sunnah* and hence the responsibility of every parent to see that it is followed within an Islamic framework. Any value system or behavioural norms that in any way jeopardize the smooth functioning of the tradition are perceived as a threat. However, the situation becomes complicated as a result of the interplay between Islamic teachings and traditions and regional and local subcultures. It often introduces a rigidity and oppression which closes options, and deprives the girls of their

legitimate religious rights, thus setting in motion a chain of reactions leading towards extreme positions. If, in the opinion of the extended family, a
girl indulged in 'immoral activities or behaviour' because of her experiences
in school, or there had been a rumour to that effect, it would certainly mean
the end of her post-compulsory education, as well as curtailing her chances
of contracting a 'good marriage'. The *bradari* gaze disciplines the girls, like
a Foucauldian Panopticon (see p. 3).

These girls exist in a Panopticon, and wherever they move they are
watched by the invisible 'gaze', which only 'frames', and any 'captions' can
be put onto those 'frames' by the watching eyes. A girl may not know anything about Islam or may not even perform *faraz abadah* such as five prayers
a day and not invite any reprimands; but in talking to a male classmate she
may cause comments like 'we are Muslims and it is not appropriate for us'.
The context of the conversation would not be considered. What is Islamic
and what is un-Islamic is currently determined by cultural considerations,
and enforced in the name of religion.

Further, Islamic teachings and values pertaining to morality are similar for
men and women. Significantly, boys are not being stopped from manifest
violations of Islamic teachings. They, it seems, are forgiven for keeping girl-
friends, indulging in dating, illicit sex,[4] alcohol and gambling (the last three
explicitly forbidden in the Qur'an), and what they do does not seem to be
perceived as a threat to Islam by the community. These different moral standards for girls and boys are used for the suppression of girls, ultimately
acting as barriers to their educational achievements and career aspirations.
These contradictions create 'tension and conflict'. Any efforts to minimize
barriers for Muslim girls in the British school context can only be effective
if religious and cultural issues are also addressed.

As I perceive it, the main issue at present for the Muslim community in
Britain is not the education of girls or concern for their careers, but the
unproblematic movement towards marriage. The girls are allowed access to
education and to career only as long as these do not disturb institutions like
marriage and family. In Muslim girls' schools there is a safe environment,
devoid of any explicit threats to their value system. Parents, even under
economic constraints, would pay for their daughters to study in these relatively poorly resourced schools if they believed that these schools were the
only safe, infiltration-free zones. However, I would argue that these 'infiltration-free zones' are not always 'Islamic zones'. From my knowledge of
Muslim girls' schools in Britain, in general, I would rather call them 'community zones' where there is a focus on rituals and cultural practices, in
addition to the formal National Curriculum. The need for the development
of **a Muslim female identity** is not generally recognized.

In Islam, a woman is not an unpaid servant as a housewife but, according
to the Qur'an, claims equal rights as a *zouj* (one of a pair) and commands
highest respect and authority as a mother. I would argue that the majority of

Muslim girls are not being educated in keeping with the Islamic philosophy which links education with 'self-completion'. Providing girls with 'uncontrolled' access to Islamic knowledge and an understanding of Islam *rasalah* (Mernissi 1993) would not favour feudal and patriarchal practices. Subsequent interpretations of the Qur'an by women religious scholars could demolish vested constructions and liberate the suppressed.

In summary, I agree that an understanding and accommodation of such socio-cultural needs as pointed out by Parker-Jenkins (1995) would ease certain barriers, but I also argue with Kaye Haw that the whole issue needs to be considered from different angles. My perspective is one which argues that the conflict between the 'two cultures' and 'ways of life' is reinforced by the tensions within the community between the Islamic spirit of justice and equality, and cultural/patriarchal practices. It is not simply a question of 'how to best educate the Muslim girls in a non-Muslim context'. It is an interplay of very serious and calculated efforts to maintain the power balance in favour of patriarchy.

Conclusion

Saeeda Shah's perspective as a high-'caste' Muslim woman who works in Pakistan and stays in Britain for periods of time provides a useful and additional angle to this work. As I argued in Chapter 5, there are some stories that I can recognize and give due consideration to, but which I cannot tell because of my own positioning and background. These are the stories concerned with identity, religion, *bradari* gaze and inter-community tensions between Islamic precepts and cultural/patriarchal practices, and an analysis that other individuals of these communities might wish to take issue with.

On a more general note it is important to recognize that the common themes which have emerged so far are also fragmented by areas of difference and fractures. This is evidenced by the selection of Nazrah stories, which serve to highlight the different discourses of 'Muslimness' operating within these groups of students and their familial contexts. It is inevitable in a piece of research working with sensitive and very personal issues that not only commonalities, but also differences and fragmentations, will be evident. However, this also means that it is at the interstices of difference that spaces can be created in which these areas of disagreement and difference can provide new ways of theorizing and perceiving lived situations and hence, new ways of working and understanding.

The Nazrah stories have raised several issues, many of which have also been highlighted in the first four chapters of this book. There are issues such as racism and a sexism founded on a particular discourse of femininity, and those which are specific to Pakistani Muslim communities in Britain and the discourses of 'Muslimness' to be found within them. These more specific issues include parental attitudes to the education of their daughters and the role of women in this particular Islamic community, as well as issues which can be placed within the discourses of culture and religion such as arranged marriage, honour within the *khandan* or *bradari* network, and the Islamic concept of the private and public spheres.

More specifically, up to this point a difference has emerged between the Muslim girls in the state school (City State) and the Muslim girls in the private school (Old Town High). It is the Muslim students in Old Town High who are more positive both to the academic achievement of Nazrah and towards her as a person. Additionally there emerges a marked difference between the Muslim girls in City State and the Muslim girls in Old Town High in terms of feeling confident, assertive; being able to question and to challenge; pioneering feelings as a Muslim woman; and academic aspirations. This prompts the question, why? What is the difference between the two schools?

Tensions have also been identified in the responses of the staff of City State as they try to reconcile their desire to encourage the students to challenge and question the stereotypes of women, their rights and their roles in contemporary society on the one hand, whilst giving due consideration to what they understand to be the religious/cultural beliefs of the Muslim students on the other hand. These tensions are not detectable in the responses of the staff or students in Old Town High. For me, this analysis begs three questions. First, do the Muslim students in Old Town High school feel 'comfortable' in their environment, where being a woman is not an issue and being a Muslim is not an issue? Second, from this basis do they feel free to question, challenge and assert their own agendas for an exploration of what it means to be a Muslim woman, and to pursue academic success and further or higher education from the safety of feeling secure in their own identity? Finally, is this the case for the Muslim students in City State? It is these questions which are explored and discussed in the next, concluding chapter.

Notes

1 This is discussed in detail in Haw 1995a.
2 In feudal patriarchal societies of the sub-continent, child marriage has been a common phenomenon, irrespective of religion. It is still a practice in certain parts of India and Pakistan, among the Muslims and Hindus as well. It is a regional practice determined by complex socio-economic elements. The multiplicity of reasons behind this practice are beyond the scope of this book. However in the case of this immigrant community, the dominant factor can be to contract an 'appropriate marriage' and transfer the responsibility and '*izzat*' of the young girl to her husband.
3 There is difference of opinion between the Malki and the Hanfi Fiqa regarding the *wali* (father/guardian)'s consent to a girl's marriage in a Muslim society, which

itself is a proof of flexibility of interpretation inherent therein, in keeping with the spirit of Islam. For a further discussion of the various major *fiqas* see Abd al Ali-Hammudah (1977).

4 According to Islamic *Shari'ah*, sex should conform to its laws. Whenever it violates any of the Qur'anic injunctions it is declared illicit.

8 Dancing with the discourses: re-searching the research

Kaye Haw

Introduction

This chapter revisits those points which I consider to have relevance to my current thoughts regarding issues of education, education for girls and education for Muslim girls. Some of the ideas in this chapter owe a great deal to the work of Kenway *et al.* (1994). In one sense their work was like footsteps in the snow for me. This is not surprising given that they too have been working within a post-structuralist framework seen through the lens of feminism, in the belief that this provides a 'better understanding of what actually happens in schools'. I have applied similar ideas in an attempt to explore the educational experiences of Muslim girls in Britain through the perspectives of gender, 'race', religion, culture and ethnicity. The chapter is presented in three sections.

The first section returns to the theoretical framework offered in the Introduction and Chapter 1. This provides the context for the further analysis of the subsequent two sections. The concern of the second section is to go back to the initial areas of interest with regard to Muslim girls' schools: whether there are any areas of agreement between Muslims and feminists concerning the ethos and purpose of single-sex schools and the issue of educational opportunity in Muslim schools. These questions masked other, deeper questions concerning the relationships of the staff and their students in both schools and the discursive positionings offered to the students. This section therefore goes on to discuss these relationships through a consideration of how the discourses of education, gender, religion, culture, 'race' and age articulate in the social construction of Muslim girls.

The third section examines the implications that this research has for social justice issues and the equal opportunity initiatives implemented in state schools. It looks at education for girls generally and Muslim girls in particular through the concept of equality in difference. Chapters 2 and 4 have already pointed out that Muslims argue that the principle of equality is not necessarily satisfied by identity of treatment and that there is injustice in treating people the same when in relevant respects they are different. Theirs is an argument for equality in diversity. It is in this chapter that the 'voices' which have contributed to this book come together once more.

The theoretical framework revisited

Several theoretical considerations have to be kept in mind at this point: first, the heterogeneous and relational nature of power. Power is to be understood in a number of ways. It is exercised over individuals who are free and only insofar as they are free, through modes of action which are indirect, that act upon actions and upon acting subjects who are capable of action (Foucault 1982). A Foucauldian interpretation of power uses discourse to examine those practices through which power is exercised by asking the questions: where is discourse, how does discourse operate, what does discourse do? The aim of these questions is to uncover the connections, forces, strategies, forays and barriers which in any given period establish what is said or unsaid, who speaks, in what context and with what authority. Practices are the sites where what is said and what is done are united. They are the sites where discursive and non-discursive acts operate so that these acts are shown to rely on and exist essentially in the other. Therefore, practices provide the context for discourse and discourse feeds back regimes of 'truth' (statements) that facilitate practice and make practices credible. Schools do not simply reflect society but are centrally involved in the re-articulation, selective dissemination and social appropriation of discourse which both contribute to, and are a result of, wider social forces.

Second, the theoretical framework offered in this book asserts that the educational experiences of the Muslim students in each school can be seen as a set of discursive relationships (discursive fields) consisting of a number of different and **sometimes** contradictory discourses, such as those of 'race', gender, class, culture and religion. These discourses are not governed by rules which individuals consciously follow, but provide the necessary context and preconditions for the making of meaning. In school these discourses are set within the discourse of education. **These can be considered as 'framing discourses' or 'primary' discourses**. Each of these discourses can themselves be considered as a discursive field, consisting of its own different discourses. Impacting on these discourses is a myriad of other discourses, **'fleshing discourses' or 'secondary discourses'** to do with, for example, age, competence, personality, physicality, attractiveness and sexuality. At any one time these framing discourses can shift and change places with other framing discourses and any of the myriad of other 'fleshing' discourses and vice versa, just as the pattern of a kaleidoscope shifts and changes with a twist of the eyepiece. As the pieces which go to make up the patterns of the kaleidoscope remain the same but take their meaning (their perceived colour and shape) from the places that they hold, so also for individuals. The pattern can remain static before it is shifted again in an endless variation of combinations over time which are always subtly different for each individual, even while they belong to groups. At the interstices of these patterns (discursive formations) are the sites where space is opened up allowing room for manoeuvre, or in Foucauldian terms 'a field of possible options' (Foucault 1972).

The discursive positionings taken up and adopted by the Muslim students in the schools involved in the study are dependent on a number of factors which position these students across the various 'framing' and 'fleshing' discourses which historically and presently constitute them as individuals and as a group of individuals. These are the discourses in school associated with the culture and subcultures of the school and the political contexts which inform and influence them; the teaching/learning relationships **and the relationships amongst and between** the staff and students. Those out of school will include the discourses of the family, the *bradari*/kinship network, the local community, local and national politics and those associated with the student's ethnic/racial/class/cultural/religious positionings. They also include the discourses of both Asian and western fashion, pop music, magazines and books, television and films, which influence the girls in terms of how to present themselves, how to make themselves attractive and how to find pleasure, power and fulfilment through consumerism, career, ideals and relationships (see also Kenway *et al.*, 1994).

Third, the relationships between the Muslim students and their teachers, the latter of whom are often white and non-Muslim, are inscribed by a series of power differentials which are focused around, and set up by, a number of competing 'framing' and 'fleshing' discourses such as 'race', ethnicity, religion, class, personality and age. Foucault maintains that these discourses seek to form 'the subjects about which they speak', so that the relationships between Muslim students and their teachers can be analysed through uncovering those rules which govern discourse. These are the rules which permit certain statements to be made while disallowing others, which decide what is desirable and what is not, what is 'normal' and what is not, and which divide individuals from each other while fragmenting them within themselves. They are the rules which regulate and discipline, the surveillance system through which we produce ourselves as 'normalized' individuals so that every one of our actions as individuals is intentional. These actions are derived from an indication of how we would like to be treated so that our actions are determined by our **desire** for social interaction with others. They are not, and never can be, derived from the notion of an essential nature, because for each individual this is fractured by a variety of accidental and relational features brought about by social forces and motivated by desire. This is where discourses operate.

Fourth is the idea of a 'changing same' (Gilroy 1993), a sameness bound by the tensions of difference; where fractures at one level are transcended by this 'sameness' at another level in a mutual and perpetual dependence. This allows for an exploration of the relationship between gender sameness and gender differentiation, for holding onto commonalities while giving due consideration to the tensions of difference. It also allows for the commonalities themselves to shift and change, again in a mutual and perpetual, relational dependence so that they are not the same over here as they are over there. They can relate to class or 'race' or culture or community, which transcend each other and are transcended by each other in a perpetual wave-like motion. Each wave is the same and different, and with and through these, meaning is taken up, rolled over and circulated in a perpetual motion which is neither fixed nor immutable. This is a view of relativism which is not nihilistic but which is relational and dependent because the 'samenesses' and the tensions of difference **rely on and exist essentially in the other.**

Fifth and more specifically, is the importance of exploring how the participants as a group or community are constructed, to understand the dominant patterns of attitudes and behaviour, and to appreciate the variations. This is because education cannot be separated from other social processes. The educational needs of a people can only be understood and realized in an interplay with the wider social context, so that a discussion of the term 'Pakistani community' is pivotal to any work which focuses on the educational experiences of Muslim girls in this country. The concept of a Muslim, Pakistani immigrant community in Britain, and the influences and processes contributing to its constructions as influenced by Islam, the Islamic concept of emigration and the consequent shaping of a Pakistani community in Britain with a particular socio-economic background, are seen as a crucial dimension to be considered. This is the third interacting angle of the triangle which Saeeda Shah notes is missing.

These are the theoretical positions in which this book is located, and it is these concepts which are used to examine the evidence regarding the differing experiences of the Muslim students in City State and Old Town High and the heterogeneous nature of power as it impinges on the lives of Muslim girls in these schools.

Outwardly accommodating, inwardly questioning: single-sex schooling and educational opportunities

With regard to the issue of single-sex schooling, there is one major difference between Muslims and western feminists. Some Muslims express a belief that their support for single-sex education is deeply rooted in their religious faith, although this is disputed by Saeeda Shah (in Chapter 2), who instead perceives it to be due to a nexus of sociocultural/political manoeuvres bound up with colonialism and reinforced by the active and effective traditions within subcultures as well as the religious Islamic discourses.

The practices in both schools emphasized commonalities in their approach to the education of girls in a single-sex setting through the selective mobilization of the discourses of liberal and radical feminisms (see also Chapter 4). This was expressed in terms of equal access to the curriculum, the questioning of gender stereotypes, the pleasure of working in a predominantly female environment, the employment of female staff as role models and the adoption of an approach which seeks to make the actual experiences of women more central to the education of the students.

Although a similar set of discourses concerning the education of girls in a single-sex setting appears to be operational in both schools, in City State the sharing breaks down for the many reasons already examined. The teachers here have to speak to a disparate audience. They do so anyway in terms of class, age, power differentials, sexual orientation and physical ability, but these fracturings are not so clearly evident as the difference embodied by their Pakistani Muslim students. The fact that the teachers believe they share a similar cultural experience as women renders such differences apparently less relevant than their shared experience of being women. However, stereotyped images of what it means to be a woman and Muslim appear to have an additional relevance which sets up tensions within the shared discourse of being a woman. To put it another way, in terms of Gilroy's 'changing same', the tensions between the claims of gender variations on one side and the comfort of those modern 'normalizing' universals, in this case 'woman', that appear to transcend gender variation on the other, arises in the sharpest possible form.

At any given moment it is shared experience, shared knowledge and shared culture which is built on. This is the case on one level for the students in Old Town High but not for the Muslim students in City State. In Old Town High the students feel comfortable and confident in their more monocultural setting and are therefore enabled, if they are given the opportunity, to pursue explorations of what it means to be a Muslim woman operating within the Muslim community. In this environment being a woman and a Muslim is not an issue. However being a **Muslim woman** is an issue. It is the raison d'être of the school. Although in Old Town High there is the **possibility** for the processes of exploration and questioning and challenging from within an Islamic framework, this is constrained by the discourses of 'Muslimness' that operate both within and outside the school which, as Saeeda Shah makes clear, revolve around 'the tensions within the community between the Islamic spirit of justice and equality, and cultural/patriarchal practices'.

The Muslim students of City State are marginalized **because of the multicultural nature** of the school. Here the staff felt confident in their abilities to deal with the common issue of being female, but not confident in their abilities to deal with the complexities of difference because they felt they had no deeper understanding of their Muslim students and certainly no understanding of their parents or their context of origin as an immigrant community. Although they had some ideas of the tenets of Islam and realized the importance of 'community', the role of kinship networks and *bradari* gaze was not fully appreciated. This meant that the possibilities for 'dialogue' between them and their Muslim students closed down and the consequence is that the Muslim students in City State are less confident about being a Muslim student in an environment where being a Muslim and a woman are both issues. The effect of the resulting practices is a system of disavowals and denials, and consequently the very practices themselves help create and read back the effects as 'other', as pathology (Walkerdine 1990). In City State the effect of these practices can be outwardly accommodating, inwardly resisting Muslim students, a 'withdrawal as silence'.

In Old Town High the lack of equipment, resources, subject options and extra-curricular activities is more than made up for by the value and experiences of sharing a common background and **cause** so that 'they feel valued and if they feel valued then they will do their best to learn'. Here, there is an atmosphere of wanting to achieve and wanting to do well which is infectious, just as the opposite attitude of 'so what it's all rubbish' is equally infectious. The girls come out from this school feeling self-confident even 'though they haven't had all the equipment and resources'. They feel that they can do well and 'no resources in the world can give that sort of attitude'.

It is the Muslim students in Old Town High who are encouraged to concentrate on educational achievement and academic success because of the belief that this is one way to combat the stereotype of what it is to be a Muslim woman and one who attended a Muslim school. It is also a means of proving the academic worth of the school both to the local Muslim community and to the wider indigenous community. In this school the students do achieve academically and are encouraged to believe in themselves and the value of academic qualifications within the academic capabilities of each individual. In this sense therefore it cannot be said that the school reduces educational opportunities, although they could be enhanced if the school had the resources to refurbish its building, extend its staffing, widen subject choices, provide better equipment and thus broaden the educational and extra-curricular educational experience of its students. On the other hand, although the students of Old Town High are enabled and encouraged to achieve academically despite the facilities and resources, the possibility for them to explore their identity as Muslim women is framed by the very specific discourses of 'Muslimness' operating within and outside this school, discourses which are not operational to the same degree in City State because of the multicultural background of its staff and students.

Comparison of the practices in both schools indicates that City State has the difficulties it has because it is multicultural, while Old Town High is more monocultural. This means that City State has had to explore and initiate means of equipping its students to be educated, and consequently to live, in an increasingly culturally and racially complex society. It then becomes a question of weighing up the advantages of a more socially complex but not necessarily academically successful educational experience over a perhaps less socially complex and 'comfortable' educational experience, and one which concentrates on dealing with fewer issues. In Old Town High this means the freedom to encourage and concentrate on academic success but not necessarily the freedom to explore their identity as **Muslim women** outside of the discourses of 'Muslimness' operational in the school.

These points are usefully discussed through a more detailed exploration of the discourses operational in each school and how they affect the students. This can provide insights for 'race' and gender policy initiatives in state schools which enable minority groups, in this case Muslim girls, to take advantage of the educational experience offered in these schools so that all children benefit from being educated together in ways which enhance their ability to live in a fragmented, fractured society and to confidently deal with hybridity, fragmentation and pluralism. Such a discussion can also provide insights into the educational experiences of Muslim girls in Muslim girls' schools.

Re-searching the feminist discourses operational in each school

The staff at both schools were not conscious of all the aspects of the preferred discourses within which they operated and the implications that this had for their students. This was particularly clear when the relationships between the non-Muslim staff and the Muslim students in City State were considered.

The teachers of both schools voiced a commitment to overturn gender stereotypes. This led to a set of discursive practices designed to enhance the options of the students while in school and on leaving school. These discursive practices consist of a number of different and often competing discourses. I have already identified the main discourses operational in each school concerning gender stereotypes as being, first, the discourse which has its roots in liberal feminism designed to influence and/or widen girls' choices of subject and career; and second, the discourse which has its roots in radical feminism designed to influence the girls themselves and place the experiences of women more firmly at the centre of their school experience (see also Kenway *et al*. 1994).

These are the discourses which the staff of both schools made explicit in their interviews. They can therefore be considered as ones which are deliberately wielded by the teachers in both schools to change things and people.

The interest here is twofold. First, how do these two discourses relate to the other discourses which perpetuate regimes (the sort that Foucault was so interested in)? Second, what meanings did these discourses offer the students, and particularly the Muslim students in the case of City State; and how did the girls position themselves and rework these meanings?

The discourse to influence girls' choices in these areas of curriculum and career drew on aspects of liberal feminism in its concern to encourage the students to take up forms of knowledge and work most often associated with males and/or a career and in this way to enhance girls' economic independence and career and social mobility. In City State the girls who were enabled to take up discursive positionings in this discourse, and who might thus have already had access to these discursive positionings, tended to be those who were middle class and/or academically bright, and those who saw their future as participants in the job market.

The staff at City State seemed to have fewer concerns or hesitations about offering this discourse to their non-Muslim students regardless of their class or academic ability, even though this discourse implicitly marginalized other preferences for knowledge and work shared by many of the students from a variety of racial, religious, ethnic and class backgrounds. Feelings of conflict and tension surfaced with regard to their Muslim students because here the 'framing' discourses of 'race' and gender were perceived as contradictory rather than as ones which rely on and exist essentially in the other. Because of this the staff felt they had to make either/or choices for their Muslim students. This choice often meant that it was the discourses of culture and religion within which they **assumed** Muslim girls and women are positioned which took precedence over the discourse of gender.

The staff felt that they were treading on the 'cultural toes' of the Muslim parents and perhaps, more importantly, the community, which appears to be regarded **as a group** rather than a set of individuals because the links between school and home are not strong.

Additionally, the staff of City State demonstrated a commitment to deal with the category 'woman' for two reasons: first, because of the multicultural nature and ethos of the school and because of the problems and confusion that arise in any attempt to deal with difference on an everyday and practical level. Second, they are operating from their own discursive positionings with respect to this discourse (the majority could be described as white, middle-class women who took up this discourse themselves while at school and in higher education).

The combination of these factors meant that it was felt only to be questionable to offer this discourse to their Muslim students, who they believed had religious/cultural, family and community pressures to consider. In this instance stereotyped images of what it means to be a Muslim woman have an additional relevance which sets up unresolved tensions within the shared discourse of being a woman. For the Muslim students in City State it is made clear in Chapters 6 and 7 that this is reflected in their attitudes towards high academic achievement and expectations on leaving school. It would seem that the reasons for this stem from the limited range of discursive positionings offered to them with respect to this discourse, and indeed it was likely that they were implicitly made to feel that this discourse was not available to them. The question here is whether schools can alter the range of discursive positionings to students out of school.

In City State there are Muslim girls who are prevented from taking up the option of higher education and a career because of cultural and family restrictions. Faced with this pressure from home, and implicit alienation from this discourse in school, possibilities of working round such difficulties seem insurmountable, with the result that many of these Muslim students seem to 'opt out' while at school.

This discourse was also available to the students of Old Town High, but the students in this school were offered à range of discursive positionings which they felt enabled to take up because they were offered within the 'framing' discourses in which they were already positioned with regard to 'race', culture and religion. Academic excellence was regarded as a means whereby the students could pursue higher education and careers such as medicine, pharmacy, teaching, and which would also enhance the reputation of the school. At the same time, other forms of knowledge and work such as the role in the home were also respected and accorded status within the particular religious and moral discourses of 'Muslimness' operational in the school. In this context these are also the discourses offered by the parents and reinforced by the school. Additionally, the discourse of career, breadwinner and social mobility was offered to the students in terms of their being able to take their skills back to the community (Muslim women would benefit from being treated by a Muslim woman doctor; pharmacy could be practised in family-run shops; teachers could go back and teach in Muslim schools).

In both Old Town High and City State, choice for Muslim girls is not an individual matter which can be carried out in isolation from family or community: 'I want them to be giving back [to the community] rather than just achieving academic success and getting where they need to.' But Old Town High was more able to explicitly acknowledge this. The parents of the students in this school were approached by the female Muslim head teacher personally, as individuals, with regard to the future of their daughter, and the discussion proceeded from within the framework of a shared understanding of the cultural, religious, community/*bradari* discourses which influenced the arguments. There are two issues here.

First, the question that must be asked is what is the real result of this greater discursive flexibility? For some academically successful students at Old Town High there is no doubt that it offered only an illusion of discursive repositioning. These were the academically successful students whose parents, for many religious and cultural reasons, did not allow them to go on to higher education. These students were then left with the choice of correspondence courses, the Open University, or the possibility that a future husband **might** allow them to continue with their education after marriage.

Old Town High offers educational opportunities to those Muslim girls in this community whose parents do not regard the education offered in state schools as suitable for their daughters, or who do not regard education in general as being important. However, it is arguable whether those students who did achieve academic success at Old Town High are 'better off' than their counterparts at City State who for many reasons 'opted out' of the academic discourse. This is perhaps most clearly illustrated by the frustration in Fozia's story (see p. 145) about Nazrah, which was in fact written by a student attending Old Town High.

Secondly, it could be argued that Old Town High sets out to challenge the views of the 'community', unlike City State which, rather, respects or ignores them. For the Muslim head teacher of Old Town High it is possible to work within the shared 'framing' discourses of culture, religion and community. Discussions with parents were approached by the sensitivity of familiarity. This also means that there is a shared and implicit awareness of the fragmentations within the 'community' and the discourses of 'Muslimness' are implicitly acknowledged. In contrast, the relationship between the staff of City State and their Muslim parents illustrates the dangers of reifying a 'community'. This reification is especially dangerous when it comes from those outside – and can turn into a stereotype. These are **key** points. If the sense of 'the community, out there' is not the same for each school, questions concerning whether it is the same set of discourses which Old Town High challenges and City State reifies, and whether indeed these are **always** the same for each school, need to be asked.

Initial impressions are that they do **appear** to be the same set of discourses grounded in cultural and religious restrictions of Muslim girls going into further and higher education. However, the challenge of Old Town High is from **within** and it is my belief that this alters the pattern of the discourses which are operational. It twists the eyepiece of the kaleidoscope so that the pattern is altered, although the pieces which go to make up the pattern are always the same. First, the material conditions and futures of a disempowered community become a primary and **common** concern, and therefore a discourse which has an influence over cultural and religious discourses. Effectively this is the discourse of class and socio-economic status; this twists the kaleidoscope and the pattern shifts. The majority of the parents are not formally educated and are unemployed so there is financial hardship but 'they have clear ideas and views and they are very much in favour of the girls being educated' because they 'see success in education, a good job and with this good money'. There is a realization that things are changing and the family members have to work, because although in the past one member of the family, the father, was sufficient to provide the necessities of life, 'now things have changed, we have moved from that time and there is a need for more than one breadwinner'.

These parents see education as a means of survival and they have formed these views both through living in the British context and from their visits back to (mainly) Mirpur and Pakistan. These regions are going through yet another period of economic deprivation and political instability so that the gaps between the 'haves' and the 'have nots' are becoming increasingly wider. At times such as these the survival of individual families and *bradari* becomes an overriding consideration, and the importance of maintaining kinship links in both countries and between both countries a necessity to this survival.

Second and at the same time, the pattern of the kaleidoscope is altered by the discourses of 'Muslimness' operational in the school. These are the 'preferred discourses' that Muslim staff teach with respect to Islam, the role of Muslim women both within the community and in the wider community, and the messages that they pass on about the identity of a Muslim woman. Interweaving their way through these are the discourses of 'Muslimness' wielded by the predominantly male governing body and community leaders, which influence the atmosphere, ethos and philosophy of the school; and those of the parents who choose to send their daughters to such a school, often at some financial sacrifice to themselves and their families. These are also the discourses that are not easily 'unmasked' by me as a white, non-Muslim researcher, but which are made more explicit in the contributions of Saeeda Shah.

In contrast, City State's reification is from **without** and from a discursive positioning which focuses on a presumed 'other'. The parents of the Muslim students in this school also have similar aspirations for their daughters, but in the interactions of the school with the Muslim parents the discourses of class, religion and culture are effectively substituted by the discourse of 'race', because of fear of the 'other'. This fear of the 'other' is a fear which is mobilized in **both** directions. In this sense the discourses which Old Town High challenges either knowingly or unknowingly have a flexibility which comes from already being 'positioned' within the 'framing' discourses of 'race', culture, community and religion. In contrast the same discourses that City State reifies with respect to the Muslim community operate through a series of power differentials which gag flexibility. The pattern of the kaleidoscope therefore sticks and changes. It becomes more set and rigid.

Since it is possible for the head teacher of Old Town High to work within these discourses, questions concerning her discursive positioning and role must also be asked. Is she an 'agent'? If so, what sort of agent is she? a 'double agent'? a 'secret agent'? an 'agent of change'? a 'sales agent'? a 'free agent'? Perhaps she is all of these. Some she would admit to and be comfortable with, others she would not because of the strict Islamic and 'framing' discourses within which she most usually operates. She continuously gets feedback on things that the community might disapprove: 'If I've taken a decision some father will mention it in the mosque to one of the governors and it will come back to me. That's very useful and also in a way it's good to know what they're thinking.' The parents are viewed as instrumental in the success of the school, so that it 'helps to know what their thoughts are' because 'it's no use moving too fast when the community is not yet ready for change, because that could end up being disastrous for the school and the children and the community itself.'

The roles of the head teacher of Old Town High are also fluid, as she implicitly and explicitly mediates her own discursive positioning within and between different discourses. There are times when some of these roles have more ascendancy than others. There are times when these roles compete. These roles are played with different emphases at different times as and when it is felt to be appropriate or applicable. Some of these roles are played consciously, others are played subconsciously. For some parents and the wider Muslim community, some of these roles are acceptable at any one time and some of these roles are not acceptable.

The **nature** and **result** of the knowing or unknowing challenge to the community of Old Town High is also brought into focus here. In one sense this challenge can be interpreted as one which is hiding behind the orthodoxies of the discourse it is challenging. This challenge can be construed as one which is also replicating these discourses (not just in the students but in the community at large), although the motives for this are very different from those of the indigenous community. For those students from Old Town High who achieve academically and are enabled through persuasion of the head teacher (among others) to go on to further and higher education, the outcomes for the 'community' cannot be predicted.

The second discourse which the teachers made explicit in both schools was that which was aimed at influencing the girls themselves. This discourse largely celebrates the feminine side of the male/female dualism and draws mainly from radical feminism. It sets out to enhance the girls' sense of self and self-worth and/or enhance the standing of the knowledge and work conventionally seen as feminine. 'Feelings of sisterhood', solidarity and esteem emerged very strongly in both schools with respect to this discourse, and femaleness was celebrated. In this context the future role of the students as mothers of the next generation was given due consideration in both schools.

In this discourse the students tended to be positioned as people sharing the same gender-related problems or people whose skills were unacknowledged. In City State the discursive conditions of possibility were limited for its Muslim students. These students do not always share the same gender-related problems because they are subordinated within different sets of discourses of culture, religion, community/kinship networks, overarched by parental concern for their unproblematic move towards marriage. Also in Islam the skills of women are differentially acknowledged and celebrated within the public/private domains. Consequently in City State the Muslim students needed a more complex set of discursive responses than it could offer. In Old Town High problems such as the difficulties of operating as a Muslim woman in a multicultural society and of facing parental opposition and *bradari* 'gaze' to preferred options such as going into the art world, the fashion industry, or hairdressing, or becoming an air hostess on leaving school, were shared and understood by those within the Islamic discourse in which they all operated; but their discursive responses were limited in a different way – through the discourses of 'Muslimness' operating within the school, again grounded in parental concern for an unproblematic move towards marriage.

This means that the Muslim students from both City State and Old Town High could benefit if they had a wider range of discursive positions made available to them. For the Muslim students in Old Town High this suggests perhaps a more open and critical acknowledgement and discussion of the discourses of 'Muslimness' operational within the school, and which position them as Muslim women, as well as the discourses of feminisms which they can then rework for their own particular context. For the Muslim students in City State this suggests a more open and critical acknowledgement of the feminist discourses that are operational within the school which position them in the same way but through different patterns of the kaleidoscope, as well as a better understanding of the discourses of 'Muslimness' which can also be reworked.

The learning environment of City State is multicultural and the staff here are concerned to combat gender stereotypes while trying to serve the needs of many. On a practical level this often means that they try to serve the needs of the 'normal'. Girls who are not positioned as 'normal' are positioned as 'different' and less than 'normal' girls. They are seen as **'special'**. This is the case for the Muslim students at City State. The Muslim girls in Old Town High are also seen as 'special' and 'other' by virtue of the fact that they have their own 'separate' school. The difference is that they **all share** this 'specialness' and 'otherness' **within the confines of the educational discourses of 'Muslimness'** operational in the school (and to a certain extent outside it) and this then filters through to other areas of their lives. In this environment it is 'normal' to be a Muslim girl and this fact is **celebrated**. This means again that there is a different range of discursive positions open to them than to their counterparts in City State. Here they are enabled to concentrate on academic achievement because of the 'pioneering' ethos to be found within a school which actively seeks to prove itself academically to both the parent and the host communities.

In Old Town High the interconnectedness of the discourses of 'race' and gender are more readily and implicitly interpreted by both the Muslim and the non-Muslim staff. Here there is the confidence on the part of the Muslim staff and the Muslim students to 'dance' with these discourses as and when the particular moment requires it as **women and Muslim,** and this filters through to the non-Muslim staff of this school.

The non-Muslim staff of Old Town High do not have that **same confidence,** and there are problems. Some of the non-Muslim staff have said they find it difficult when their students speak in their mother tongue to each other in classroom situations, and there are worries over curricular, cultural and religious issues. The advantage here is that these non-Muslim staff are work-ing with Muslim staff and within the 'Islamic ethos' of the school, so such issues can be confronted and discussed as and when they arise and this legiti-mates the movement between the 'race' and gender discourses even within the traditional inflexibility of educational discourses. The same cannot be said for the non-Muslim staff in City State, who do not have the same confidence as the non-Muslim staff of Old Town High and appear to be immobilized by their concerns about how to deal with their Muslim students.

It is appropriate at this point for me to critically and explicitly examine my own positioning. I am not sure that the head teacher would recognize the analysis of her role that I have offered because it belongs to an academic dis-course. It is a discourse in which I am placed but one in which I do not always feel 'comfortable' and so understandably it might well be a discourse which the head teacher would reject.

I am also aware that there are, and will continue to be, gaps in my 'know-ledge' which have a bearing on this analysis and which place limitations on this book, so that its purpose is to act as a means of developing my thinking and that of others. This is an ongoing process which involves my own criti-cal reflexivity (and that of others). To this end this book has applied the ideas of others to my own research with Muslim girls, so that I have reflected upon them, reworked them, and recycled them.

Earlier I argued that an analysis of the work involves attention to multi-plicities, contradictions and relations of power embedded in interpretive structures. It is difficult: partly because it is about critically examining why I wanted to hear the stories of the Muslim women and girls who participated in this research. I have had to ask myself whether I was asking for their accounts for **my** benefit, which I could not **hear** because of the benefit I derived from hearing them (Razack 1993). I believe that I have partly answered these issues, but for me they will never totally be resolved. My intention has been to open up spaces for voices suppressed in traditional education, but I cannot know whether that will be the outcome, nor do I think that this is enough in itself. However, following this line of thought the next section of this chapter discusses the implications which I believe this research has for social justice issues more generally.

Equal opportunities and difference

Muslims argue that equality is achieved through separation of the sexes from adolescence, an argument endorsed by those who support single-sex schooling in general. This is a belief that equality is achievable through separation, and not the same as equality achievable through the recognition of, and working through, 'difference'. I would argue that separation is something to be used judiciously and flexibly because the danger here is that it can be logically extended to mean having all monocultural schools – this one for white working class, this one for Pakistani children, another for Caribbean children of African descent – and this leaves a lot of people unaccounted for in a society which is increasingly complex culturally and racially. It also leads to social and cultural isolation.

In Old Town High there is a more monocultural environment **but** there are fragmentations and fracturings amongst the staff and students which become obvious as the discourses of 'Muslimness' are unmasked. These are the ones, as in City State, which are not **immediately obvious**. They are the fragmentations that occur within the religious, ethnic, class, caste/*bradari*, 'community' and gender discourses, and which are becoming clearer as my relationship with different Muslim communities and individuals within those communities becomes closer.

The question is whether Old Town High is able to offer 'discursive variety' to its students and to minority groups within the school as the school develops and its numbers increase, and whether indeed it will have something to learn from schools like City State which already have a wealth of experience in dealing with such issues. I will return to this point later. For now the need is to concentrate on the implications that the different educational experiences of the Muslim students in these two schools have for Muslim girls in particular.

The equal opportunities policies and practices on 'race' and gender adopted by City State, have served to promote anxiety in the staff concerning their relationships with their Muslim students and their parents. These policies appear to both promote and produce 'liberal angst' in the staff with regard to treading on 'cultural toes' because the sources and processes of their exclusion are treated as causal and linear. This effectively closes options for their Muslim students. These students appear to be less enabled to negotiate the hurdles that they face, due to some confusion as to how they are being positioned at any given moment. Linked to this is the felt lack of cultural knowledge constantly alluded to by the staff of City State.

This research offers an understanding of Muslim girls which is able to make adjustments for the complexities of being a girl and a Muslim girl by showing that they are multipositioned, fragmented subjects while acknowledging their commonalities and their many differences. Such a perspective, which recognizes girls as complex subjects, also suggests that reductionist, pragmatic approaches to social justice issues and to policy development in this area will fail them or any other minority groups. The equal opportunities policies currently practised in state schools are **visible** means of appearing to empower minority groups. They often cater for the **superficial** needs of different minority groups but fail to address the deeper changes which need to occur if we are to leave the opposite bank and adequately understand the needs of minority groups. This is also made clear in the perspective of Saeeda Shah in Chapter 7.

Policy can be viewed as operating at three levels: statutory, institutional and individual. At two of these levels, statutory and institutional, broad definitions are taken and then applied in particular ways. As these definitions are appropriated and adapted, the result is a shifting but inclusive definition in relation to different policy frameworks. These policies then fail to meet the interests of the majority of the target groups that they purport to support and 'include', because the processes through and by which groups become excluded are lost in a fog of the processes in which policy is created. Through the use of 'umbrella' definitions, groups are 'labelled' as different from the 'normal' and in these spaces other agendas are given the room to manoeuvre.

Statutory policy is rarely implemented directly into practice. It is mediated by other policy levels which necessarily influence the efficacy of statutory policy. First, this is at the institutional policy levels (for example at the level of local authorities and schools, the family and the Church), which 'translate' statutory policies into more specific policies and practices for implementation in their particular contexts. This can involve a whole range of pragmatic decisions which 'tweak' statutory policies through interpretation and which are made especially obvious when there are contradictions between different parts of statutory policy. An example of this in Britain would be the way that individual LEAs have balanced the requirements of the Children and Young Persons Act and the Education Act, which place different emphases on the rights of parents and children. Another example is the Education Act and the Race Relations Act, which again place different emphases on parental choice of school (see the Dewsbury and Cleveland affairs in England, Haw 1995a).

Second, there is the personal level. Individuals in their own institutions 'translate' both structural and institutional policy into their own practice. Equally, the young people they work with construct a series of personal policies as they respond to these policy practices, so that they reject, negotiate and adopt according to personal positionings which are influenced by a multitude of discursive practices.

Hadfield (1995) assessed 80 local education authority equal opportunities policies. While acknowledging that the publication of these landmark policies was a major achievement, taking into consideration the process of policy production and the political contexts in which many of them were created, he also argues that the increase in policy production throughout the 1980s was matched by a decreasing amount of policy innovation. This lack of innovation was in his view due to three factors: first, the degree of repetition in later policies, often marked in some instances by verbatim reproduction of whole sections of earlier policies; second, the increasingly undifferentiated application of cultural reproduction theories to policies; and third, the failure of later policies to develop more sophisticated curriculum responses throughout a decade of policy development. He argues that:

> The impression created is of policy developers happy to work within the relative safety of a theoretical rationale based upon the cultural reproduction of discrimination. Such a rationale is safe, and attractive, because it encouraged those in the education system to look inwards at their provision, it provided a simple heuristic model based on a number of general concepts and processes with which to critique their provision, and generated educational outcomes which were easily justifiable as legitimate concerns of the education system, even to the most reactionary of critiques . . . The added bonus of this rationale was that it did not make great demands on teachers' time or **radically** influence the nature of the curriculum.
>
> (pp. 85–6, emphasis added)

A policy context was therefore created, dominated by the issues of 'race', culture and gender, with other issues such as social class, age and handicap only discussed in association with this core and all treated as deriving from the same basic process of stereotyping and culturally based discrimination. The inevitable result of this is that the issues have become homogenized, with the same policy options being applied to an increasing number of issues. As far as institutional policy responses are concerned this has inevitably led to small-scale additions to existing curricula, with an emphasis on the humanities, and the removal of those organizational processes and structures which are most easily perceived as being based on, or reinforcing, stereotypical or discriminatory beliefs. Thus the outcome has been the creation of 'discrimination free zones within schools rather than fully fledged socially critical pupils' (p. 86).

Based on a post-structuralist theoretical framework informed by feminisms, this research shows how Muslim girls and women are positioned in a number of ways which mean that they are not so unambiguously powerless as policy definitions of exclusion tend to suggest. Such a framework allows for a recognition that we are all complex human beings and are active readers of our cultures. This then allows for the complicated and ambiguous ways that meaning is made with regard to policy. This is not a view of policy which is mechanistic and static; rather it is a view which is dynamic, fluid and shifting and which considers the levels at which policy is developed as interconnected. To achieve an insight into the fluid and shifting nature of these levels requires a depth of analysis such as the one offered. By this means it becomes obvious that a range of factors affect the perceptions and aspirations of ethnic minority communities. These range from their past and present experiences of migration, to the extent to which they have accommodated or rejected the values of the differing cultures which surround them. Such communities reflect the changing complexities of the inner city communities where these communities are most usually located. For now their specific configurations of social inclusions and exclusions cannot be described simply in terms of, for example, gender, race, class or age, because all of them are non-additive combinations of all, and more, of these categories. These communities do not fit into current theoretical categories, because they are based purely neither in interest nor in identity (Eade 1991; Werbner and Anwar 1991). Policy development in this field therefore requires theoretical innovation which is sophisticated enough to deal with the complexity of plurality, and the means open to individuals and groups to negotiate a role for themselves as 'actors' within society, given the practical realities of control and access to resources.

By focusing on the educational experiences of Muslim girls it has been possible to fill key gaps in our knowledge concerning the sources and processes of exclusion within school, which has implications for policy formation. In a broad sense these are gaps concerning an understanding of how Muslim girls define themselves in relation to their peers, parents, the wider ethnic community and beyond and concerning the way that this definition changes over time in response to their own socialization and shifting economic and social circumstances. From this point it has then been possible to gain some understanding of how this impacts on their expectations and aspirations. It also allows us to study the way in which they experience their own self-identities as they move through these different contexts.

In recent times Muslim communities in Britain have been at the forefront of negative media attention and negative social stereotyping (Ahmed 1992). At the same time these communities are settled and vibrant, reflecting the subtle processes of involvement in the British context over many decades, so that second and third generations are socialized differently into the host culture. Such communities then exhibit rapidly changing patterns of beliefs and behaviours, not least because of the very different social experiences of Muslim youth compared to their parents. From both this work and other work (Eade 1991; Werbner 1991; Brah 1992) we know that young British Muslims are influenced by a complex interaction of personal, community and social beliefs.

The indications are that at an institutional and personal policy level the matter of 'difference' in equal opportunity work is not addressed in any adequate way at all, and further, that the role of the student in actively engaging with and combating these issues has never been fully explored. In City State the tendency is to essentialize all girls in the terms of the 'normal' girl and in Old Town High the tendency is to essentialize all girls in terms of the 'normal' Muslim girl. But girls learn about themselves both now and for the future through contradictory and shifting patterns of discourses. For each individual the kaleidoscope is twisted by their own individual discursive positioning so that the pattern shifts subtly for them at any one time and over time. Through the kaleidoscope of discursive shifting patterns girls are taught about what is appropriate for them and how they should act as 'normalized' individuals. They make decisions from the positions made available to and by them through discursive and non-discursive acts and from controlled and often subconscious choices from their own individual perspectives. For Muslim girls the patterns of the kaleidoscope are interpreted through the lens of Islam, community and kinship networks and what it is to be a Muslim woman.

In City State there was an inclination to read the racialized and gendered aspects of the school in two ways: first, as the mirrored image of wider relationships of gender and 'race', elsewhere, 'beyond the school gates'; second, within school, where thinking about gender, 'race' and ethnicity is structured by the ways in which the cultures and practices of the schools themselves are formed. From this point in state schools the move is towards pragmatic policy making, **working in isolation** and without an in-depth knowledge of the sources and processes of the exclusions of different groups. This is a perspective which allows for dualisms to become mobilized so that at the statutory and institutional levels of policy development, broad definitions are taken and then applied in a particular way. As these definitions are appropriated and adapted, the result is a shifting but inclusive definition in relation to different policy frameworks. An example of this is the White Paper (Commission of the European Communities 1995) in the UK on Higher Education and Training, which emphasizes those disadvantaged groups who 'lack the family and social environment' to access training and education. Here social exclusion is related to the characteristics of the group, who are then defined as dysfunctional (Hadfield 1997), and this results in the kind of educational experiences of the Muslim students in City State.

Implications for social justice issues and equal opportunities – is there a way forward?

This critique of equal opportunity reform does not mean that it should be dismissed out of hand, but to date it seems that it has developed from retrospective theory. By this I mean the sort of theory which is generated when practice is analysed in such a way as to show that it 'fits' into theory. Implicit in any equal opportunity reform in school is the notion of the 'normal'. In UK society this is white, middle class and male. Those who are not positioned as 'normal' are positioned as other than and less than 'normal' girls. In City State the Muslim students are seen as 'special', and not because this is how they have been positioned by the school but by society 'outside'. This allows for two things to happen.

First, it allows the school to shift blame and responsibility for any of the problems the girls may have at school, to their home or their culture. Blame can be transferred elsewhere, and girls and their parents and their 'community' can then be asked to accept all responsibility for any problems. This relates to issues of how the discourses which were deliberately wielded by the staff of both Old Town High and City State relate to the discourses which **perpetuate** regimes. On one level the answer seems to lie in an exploration of this shifting of blame, which is a **two-way process** and which allows room for the discourses which perpetuate regimes to manoeuvre and operate **while simultaneously** unmasking and critically exploring what these discourses are. The question is whether schools can really alter the range of discursive positionings to students out of school. Again, this same two-way blame-shifting operation which is being wielded by and through masked discourses, requires further exploration and research.

Second, and/or alternatively, the school develops some sort of compensatory measures couched in terms of the 'normal' to try and reposition those students who are perceived to be 'different'. As a result the Muslim students in City State are positioned by institutional structures and practices in such a way as to marginalize and disown them. This means that schools need to **firstly** examine **themselves** rather than elsewhere, to critically examine their practices and ask questions about how some of their students are positioned at the margins of school life and how they can be repositioned **in consultation with the students themselves.**

In City State the teachers **knew** that the tendency was to reduce all girls to the 'normal' girl with the implicit assumption that all girls have similar needs, pleasures, interests and worries, that they are subordinated by one type of oppression which can be overcome by one type of 'empowerment'. Their confusion stemmed from the difficulty of what to do about it without getting caught up in the 'liberal dilemma' associated with either cultural relativism and pluralism or with the stereotypical cultural notions formed by their own discursive positionings around these discourses.

In Old Town High there is also the tendency to reduce all its students to that of the 'normal Muslim girl' as positioned by her community but this too is unacceptable in situations of fluidity, transformation and continuing social change. Schools are now responsible for educating a majority of children of Muslim parents who have been born and have grown up in Britain. This generation of Muslim students has concerns which are inevitably different from their parents who migrated to this country. 'Difference' then is seen to be problematic not only on a theoretical level but on a practical level as well.

I have already argued that there is a need for feminism to hold on to the commonalities while taking account of the differences, and that there are times when the commonalities are more important than the differences and vice versa; for a sameness bound by the tensions of difference; where fractures at one level are transcended by this 'sameness' at another level in a mutual and perpetual dependence which exist in, and rely essentially on, the other. In a practical sense this seems to require a strategy which explores how regimes of power use 'difference' to weaken opposition by isolating multipositioned individuals from each other, while looking for ways of positively harnessing 'difference' so that individual experience is appreciated together with an appreciation of our commonality. Such a complex strategy is the way forward for social justice reform.

For the teachers of City State – for any school – this implies the need for a 'knowledge' of different feminisms, for a critical examination of their different weaknesses and strengths in particular geographical, social and historical circumstances both in school and beyond, and for a view of them as strategies rather than end points. In the same but a different way, for the teachers of Old Town High it implies the need for a 'knowledge' of different discourses of 'Muslimness' and a critical re-assessment of their strengths and weaknesses. This is Trinh's 'points of departure', her ground-clearing activity. Teachers could then make these discourses of feminism and 'Muslimness' available to their Muslim students and enable them to explore different feminisms and 'Muslimness' as strategies for change to suit individuals according to their material, historical and cultural locations. This embraces Foucault's notion of freedom of being able to critically question and reassess our inherited identities and values, with its attendant consequences of **risk**. Foucault's concern is about the consequences of not risking oneself, one's truth, one's beliefs.

Earlier in the book I posed two questions that have been asked about Muslim girls' schools: whether they are a reaction to discrimination, conflict and educational failure, or whether they are a fundamentalist means of empowerment and strength which will crystallize the racial, cultural and religious issues separating some Muslims from the white indigenous British population. At the end of this book I wonder whether such questions are appropriate. I believe that these schools were established initially as a short-term defence strategy, as has been made clear by Saeeda Shah in Chapter 2. Initially, unmarried teenage daughters were not sent to the United Kingdom, but this changed with the 1962 Immigration Act and on entering this country there was a legal requirement that these school-age girls were educated. The socio-economic, cultural and religious background of some of their parents meant that initially, state schools (and particularly mixed-sex state schools) were not considered to be suitable places to educate their daughters for moral and cultural reasons, as they did not facilitate the smooth and unproblematic transition to an arranged marriage. These reasons then came to encompass the discourses of discrimination, religion, educational opportunity and the maintenance of a cultural and religious identity. A short-term defence strategy became so much more; it blossomed into discourses of rights, religion, cultural identity, morality and above all a power struggle between a now established British Muslim community with political clout and the 'host' community.

The research has made clear that each school in this study has its limitations. In City State this has to do with multicultural intake and the difficulties of putting the concept of equality in difference into practice. In Old Town High with its more monocultural intake this has to do superficially with physical environment, resources and width of curriculum as well as issues of separatism; but more importantly and on a deeper level this has to do with the 'tensions within the community between the Islamic spirit of justice and equality and cultural/patriarchal practices'.

What is needed is well theorized practices and practical theories which have the sophistication to deal with 'difference', hybridity and pluralism. This means theories which challenge practice and practices which challenge theory. In this case it means a challenge from an analysis of practices which question what a theoretical analysis of power through discourse means for practice. In this regard I have argued that a post-structural approach and analysis of the practices concerning the educational experiences of Muslim girls has relevance to future initiatives and innovations in the social justice debate, because it allows for a theory which transcends agency/structure dualisms and avoids simplistic notions of patriarchal power in understanding the complex educational experiences and (by implication) girls from a plurality of backgrounds. I hope this means there will come a time when social justice and equal opportunity reform has reached the point where Muslims (or any other minority group) do not feel the need, or indeed have the need, to educate their children in 'separate schools'.

Meanwhile the intention of this book was 'an attempt to leave the opposite bank'. Having written it I believe the potential to leave the opposite bank is there. However, this may not be at the points or crossings of our choosing. Travelling to Peshawar in Pakistan from Mirpur I crossed a bridge where the tributaries of two rivers came together. One of these tributaries had flowed through land which coloured it blue, the other had flowed through land which coloured it red. They met in one river which flowed for some way so that it was distinctly one part blue and one part red. The colours did not mix. Rather they slid past each other. They slid past each other in much the same way that many academic/theoretical debates and theoretical versus practical debates slide past each other because of a preoccupation with labels and 'naming'. The river was striking most especially as I did not have the knowledge or language to explain it, but at some point(s) and gradually the colours swirled and mixed into one. The new, larger and by this point more potent river then journeyed onwards to the sea.

Glossary

abad	'man', human being
abadah	(rituals of) worship
bradari	extended kinship group, clan
Daras	place of learning, Islamic schools
Eids	religious festivals
fajar	before sunrise, also the name for morning prayer
faraz	incumbent
fatwas	injunction
fiqas	Islamic schools of law
Hadith	sayings of the noble prophet Mohammed
hijab	veil
Imaan	faith
Imam	religious leader/one who leads prayers
izzat	honour
Jihad	struggle
Khatam-al-Qur'an	reading of complete Qur'an
Khalifah	vice-gerent
khandan	family
la ikraha fid-d-din	no compulsion in (choice of) religion
madrasahs	places of learning/schools
Milad	the prophet Mohammed's birthday
mughrab	immediately after sunset, also the name for prayers offered around that time
Ramazan	month of fasting
rasalah	very close to the spirit and teaching of the Qur'an
rizak-e-halal	honest rightful earnings
sahib-e-nisab	those in Islamic Shari'ah who have to pay Zakat
shalwar kameez	Pakistani dress – 'shalwar' equivalent to trousers and 'kameez' to shirt
Shari'ah	Islamic law

Sunnah	the prophet's acts
Suras	sections/chapters of Qur'an
ulema	religious scholars
Ummah	community of believers

References

Abd al Ali-Hammudah (1977) *The Family Structure in Islam*. Washington, IN: American Trust Publications.

Afshar, H. (1994) Muslim women in West Yorkshire, in H. Afshar and M. Maynard (eds) *The Dynamics of 'Race' and Gender: Some Feminist Interventions*. London: Taylor and Francis.

Ahmed, A.S. and Hastings, D. (eds) (1994) *Islam, Globalisation and Postmodernity*. London: Routledge.

Ahmed, L. (1992) *Women and Gender in Islam: Historical Roots of a Modern Debate*. London: Yale University Press.

Al-Ahsan, A. (1992) *Ummah or Nation: Identity Crisis in Contemporary Muslim Society*. Leicester: The Islamic Foundation.

Al-Attas, S.N. (ed.) (1979) *Aims and Objectives of Islamic Education*. London: Hodder & Stoughton.

Al-Ghazali (1995) *On Disciplining the Soul*. Cambridge: The Islamic Texts Society.

Al-Hibri, A. (ed.) (1982) *Women and Islam*. Oxford: Pergamon Press.

Alcoff, L. (1987) Cultural feminism versus post-structuralism: the identity crisis in feminist theory'. *Signs*, 13(3): 405–36.

Ali, R.E. (1996) 'The Youth Service and the young Asians in Peterborough', PhD thesis. University of Nottingham, England.

Altbach, P.G. (1982) Servitude of the mind: education, dependency, and neo-colonialism, in P.G. Altbach, R. Arnove and G.P. Kelly (eds) *Comparative Education*. London: Macmillan.

Alvarado, M. and Ferguson, B. (1983) The curriculum, media studies and discursivity. *Screen*, 24(3): 20–34.

Amos, V. and Parmar, P. (1981) Resistances and responses: experiences of black girls in Britain, in A. McRobbie and T. McCabe (eds) *Feminism for Girls: an Adventure Story*. London: Routledge and Kegan Paul.

Amos, V. and Parmar, P. (1984) Challenging imperial feminism. *Feminist Review*, 17 July: 3–19.

Anwar, M. (1979) *The Myth of Return*. London: Heinemann.

Anwar, M. (1981) Young Muslims in Britain: their educational needs and policy implications, in M.W. Khan (ed.) *Education and Society in the Muslim World*. London: Hodder and Stoughton.

Anwar, M. (1982) *Young Muslims in a Multicultural Society: Their Needs and Policy Implications*. Leicester: The Islamia Foundation.

Anzaldua, G. (1987) *Borderlands/La Frontera*. San Francisco, CA: Aunt Lute Foundation Books.

Arnot, M. and Weiner, G. (eds) (1987) *Gender and the Politics of Schooling*. London: Hutchinson in association with the Open University.

Ashraf, S.A. (1986) Foreword to J.M. Halstead *The Case for Muslim Voluntary Aided Schools: Some Philosophical Reflections*. Cambridge: The Islamic Academy.

Ashraf, S.A. (1992) Open house: defining education. *Islamia*, July (19): 13.

Association of Educational Psychologists (1988) *Sexism in Schools*. Durham: AEP.

Balkin, J. (1987) Contribution of friends to women's fear of success in college. *Psychological Reports*, 61(1): 39–42.

Ball, S.J. (1990) Introducing Monsieur Foucault, in S. Ball (ed.) *Foucault and Education: Disciplines and Knowledge*. London: Routledge.

Banton, M. (1972) *Racial Minorities*. London: Fontana.

Barrett, M. (1980) *Women's Oppression Today: Problems in Marxist Feminist Analysis*. London: Verso.

Basit, T. (1995) 'I want to go to college': British Muslim Girls and the Academic Dimension of Schooling. *Muslim Education Quarterly*, 12(3): 55–61.

Beddard, A. (1980) *Human Rights and Europe* (2nd edition). London: Sweet and Maxwell.

Benhabib, S. (1992) *Situating the Self: Gender, Community and Postmodernism*. Cambridge: Polity Press.

Berliner, W. (1993) Muslims stand their ground, *Education Guardian*, 23 March.

Best, S. and Kellner, D. (eds) (1991) *Postmodern Theory: Critical Interrogations*. London: Macmillan.

Bhatti, G. (1995) A journey into the unknown: an ethnographic study of Asian children, in M. Griffiths and B. Troyna (eds) *Antiracism, Culture and Social Justice in Education*. Stoke-on-Trent: Trentham Books

BMMS (1993) *Meeting of the Muslim Parliament*, Vol. 1, No. 1. Centre for the Study of Islam and Christian-Muslim relations, Selly Oak Colleges, Birmingham.

Bone, A. (1983) *Girls and Girls-Only Schools*. Manchester: EOC.

Boudhiba, A. (1985) (trans. Alan Sheridan) *Sexuality in Islam*. London: Routledge and Kegan Paul.

Bradley, H. (1996) *Fractured Identities: Changing Patterns of Inequality*. Cambridge: Polity Press.

Bradney, A.G.D. (1987). Ethnic minorities and the law. *New Community*, X113(3): Spring.

Brah, A. (1991) Questions of difference and international feminism, in J. Aaron and S. Walby (eds) *Out of the Margins*. London: Falmer Press.

Brah, A. (1992) Difference, diversity and differentiation, in J. Donald and A. Rattansi (eds) *'Race', Culture and Difference*. London: Sage Publications in association with the Open University.

Brine, J. (1993) 'The European Social Fund and the vocational training of unemployed women: policy aims and implementation', unpublished PhD thesis. University of Nottingham.

Broverman, I.K.,Vogel, S.R., Broverman, D.M., Clarkson, F.E. and Rosenkranz, P.S. (1970) Sex-role stereotypes and clinical judgements of mental health. *Journal of Consulting and Clinical Psychology*, 34(1): 1–7.

Bunch, C. (1987) *Passionate Politics: Feminist Theory in Action*. New York: St Martin's Press.

Burgess, A. (1990) Co-education – the disadvantages for schoolgirls. *Gender and Education*, 2(1): 91–5.

Burris, B. (1973) The fourth world manifesto, in A. Koedt, E. Levine and A. Rapone (eds) *Radical Feminism*. New York: Quadrangle Books.

Byrne, E. (1978) *Equality of Education and Training for Girls (10–18 Years)*. Collection Studies: Education Series No.9. Brussels: Commission of the European Communities.

Cherryholmes, C. (1988) *Power and Criticism: Poststructural Investigations in Education*. New York: Teacher's College Press.

Choudury, M.A. (1993) A critical examination of the concept of Islamisation of knowledge in contemporary times. *Muslim Education Quarterly*, 10(4): 3–34.

Christian, B. (1987). The Race for Theory. *Cultural Critique*, Spring 1987, pp. 51–63.

Christie, C.J. (1991) The rope of God: Muslim minorities in the West and Britain. *New Community*, 17(3): 457–66.

Coard, B. (1971) *How the West Indian is Made ESN in the British School System*. London: New Beacon Books.

Cockburn, C. (1991) *In the Way of Women: Men's Resistance to Sex Equality in Organisations*. London: Macmillan.

Commission of the European Communities (1995) White Paper on Education and Training. *Teaching and Learning: Towards the Learning Society*. COM/95/590/ fin.

Connolly, P. (1994) Theorising racism in educational settings: reintroducing the work of Pierre Bourdieu. Working paper presented to *BERA*, 8–11 September, St Anne's College, Oxford.

Connolly, P. (1995) Boys will be boys? Racism, sexuality and the construction of masculine identities amongst infant boys, in J. Holland, M. Blair and S. Sheldon (eds) *Debates and Issues in Feminist Research and Pedagogy*. Clevedon: Multilingual Matters.

Cotterill, P. (1992) Interviewing women, issues of friendship, vulnerability and power. *Women's Studies International Forum*, 15: 593–606.

Craft, A. and Bardell, G. (eds) (1984) *Curriculum Opportunities in a Multicultural Society*. London: Harper Educational.

CRE (1990) *Schools of Faith: Religious Schools in a Multicultural Society*. London: CRE.

Crompton, R. and Sanderson, K. (1987) Where did all the bright girls go? *Quarterly Journal of Social Affairs*, 3(2): 135–47.

Cruickshank, M. (1963) *Church and State in English Education: 1870 to the Present Day*. London: Macmillan.

Curtain, P.O. (ed.) (1971) *Imperialism: The Documentary History of Western Civilization*. New York: Walker and Co.

Dale, R.R. (1969, 1971, 1974) *Mixed or Single Sex Schools?* Vols 1, 2 and 3. London: Routledge and Kegan Paul.

Daly, M. (1978) *Gyn/Ecology: The Meta-ethics of Radical Feminism*. Boston: Beacon Press.

Davies, L. (1984) *Pupil Power: Deviance and Gender in School*. Lewes: Falmer Press.

Davis, A. (1981) *Women, Race and Class*. London: The Women's Press.

Dean, C. (1992) A-level triumph for girls' schools', *Times Educational Supplement*, 13 November.

Deem, R. (ed.) (1984) *Co-education Reconsidered*. Milton Keynes: Open University Press.

Delamont, S. (1980) *The Sociology of Women*. London: George Allen & Unwin.

Department for Education (1981) *The Rampton Report. West Indian Children in Our Schools*. London: DES.

Department for Education (1985) *Education for All. Report of the Committee of Enquiry into the Education of Children from Ethnic Minority Backgrounds* (The Swann Report). London: HMSO.

Derrick, J. and Goodall, J.R. (1968) School – the meeting point and the Pakistani background in R. Oakley (ed.) *New Backgrounds*. London: Oxford University Press for the Institute of Race Relations.

Derrida, J. (1973) *Speech and Phenomena, and Other Essays on Husserl's Theory of Signs*. Evanston, IL: Northwestern University Press

Derrida, J. (1976) *Of Grammatology*. Baltimore and London: Johns Hopkins University Press.

Derrida, J. (1978) *Writing and Difference*. London: Routledge and Kegan Paul.

Desai, R. (1963) *Indian Immigrants in Britain*. Oxford: Oxford University Press for the Institute of Race Relations.

Donald, J. and Rattansi, A. (eds) (1992) *'Race', Culture and Difference*. Sage Publications in association with the Open University.

Durham, M. (1989) The religious issue that will not go away, *Guardian*, 14 March.

Durkee, N. (1990) Marriage for a Muslimah. *Muslim Educational Quarterly*, 7(3): 65–71.

Dworkin, A. (1981) *Pornography: Men Possessing Women*. London: Women's Press.

Eade, J. (1991) in P. Werbner and M. Anwar (eds), *Black and Ethnic Leadership: The Cultural Dimensions of Political Leadership*. London: Routledge.

Edwards, R. (1990) Connecting method and epistemology: a white woman interviewing black women. *Women's Studies International Forum*, 13(5): 477–90.

Eggleston, J. (1990) Can antiracist education survive the 1988 ERA? *Multicultural Teaching*, 8(3): 9–11.

Eisenstein, H. (1984) *Contemporary Feminist Thought*. London: Unwin.

El Sadaawi, N. (1980) *The Hidden Face of Eve*. London: Zed Press.

Farah, M. (1984) *Marriage and Sexuality in Islam*. Salt Lake City, UT: University of Utah Press.

Faulkner, J. (1989) 'Attitudes to high academic achievement in girls: a comparative study of the attitudes of second, third and fourth year pupils attending mixed-sex and single sex comprehensive schools', unpublished PhD thesis. University of Birmingham.

Faulkner, J. (1991) Mixed-sex schooling and equal opportunities for girls: a contradiction in terms? *Research Papers in Education*, 16(3): 197–223.

Fernea, E. (ed.) (1985) *Women and the Family in the Middle East: New Voices of Change*. Austin: University of Texas Press.

Flax, J. (1987) Postmodernism and gender relations in feminist theory. *Signs* 12(4): 621–43.

Foucault, M. (1967) *Madness and Civilization. A History of Insanity in the Age of Reason*, trans. R. Howard. London: Tavistock.

Foucault, M. (1971) *L'Ordre du Discours*. Paris: Gallimard.

Foucault, M. (1972) *Histoire de la folie*. Paris: Gallimard.

Foucault, M. (1974) *The Archaeology of Knowledge*. London: Tavistock.

Foucault, M. (1979) *Discipline and Punish: The Birth of the Prison*, trans. A. Sheridan. New York: Vintage.

Foucault, M. (1980a) *Power/Knowledge: Selected Interviews and Other Writings, 1972–77*, ed. C. Gordon. New York: Pantheon.

Foucault, M. (1980b) *History of Sexuality Volume 1*. New York: Vintage.

Foucault, M. (1982) The subject and power, in H. Dreyfus and P. Rabinow (eds) *Michel Foucault: Beyond Structuralism and Hermeneutics. With an Afterword by Michel Foucault*. New York: Harvester Press.

Foucault, M. (1984) What is enlightenment?, in P. Rabinow (ed.) *The Foucault Reader*. New York: Pantheon.

Fuss, D. (1989) *Essentially Speaking*. London: Routledge.

Gilroy, P. (1987) *There Ain't No Black in the Union Jack*. London: Hutchinson.

Gilroy, P. (1992) The end of antiracism, in J. Donald and A. Rattansi (eds) *'Race', Culture and Difference*. London: Sage Publications in association with the Open University.

Gilroy, P. (1993) *The Black Atlantic*. London: Verso.

Giroux, H. (1983) *Theory and Resistance in Education: A Pedagogy for the Opposition*. London: Heinemann Educational Books.

Giroux, H. (1988) *Schooling for Democracy: Critical Pedagogy in the Modern Age*. London: Routledge.

Griffiths, M. (1992) *Self-Identity, Self-Esteem and Social Justice*. Nottingham: School of Education, University of Nottingham.

Griffiths, M. (1995a) Making a difference: feminism, postmodernism and the methodology of educational research. *British Educational Research Journal*, 21(2): 219–35.

Griffiths, M. (1995b) *Feminisms and the Self: The Web of Identity*. London: Routledge.

Griffiths, M. and Davies, C. (1995) *In Fairness to Children*. London: David Fulton.

Griffiths, M. and Haw, K.F. (1996) Equity and quality for Asian schoolchildren. Report for City Challenge and Project Azadi.

Haddad, Y.Y., Haines, B. and Findly, E. (1984) *The Islamic Impact*. Syracuse, New York: Syracuse University Press.

Hadfield, M. (1995) 'Conceptualising equal opportunities in primary schools', unpublished PhD thesis. Nottingham Trent University.

Hadfield, M. (1997) The TIME project: communities, commercialism and continuing education. Paper presented to European Educational Research Association, September, Frankfurt.

Hakim, C. (1979) *Occupation Segregation*. London: Department of Employment.

Hall, S. (1992) New ethnicities, in J. Donald and A. Rattansi (eds) *'Race', Culture and Difference*. London: Sage Publications in association with the Open University.

Hall, S. (ed.) (1997) *Representation: Cultural Representations and Signifying Practices*. London: Sage.

Hall, S. and de Gay, P. (eds) (1996) *Questions of Cultural Identity*. London: Sage.

Halstead, M. (1986) *The Case for Muslim Voluntary-Aided Schools: Some Philosophical Reflections*. Cambridge: The Islamic Academy.

Halstead, M. (1988) *Education, Justice and Cultural Diversity. An Examination of the Honeyford Affair, 1984–85*. Lewes: Falmer Press.

Halstead, M. (1991) Radical feminism, Islam and the single-sex school debate. *Gender and Education*, 3(3): 263–78.

Hamilton, M. and Hirszowicz, M. (1987) *Class and Inequality in Pre-Industrial Capitalist and Communist Societies*. Brighton: Wheatsheaf Books.

Haneef, S. (1979) *What Everyone Must Know About Islam*. Chicago: Kazi Publications.

Haraway, D. (1988) Situated knowledges: the science question in feminism and the privilege of partial perspective. *Feminist Studies*, 14(3): 575–99.

Harding, S. (1986) *The Science Question in Feminism*. Milton Keynes: Open University Press.

Harding, S. (ed.) (1987). *Feminism and Methodology*. Milton Keynes: Open University Press.

Hargreaves, D.H. (1967) *Social Relations in a Secondary School*. London: Routledge and Kegan Paul.

Hartsock, N. (1987) Rethinking modernism: minority vs. majority theories. *Cultural Critique*, 7, 187–206.

Hassan, R. (1995) The development of feminist theology as a means of combating injustice towards women in Muslim communities and culture. Paper delivered to the 22nd International Student Conference of Jews, Christians and Muslims, 6–13 March.

Haw, K. (1990) 'Muslim girls' schools: a question of race, gender or religion?', unpublished MA dissertation. Sussex University.

Haw, K. (1994) Muslim girls' schools – a conflict of interests? *Gender and Education*, 6(1): 63–77.

Haw, K. (1995a) 'Education for Muslim girls in contemporary Britain: social and political dimensions', unpublished PhD Thesis. University of Nottingham.

Haw, K. (1995b) Why Muslim girls are more feminist in Muslim schools, in M. Griffiths and B. Troyna (eds) *Antiracism, Culture and Social Justice in Education*. Stoke-on-Trent: Trentham Books.

Haw, K. (1996) Tales told to tourists: should the white researcher stay at home?. *British Educational Research Journal*, 22(3): 319–30.

Hill, C. (1970) *Immigration and Integration: A Study of the Settlement of Coloured Minorities in Britain*. Oxford: Pergamon.

hooks, b. (1984) *Feminist Theory: From Margin to Centre*. Boston: South End Press.

hooks, b. (1993) bell hooks speaking about Paulo Freire – the man and his work, in P. Mclaren and P. Leonard (eds) *Paulo Freire: A Critical Encounter*. London: Routledge.

Horner, M.S. (1969) Women's will to fail. *Psychology Today*, 3: 6, 36–8.

Horner, M.S. (1972) Towards an understanding of achievement related conflicts in women. *Journal of Social Issues*, 28(2): 157–75.

Husain, S.S. and Ashraf, S.A. (1979) *Crisis in Muslim Education*. London: Hodder and Stoughton.

Hussain, F. (ed.) (1984) *Muslim Women*. New York: St Martins Press.

Hutcheon, L. (1989) *The Politics of Postmodernism*. New York: Routledge.

Iqbal, M. (1975) *Islamic Education and Single-Sex Schools*. London: Union of Muslim Organisations.

Iqra Trust (1991) *Meeting the Needs of Muslim Pupils*. London: Iqra Trust.

The Islamic Academy (1985) *The Swann Committee Report: An Evaluation from the Muslim Point of View. An Agreed Statement*. Cambridge: The Islamic Academy.

Jacobs, S.G. (1975) *European Convention on Human Rights*. Oxford: Clarendon Press.

Jaggar, A.M. (1983, reprint 1988) *Feminist Politics and Human Nature*. New Jersey: Rowan and Littlefield Publishers Inc.

Jeffery, P. (1976) *Migrants and Refugees: Muslim and Christian Migrant Families in Britain*. Milton Keynes: The Open University.

Joly, D. (1989) Muslims in Europe. Ethnic minorities and education in Britain: interaction between the Muslim community and Birmingham schools. *Research Papers* No. 41. Centre for the Study of Islam and Christian-Muslim relations. Birmingham: Selly Oak Colleges.

Jones, A. (1993) Becoming a 'girl': poststructuralist suggestions for educational research. *Gender and Education*, 5(2): 157–66.

Jones, C. and Mahony, P. (eds) (1989) *Learning Our Lines: Sexuality and Social Control in Education*. London: Women's Press.

Kabbani, R. (1986). *Europe's Myths of Orient*. Basingstoke: Macmillan.

Kadar, M. (1988) Sexual harrassment as a form of social control, in A.T. McLaren (ed.) *Gender and Society: Creating a Canadian Women's Sociology*. Ontario: Copp Clark Pitman.

Kandiyoti, D. (1991) Islam and patriarchy: a comparative perspective, in N. Keddie and B. Baron (eds) *Women in Middle Eastern History*. New Haven: Yale University Press.

Kandiyoti, D. (1996) Islam and feminism: a misplaced polarity? *Women Against Fundamentalism Journal*, 8: 10–14.

Kavanagh, D. (1987) *Thatcherism and British Politics: The End of Consensus*. New York: Oxford University Press.

Kenway, J. and Willis, S. (1986) Feminist single-sex educational strategies: some theoretical flaws and practical fallacies. *Discourse*, 7(1): 1–30.

Kenway, J., Willis, S., Blackmore, J. and Rennie, L. (1994) Making 'hope practical' rather than despair 'convincing': feminist post-structuralism, gender reform and educational change. *British Journal of Sociology of Education*, 15(2): 187–210.

Kirkwood, G. and Kirkwood, C. (1989) *Living Adult Education: Freire in Scotland*. Milton Keynes: Open University Press in association with Scottish Institute of Adult and Continuing Education.

Kremer, J. and Curry, C. (1986) *Attitudes Towards Women in Northern Ireland*. Belfast: Equal Opportunities Commission for Northern Ireland.

Lacey, C. (1970) *Hightown Grammar*. Manchester: Manchester University Press.

Laclau, E. and Mouffe, C. (1985) *Hegemony and Socialist Strategy: Toward a Radical Democratic Politics*. London: Verso Books.

Lamb, F. and Pickthorne, H. (1968) *Locked-up Daughters: A Parents' Look at Girls' Education and Schools.* London: Hodder and Stoughton.

Lather, P. (1988) Feminist perspectives in empowering research methodologies. *Women's Studies International Forum,* 11(6): 569–81.

Lather, P. (1991) *Getting Smart: Feminist Research and Pedagogy with/in the Postmodern.* New York: Routledge.

Lawson, J. and Silver, H. (1973) *A Social History of Education in England.* London: Methuen & Co.

Lee, V.E. and Bryk, A.S. (1986) Effects of single-sex secondary schools on student achievement and attitudes. *Journal of Educational Psychology,* 78(5): 381–95.

Little, A. and Willey, R. (1981) Multi-ethnic education: the way forward. *Schools Council Pamphlet 18.* London: Schools Council.

Little, A. and Willey, R. (1983) Studies from the multi-ethnic curriculum. Full Report from the Schools Council Project on Studies in the Multi-ethnic Curriculum based at Goldsmith's College, University of London (1978–80). London: Schools Council.

Llewellyn, M. (1980) Studying girls at school: the implications of confusion, in R. Deem (ed.) *Schooling for Women's Work.* London: Routledge and Kegan Paul.

Lodge, B. (1990a) Veto could cost votes, warns Muslim leader, *Times Educational Supplement,* 8 June.

Lodge, B. (1990b) Muslim body asks schools to shut on holy days, *Times Educational Supplement,* 6 July.

London Lesbian Offensive Group (1984) Anti-lesbianism in the Women's Liberation Movement, in A. Kanter, S. Lefanu, S. Shah and C. Spedding (eds) *Sweeping Statements. Writings from the Women's Liberation Movement 1981–1983.* London: Women's Press.

Mabud, S.A. (1992) A Muslim response to the Education Reform Act of 1988. *British Journal of Religious Education,* 14 (Spring): 88–98.

Macdonald, I., Bhavnani, R., Khan, L. and John, G. (1989) *Murder in the Playground.* London: Longsight Press.

Mahony, P. (1985) *Schools for the Boys? Co-education Reassessed.* London: Hutchinson.

Marsh, H.W. (1989) Effects of attending single-sex and co-educational high schools on achievement, attitudes, behaviours and sex differences. *Journal of Educational Psychology,* 81(1): 70–85.

Mawdudi, S.A.A. (1985) *Let Us Be Muslims* (ed. K. Murad). Leicester: The Islamic Foundation.

McClelland, D.C. (1953) *The Achieving Society.* Princeton, NJ: Van Nostrand.

McLaughlin, E. (1991) Oppositional poverty: the quantitative/qualitative divide and other dichotomies. *The Sociological Review,* 39(2): 292–309.

McRobbie, A. and Garber, J. (1976) Girls and subcultures, in S. Hall *et al., Resistance Through Rituals.* London: Hutchinson.

Measor, L. and Sikes, P. (1992) *Gender and Schools.* London: Cassell.

Mernissi, F. (1975) *Beyond the Veil: Male-Female Dynamics in Modern Muslim Society.* Cambridge, MA: Schenkman.

Mernissi, F. (1991) *Women and Islam: An Historical and Theological Enquiry.* Oxford: Basil Blackwell.

Mernissi, F. (1993) *The Forgotten Queens of Islam.* Cambridge: Polity Press.

Midgley, S. (1989) Muslims turn to separate schools to preserve Islamic faith, *Independent*, 30 January.

Mirza, H.S. (1992). *Young Female and Black*. London: Routledge.

Mirza, M. (1995) Some ethical dilemmas in fieldwork, in M. Griffiths and B. Troyna (eds) *Antiracism, Culture and Social Justice in Education*. Stoke-on-Trent: Trentham Books.

Modood, T. (1992) *Not Easy Being British: Colour, Culture and Citizenship*. Stoke-on-Trent: Trentham Books.

Mohamed, Y. (1991) Knowledge in Islam and the crisis in Muslim education. *Muslim Educational Quarterly*, 8(4): 13–32.

Morgan, R. (1984) *Sisterhood is Global*. New York: Anchor Press/Doubleday.

Morris, M. (1988) *The Pirate's Fiancee: Feminism Reading Postmodernism*. London: Verso.

Mullard, C. (1985) Multiracial education in Britain: from assimilation to cultural pluralism, in M. Arnot (ed.) *Race and Gender. Equal Opportunities Policies in Education*. Oxford: Butterworth Heinemann.

Nehaul, K. (1995) *The Schooling of Children of Caribbean Heritage*. Stoke-on-Trent: Trentham Books.

Nicholson, N. (ed.) (1990) *Feminism/Postmodernism*. London: Routledge.

Nielsen, J. (June/September 1986) A survey of British local authority response to Muslim needs. *Research Papers: Muslims in Europe*, 30/31. Centre for the Study of Islam and Christian/Muslim Relations, Selly Oak Colleges, Birmingham B29 6LE.

Nielsen, J.S. (1992) *Muslims in Western Europe*. Edinburgh: Edinburgh University Press.

Oakley, A. (1981) Interviewing women: a contradiction in terms. in H. Roberts (ed.) *Doing Feminist Research*. London: Routledge and Kegan Paul.

Oakley, A. (1982) *Subject Women*. London: Fontana.

Opie, A. (1992) Qualitative research, appropriation of the 'other' and empowerment. *Feminist Review*, 40 (Spring): 52–69.

O'Rourke, D., Henderson, L. and Owen, J. (producers) (1993) *Cannibal Tours*. Channel Four.

Parker-Jenkins, M. (1995) *Children of Islam*. Stoke-on-Trent: Trentham Books.

Parkin, M. (1984) Muslim school's accommodation and teaching fail to pass inspectors' test; Muslim pupils kneel to work – report in school for Muslim girls Dewsbury, *Guardian*, 26 November and 17 December.

Payne, I. (1980, reprinted 1988) Sexist ideology and education, in D. Spender and E. Sarah (eds) *Learning to Lose: Sexism and Education*. London: The Women's Press Ltd.

Pignatelli, F. (1993) What can I do? Foucault on freedom and the question of teacher agency. *Educational Theory*, 43(4): 411–32.

Prosser, J. (1992) Personal reflections on the use of photography in an ethnographic case study. *British Educational Research Journal*, 18(4): 397–413.

Rabine, L. (1988) A feminist politics of non-identity. *Feminist Studies*, 14(1): 11–31.

Rafferty, F. (1993) Girls outstrip boys in English exams, *Times Educational Supplement*, 12 March.

Ramazanoglu, C. (1986) Gender and Islam – the politics of Muslim feminism. *Ethnic and Racial Studies*, 9(2): April.

Ramazanoglu, C. (1989) *Feminism and the Contradictions of Oppression*. London: Routledge.

Rattansi, A. (1992) Changing the subject? Racism, culture and education, in J. Donald and A. Rattansi (eds) *'Race', Culture and Difference*. London: Sage Publications in association with the Open University.

Razack, S. (1993) Story-telling for social change. *Gender and Education*, 5(1): 55–70.

Rendel, M. (1992) European law: ending discrimination against girls in education. *Gender and Education*; 4(1/2): 163–73.

Rex, J. (1989) Equality of opportunity, multiculturalism, anti-racism and 'Education for All', in G.K. Verma (ed.) *Education for All: A Landmark in Pluralism*. London: Falmer Press.

Rich, A. (1980) Compulsory heterosexuality and lesbian existence. *Signs*, 5: 631–60.

Risalludin, S. (1996) Is there a space for feminism in Islam? *Women Against Fundamentalism Journal*, 8: 4–5.

Robertson, A.H. (1982) (2nd ed.) *Human Rights in the World: An Introduction to the Study of International Protection in Human Rights*. Manchester: Manchester University Press.

Rowland, J. (1987) Technology and motherhood: reproductive choice reconsidered. *Signs*, 12(3): 512–28.

Said, E. (1978) *Orientalism: Western Conceptions of the Orient*. London: Routledge and Kegan Paul.

Said, E.W. (1981) *Covering Islam: How the Media and the Experts Determine How We See the Rest of the World*: New York: Pantheon Books.

Saifullah Khan, V.J. (1977) The Pakistanis: Mirpuri villagers at home and in Bradford, in J.L. Watson (ed.) *Between Two Cultures*. Oxford: Blackwell.

Saifullah Khan, V.J. (1992) *Muslims in Western Europe*. (ed. J.S. Nielsen). Edinburgh: Edinburgh University Press.

Sarwar, G. (1991) *British Muslims and Schools*. London: Muslim Educational Trust.

Sawicki, J. (1991) *Disciplining Foucault: Feminism, Power and the Body*. London: Routledge.

Scott, J. (1988) Deconstructing equality-versus-difference: or, the uses of poststructuralist theory for feminism. *Feminist Studies*, 14(1): 33–50.

Segal, L. (1987) *Is the Future Female?: Troubled Thoughts on Contemporary Feminism*. London: Verso.

Seller, A. (1993) Should the feminist philosopher stay at home? in J. Lennon and C. Whitford (eds) *Knowing the Difference: Feminist Perspectives in Epistemology*. London: Routledge.

Shackleton, J. (1993) USA community colleges and further education in Britain, in D. Finegold *et al.* (eds) *Something Borrowed, Something Blue?* Oxford Studies in Comparative Education Vol. 3, no. 1.

Shah, N. (1989) *Pakistani Women: A Socio-economic and Demographic Profile*. Islamabad, Pakistan: Pakistan Institute of Development Economics.

Sharpe, S. (1976) *Just Like a Girl: How Girls Learn to be Women*. London: Penguin.

Shaw, A. (1988) *A Pakistani Community in Britain*. Oxford: Blackwell.

Siddiqi, M.M. (1982) *Women in Islam*. Lahore: Institute of Islamic Culture.

Skeggs, B. (1991) Postmodernism: what is all the fuss about? *British Journal of Sociology of Education*, 12(2): 255–67.

Smith, D. (1988) Institutional ethnography: a feminist method, in A.T. McLaren (ed.) *Gender and Society: Creating a Canadian Women's Sociology*. Oxford: Capp Clark Pitman.

Smith, J. (1984) The experiences of Muslim women: considerations of power and authority, in Y. Haddad, B. Haines and E. Findly (eds) *Islamic Impact*. Syracuse, New York: Syracuse University Press.

Spence, J.T., Helmreich, R. and Stapp, J. (1973) A short version of the Attitude Towards Women Scale (AWS). *Bulletin of the Psychonomic Society*, 2: 219–20.

Spender, D. and Sarah, E. (eds) (1980) *Learning to Lose: Sexism and Education*. London: The Women's Press.

Spivak, G.C. (1987) *In Other Worlds: Essays in Cultural Politics*. London: Methuen.

Spivak, G.C. with Rooney, E. (1989) In a word. Interview. *Differences*, 1(2): 124–56.

Spivak, G.C. (1990) *The Post-Colonial Critic. Interviews, Strategies, Dialogues* (ed. Sarah Harasym). London: Routledge.

Stanley, L. (ed.) (1990). *Feminist Praxis. Research, Theory and Epistemology in Feminist Sociology*. London: Routledge.

Stanley, L. and Wise, S. (1990) Method, methodology and epistemology in feminist research processes, in L. Stanley (ed.), op. cit.

Steedman, J. (1983) *Examination Results in Mixed and Single Sex Schools*. Manchester: Equal Opportunities Commission.

Swann, M. (1985) *Education for All: The Report of the Committee of Inquiry into the Education of Children from Ethnic Minority Groups*, Cmnd 9453. London: HMSO.

Taylor, S. (1993) *A Land of Dreams: A Study of Jewish and Caribbean Migrant Communities in Britain*. London: Routledge.

Tomlinson, S. (1984) *Home and School in Multicultural Britain*. London: Batsford.

Tong, R. (1988) *Feminist Thought: A Comprehensive Introduction*. London: Unwin Hyman.

Townsend, H.E.R. and Brittan, E.M. (1972) *Organisation in Multicultural Schools*. Windsor: NFER-Nelson.

Townsend, H.E.R. and Brittan, E.M. (1973). *Multiracial Education: Need and Innovation*. Schools Council Working Paper 50. London: Evans/Methuen Educational.

Trinh, Minh-ha, T. (1989) *Woman, Native Other*. Bloomington: Indiana University Press.

Trivedi, P. (1984) To deny our fullness: Asian women in the making of history. *Feminist Review*, 17 (July): 37–50.

Troyna, B. and Carrington, B. (1987) Anti-sexist/anti-racist education – a false dilemma: a reply to Walkling and Brannigan. *Journal of Moral Education*, 16(1): 60–5.

UNESCO, (1984) *Social Science Research and Women in the Arab World*. Paris: UNESCO; London: Frances Pinter.

Union of Muslim Organisations Youth Council of UK and Eire (June 1989). Seminar on ERA 1988.

Verma, G.K. and Bagley, C. (eds) (1975) *Race and Education Across Cultures*. London: Heinemann.

Verma, G.K. (ed.) (1989) *Education for All: A Landmark in Pluralism*. London: Falmer Press.

Walker, R. and Weidel, J. (1985) Using pictures in a discipline of words, in R. Burgess (ed.) *Field Methods in the Study of Education*. Lewes: Falmer Press.

Walkerdine, V. (1990) *Schoolgirl Fictions*: London: Verso.

Walkling, P.H. (1980) The idea of a multicultural curriculum. *Journal of Philosophy of Education*, 14: 87–95.

Walkling, P.H. and Brannigan, C. (1986) Anti-sexist/anti-racist education: a possible dilemma. *Journal of Moral Education*, 15.

Watling, R (1995) 'Practical media work and education', unpublished PhD thesis. University of Nottingham.

Weedon, C. (1987) *Feminism Practice and Post Structuralist Theory*. Oxford: Basil Blackwell.

Weiner, G. (1994) *Feminisms in Education: An Introduction*. Buckingham: Open University Press.

Weiss, A. (1994) Challenges for a Muslim woman in a post-modern world, in A.S. Ahmed and D. Hastings (eds) *Islam, Globalization and Postmodernity*. London: Routledge.

Werbner, P. and Anwar, M. (eds) (1991) *Black and Ethnic Leadership: The Cultural Dimensions of Political Leadership*. London: Routledge.

West, C. (1987) Postmodernism and black America. *Zeta Magazine*, 1(6): 27–9.

Weston, C. (1989). Separate schools debate offers test, *Guardian*, 22 July.

Whitehorn, K. (1997) Blaming the Asians: whatever happened to the melting pot? *The Observer Review*, 9 March.

Williams, J. (1986) Education and race: the racialisation of class inequalities? *British Journal of Sociology of Education*, 7(2): 135–54.

Williams, J. (1987) The construction of women and black students as educational problems: re-evaluating policy on gender and race, in M. Arnot and G. Weiner (eds) *Gender and the Politics of Schooling*. London: Hutchinson in association with the Open University.

Willis, P. (1977). *Learning to Labour: How Working Class Kids Get Working Class Jobs*. Farnborough: Saxon House.

Wood, D. (1985) An introduction to Derrida, in R. Edgley and R. Osborne (eds) *Radical Philosophy Reader*. London: Verso.

Wright, C. (1987) Black students – white teachers, in B. Troyna (ed.) *Racial Inequality in Education*. London: Allen and Unwin.

Index

FEMINISMS IN EDUCATION
AN INTRODUCTION

Gaby Weiner

Gaby Weiner presents an overview of recent developments in feminist educational thinking and practice in Britain, exploring the ethical and professional challenges which now face feminist teachers and educators. She relates feminist thinking and practice to her own autobiographical experiences, to research and practitioner perspectives on gender, and to a variety of teacher and policy gender initiatives. She examines how the curriculum is implicated in the construction of gender relations, for example, in defining gender appropriate behaviour and/or in shaping perceptions of the appropriate place for girls and women in the family, school and employment. Throughout, she offers suggestions for feminist practice and the book concludes with specific proposals for developing an educational politics out of post-structural feminism, and for creating a feminist praxis as a basis for feminist action in education.

> This timely book takes stock of past and present feminist educational thinking and practice in Britain. It is the range and clarity of the descriptions of past feminist activities in education, combined with an unflinching engagement with the complexities of contemporary feminist ideas, that make this book essential reading for a wide range of people. Weiner's style is direct and intellectually interactive.
>
> *Gender and Education*

Contents
Preface – Introduction – From certainty to uncertainty: an autobiographical narrative – Teacher-proof or teacher-led: universal or specific (discourses on the curriculum) – Feminisms and education – Eradicating inequality: feminist practitioners and educational change – The gendered curriculum: producing the text – Developing a feminist praxis in pedagogy and research – References – Index.

176pp   0 335 19052 9 (Paperback)   0 335 19053 7 (Hardback)